POPULAR
PRINT AND
POPULAR
MEDICINE

POPULAR PRINT AND POPULAR MEDICINE

Almanacs and Health Advice in Early America

THOMAS A. HORROCKS

University of Massachusetts Press

Amherst

Copyright © 2008 by University of Massachusetts Press
All rights reserved
Printed in the United States of America

LC 2008003103
ISBN 978-1-55849-657-6 (paper); 656-9 (library cloth)

Designed by Dennis Anderson
Set in Sabon and Berthold Walbaum Book by dix!
Printed and bound by The Maple-Vail Book Manufacturing Group

Library of Congress Cataloging-in-Publication Data
Horrocks, Thomas A.
Popular print and popular medicine :
almanacs and health advice in early America / Thomas A. Horrocks.
p. cm.
Includes bibliographical references and index.
ISBN 978-1-55849-657-6 (pbk. : alk. paper)—
ISBN 978-1-55849-656-9 (library cloth : alk. paper)
1. Almanacs, American—History—18th century.   2. Almanacs,
American—History—19th century.   3. Medicine, Popular—History—18th
century.   4. Medicine, Popular—History—19th century.   5. Social medicine—
United States—History—18th century.   6. Social medicine—United States—
History—19th century.   7. Medical literature—United States—
History—18th century.   8. Medical literature—United States—History—19th
century.   9. Astrology, American—History—18th century.   10. Astrology,
American—History—19th century.   I. Title.
AY31.A1H67 2008
031.02'09033-dc22   2008003103

British Library Cataloguing in Publication data are available.

In memory of my parents,
Charles and Augusta,
and for Beth

CONTENTS

ILLUSTRATIONS

ACKNOWLEDGMENTS

I HAVE been fortunate in having the assistance and support of numerous colleagues, friends, and family members over the course of my work on this book, and it is with pleasure that I acknowledge them here. First, for guidance at early stages, I thank Richard Beeman, Kathleen Brown, the late Edward C. Carter II, and Charles Rosenberg. I am honored to have had the opportunity to work with Charles Rosenberg, who encouraged my interest in early American popular medicine and fostered my ensuing work. Ted Carter was always there with a wise suggestion, a word of encouragement, and, when needed, a reality check; with his sudden death, I lost a friend, mentor, and teacher. Finally, I want to thank James N. Green for his invaluable guidance and insights.

My interest in book history, and almanacs in particular, was inspired by three summer seminars at the American Antiquarian Society in the early to mid-1990s led by Michael Winship and the late William Gilmore-Lehne, both of whom had a role in shaping my work. My fellow seminar participant Russell Martin deserves special thanks for bringing to my attention the vast array of health advice contained in early American almanacs. The collections and staff of the American Antiquarian Society—a home away from home for historians of the book in American culture—are unsurpassed. Joanne Chaison, Nancy Burkett, John Hench, and Richard Anders were especially generous with their ideas and assistance.

I am very grateful for the encouragement and support provided by the institutions for which I have worked full-time during the course of this project: the College of Physicians of Philadelphia, the Francis A. Countway Library of Medicine (Harvard Medical School), and Houghton Library (Harvard University). Special thanks are due to John O'Donnell, Marc Micozzi, Judith Messerle, and William Stoneman.

I thank Paul Wright, former editor at the University of Massachusetts Press, for supporting this project in its early stages. Managing editor Carol Betsch and copy editor Deborah Smith deserve plaudits for their skill and patience. The two outside readers for the University of Massachusetts Press provided welcome criticism and recommendations which made this a better book. Whatever faults may be found in it are due to my having failed to listen to the good advice I received along the way.

Johns Hopkins University Press has graciously given me permission to reprint passages from my earlier article "Rules, Remedies, and Regimens: Health Advice in Early American Almanacs," in *Right Living: An Anglo-American Tradition of Self-Help Medicine and Hygiene,* ed. Charles E. Rosen (2003). I also wish to thank the Boston Medical Library in the Francis A. Countway Library of Medicine (Boston) for permission to quote from the Moses Appleton receipt book.

I regret that my father, Charles, and my mother, Augusta, did not live to see the birth of this book. I am forever grateful for their tireless encouragement and unwavering support of my educational and career aspirations. I thank my sister, Mary Horrocks Donohue, and my brother-in-law, Douglas Donohue, for their interest and support. Joan Carroll and the late Robert Carroll helped sustain me during the writing with their confidence and enthusiasm. Their daughter Beth is the love of my life. When we married, neither Beth nor I envisioned my writing this book. She has had to live through too many years of marriage shared with this project. For this and the happiness she brings to my life, I owe her my deepest gratitude and give her my enduring love.

POPULAR PRINT AND POPULAR MEDICINE

ALMANACS AND THE LITERATURE OF POPULAR HEALTH IN EARLY AMERICA

A HISTORIAN of early American almanacs once lamented that modern versions of the genre are the "degenerate offspring of respected ancestors whose contents were not primarily advertisements for hair-growing and itch-relieving potions." Marion Barber Stowell's critical remarks, expressed in a 1983 article, echo those made almost a century earlier by another historian of almanacs, Samuel Briggs. The almanac's columns abound with "the virtues of pills, potions and plasters," Briggs complained, "interspersed with views of our internal economy calculated to make the well man ill, and the invalid to relax his grasp on the thread of life." [1] Stowell's assessment of almanacs in the 1980s is exaggeration, but Briggs's review of the genre in the late nineteenth century is less so. By the time Briggs issued his searing indictment, the almanac trade was dominated by proprietary medicine firms and pharmaceutical companies.

Briggs and Stowell wrote wistfully of a world that had been lost, a pre–Civil War world in which almanacs offered their readers not various brands of hair-growing and itch-relieving nostrums but advice, enlightenment, and entertainment. It was a world in which Poor Richard, Merry Andrew, Timothy Telescope, Abraham Weatherwise, Copernicus Weatherguesser, and Dick Astronomer passed along farming tips, anecdotes, astrology, humor, maxims, weather predictions, and health advice. Because the almanac of this world offered something for almost everyone and almost everyone could afford to purchase one, it was, in the words of Briggs, an "honored guest at every fireside." [2]

Briggs and Stowell—as well as others—have ardently proclaimed the almanac's importance as a valuable resource for the study of popular culture in America from the colonial period to the Civil War.[3] While I disagree with Briggs and Stowell's apparent dismissals of later almanacs—specifically proprietary medicine almanacs—as unworthy of scholarly attention, I heartily concur with their shared belief in the value to historians of those published before 1860.[4] Because its popularity spread through almost every level of American society, the almanac was, in effect, a microcosm of that society. The almanac, more than any other genre of print (with the possible exception of the newspaper), provides a lens through which scholars can examine American popular culture of the seventeenth and eighteenth centuries and the first half of the nineteenth.[5]

Almanacs are indispensable resources for the study of lay medical beliefs and practices in early America. I argue in this study that a better understanding of popular attitudes concerning the body, health, and disease and the behaviors and practices these attitudes informed can be achieved by examining health advice presented in American almanacs published before the Civil War. American almanacs contained several forms of health and medical information, such as descriptions of various herbs and plants and explanations of how to use them, essays on current and recent epidemics, extracts from lay and professional medical publications, proprietary medical advertisements, and health advice. In the chapters that follow, I examine the three main categories of health advice presented in early American almanacs: astrological guidance, "cures" or remedies for various ailments, and prescribed or proscribed behaviors (regimen advice) for preserving health and ensuring long life.

The genre already had a long history by 1639, the year this country's first almanac was printed in Cambridge, Massachusetts. The almanac in its seventeenth-century guise was a composite of three chronological devices that dated to antiquity. It was a *calendar* or list of days of the week and months that noted church festivals and saints' days, an *almanac* consisting of astronomical and astrological compilations of the passage of time, and a *prognostication* comprising astrological predictions of political and social events. America's first almanacs, sometimes referred to as "Cambridge" or "Harvard" almanacs because they were compiled by

Harvard graduates or graduate students and printed in Cambridge, Massachusetts, by a press controlled by Harvard College, resembled English almanacs in certain ways. Like their English counterparts, most American almanacs issued during the seventeenth century included a preface, a calendar, information on eclipses and other astronomical phenomena, and a list of local court and fair dates.[6]

There were significant differences, however, between Harvard and English almanacs. The former, compiled by staunch supporters of Puritan orthodoxy, replaced saints' and feast days with important historical dates and identified months with numbers rather than with traditional names, which were considered pagan in origin. More important, English almanacs devoted much attention to astrology, while Harvard almanacs emphasized astronomy, learning, and Puritan doctrine over what their compilers considered heathenish prognostications of health, weather, or both. The Harvard astronomer William Brattle, for example, omitted any mention of astrology in his 1694 almanac because it would only "Delude and Amuse the Vulgar." In 1721, Cotton Mather, who, among his many ventures, compiled an almanac, vigorously condemned the "foolish *Astrology* of the *Star-gazers*" who attempt to read from the stars "what the Great GOD that made them has not *written* there." Concerning the supposed influence of the planets over plants, herbs, and certain diseases, he harshly denounced such belief as a "Folly akin to the Idolatry and the Superstition of the *Roman-Catholicks*, in looking to *Saints*, for their Influences on our Several *Diseases*." Mather was appalled that mankind had become so "*Planet-Struck*."[7] While their English counterparts sought to entertain a general audience of readers for profit, Harvard almanacs sought to edify and instruct an audience of readers as well educated as their compilers.

By the last decades of the seventeenth century American almanacs began to offer their readers more variety, and Harvard almanac makers were losing their hold on the market to competitors who correctly sensed that almanac readers wanted more predictions, less piety, and some levity along with their learning. And readers wanted astrology. By the end of the century the almanac had assumed the basic form with which Americans of the eighteenth century were familiar: a publication consisting of a calendar, astronomical and astrological compilations of time, and weather predictions.[8] During the eighteenth century other elements were added to the almanac, such as extracts from literature, poetry, lists of roads, local and federal court dates, postage and currency information, farming advice, essays on various subjects, humor, and health information. By the end of the century the almanac had become the most popular secular publication in America. For many Americans it was a fount of information and entertainment; a repository of vital facts for the farmer, merchant, and seaman; and a place where one could seek respite from the unchanging routines of everyday life.[9]

The format that almanacs assumed during the early decades of the eighteenth century remained consistent throughout that century and well into the nineteenth. Ranging in length from twenty-four to forty-eight pages, almanacs generally included three main sections. (Almanacs that were also city or state directories often contained more than a hundred pages.) The first section, or front matter, consisted of a preface or introductory statement by the almanac maker, eclipses for the coming year, names and symbols of the planets, a list of the five aspects,[10] a list of the twelve signs of the zodiac or a woodcut of the "Anatomy" or both,[11] and other astronomical and astrological information.[12] Occasionally, the first section contained an explanation of the astronomical and astrological symbols and terms that appeared in the almanac. The second section, which made up the bulk of the almanac, contained the calendar. Each month's calendar was divided into seven or eight columns, listing the days of the month and facts such as times of the rising and setting of the sun and moon, times of high tide, the moon's place in the zodiac, feast days and other days of historical significance, and weather predictions. The information provided in the calendar pages enabled readers to mark passages of the seasons as well as passages of time in the days before the advent of wall calendars and wristwatches.[13] The calendar pages also included the phases of the moon for each month, poetry, and sometimes maxims or proverbs, as well as short essays on farming, health, and the virtues of honesty, morality, and thrift. The third section comprised interest and currency tables, local and federal court schedules, a list of local roads, which included the distance between towns, essays on various subjects, humor and anecdotes, and, beginning around the 1830s, proprietary medicine advertisements. Generally, the reader would encounter farming tips and health advice in this section of the almanac.

Almanacs posed minor risks for early American printers. Colonial printers, according to one historian, "had to cope with weak markets, tight credit, restive labor, poor transportation, and political interference—all serious problems but none rivaling the fundamental difficulty of obtaining basic manufacturing materials." For example, a printer's annual expenditure on paper could equal or exceed his initial capital investment. Colonial printers could ill afford the financial risk of producing full-length books for a limited market. Books, be they original American works or reprints of English or European publications, were expensive to produce and thus their price was beyond the financial reach of many Americans. This situation, for the most part, had not changed by the early years of the nineteenth century. For example, Caleb P. Wayne, the Philadelphia publisher of John Marshall's *Life of George Washington*, issued in five volumes between 1804 and 1807, garnered more than seven thousand subscribers from over 650 cities. Yet, despite these impressive numbers and the widespread popularity of the biographer's subject, Wayne lost money on the work. A large majority of early American printers made a living not by producing large, expensive books but by selling such things as stationery and proprietary medicines, serving as bookbinders and as postmasters, and printing small, cheap publications, such as blank forms, single-sheet newspapers, primers, spelling books, broadsides, chapbooks, and almanacs.[14]

Because of low production costs and a ready market, almanac production was a profitable venture for many early American printers. Their affordability (ranging from six to twelve cents an issue from the 1780s through the 1850s) made almanacs accessible to Americans at the lower end of the economic scale, although it must be stressed that almanacs circulated widely in—and were popular with—all economic classes.[15] One almanac maker wrote in 1705 that his publication was "Plain enough for the Meanest Capacity." "B. A. Philo-Astro," the compiler of a 1723 almanac, claimed that he directed his publication to the "unlearned," so they would "know the general Opinion of the Learned World." In his *Autobiography*, Benjamin Franklin refers to his *Poor Richard* almanac "as a proper Vehicle for conveying Instruction among the common people." Another almanac maker, Nathanael Low, asserted that he did not design his publication "to inform the learned" but rather for the "few Poor and Illiterate" who were "not so biased against the arts as the multitude are." And Nathaniel Ames was blunt when writing about his almanac's intended audience: "This Sheet enters the solitary Dwellings of the Poor & Illiterate, where the studied Ingenuity of the learned Writer never comes."[16]

Despite the implications of passages such as those quoted in the pre-ceding paragraph and the almanacs' affordability and small size (most could fit into a person's pocket), these publications were not issued solely for the poor and semi-literate.[17] Many almanacs, particularly those is-sued in New York, Pennsylvania, and New Jersey, contained philosophi-cal essays, extracts from medical and scientific treatises, references to classical literature, the poetry of Dryden, Pope, and Shakespeare, and selected passages from contemporary works of fiction, suggesting that early American almanac makers—at least those from the mid-Atlantic region of the country—were targeting the widest possible audience.[18]

Clark Elliott's boast that people of "every Rank and Character" read his *Connecticut Almanack* may have been self-serving. Yet his confident assertion that his annual was "absolutely necessary to the Clergyman, the Lawyer, the Physician, the Merchant, the Husbandman, the Soldier, the Sailor, and every occupation of human Life" indicates that his in-tended audience included all levels of society. Like Elliott, Benjamin West directed his *Bickerstaff's Boston Almanac* to those "intelligent and chari-table persons, who live in the country, and who seem to have . . . a call from Providence to assist their less intelligent poor readers with advice." William Goddard, too, had a broad audience in mind when in 1787 he stated that his almanac was "highly useful, pleasing, and interesting" to the gentry, merchants, planters, farmers, and mechanics, "for whose use it hath been compiled, and under whose patronage it is intended to be continued." The intended audience for Isaiah Thomas's almanac was "all classes of men." And Daniel George, in the preface of his 1786 almanac, waxes somewhat inelegantly about the wide range of readers who would profit from almanacs, especially his own.

Into what inextricable perplexity would the most experienced seaman be frequently led, were it not for the seasonable information, and friendly admonition of the Almanac-maker. And even the most illiterate tarpawling (if he be able to read plain English) may, by consulting one of these use-ful pamphlets, learn to a mathematical nicety, the time of high water, and manage his business accordingly. And not only are we vastly serviceable to the rough sons of *Neptune*, but gentleman of the Faculty, the disciples of *Aesculapius* are greatly indebted to us for, without a previous consulta-tion of our productions, the single operation of venesection can scarcely be performed with safety. . . . Lawyers . . . will be ready to acknowledge themselves under almost infinite obligation to the Almanack, without whose assistance their clients would seldom be able to determine the time of attending Court. . . . Ladies will scarcely venture abroad, even on a summer's day, without first examining the Almanack, to know whether a *shower* or *wind* be predicted.[19]

A review of the contents of early American almanacs reveals that there was more in terms of subject matter of interest to women than the weather cited by George. Whereas such things as currency exchange and interest tables, farming advice, and court schedules might have been directed more to male readers, such items as gardening tips, cooking recipes, advice concerning the education of children, and remedies for various ailments would have been directed more to female readers (who assumed much of the health care responsibilities in the early American home). Some early nineteenth-century almanac makers openly courted female readers by using titles such as "The Lady's Almanac" and "The Lady's Astronomical Diary." [20] It should be noted here that, despite their appeals to female readers, almanac makers rarely included articles on childbirth or child rearing.

By attracting a readership that included men and women, the affluent and the poor, the learned and the semi-literate, the artisan and the farmer, and the urban as well as the country resident, almanac makers, like American printers in general, were, in many ways, acting as cultural mediators. Historians have shown that, generally, early American almanac makers and printers came from the artisan class—the same strata, for example, as surveyors and ship captains. Literate but not overly learned, almanac makers to be successful had to know the literary tastes of readers from different social and economic groups. In short, almanac makers had to select material for their publications that would meet the needs of—and not offend—a diverse readership, ranging from the affluent, learned reader to the poor, semi-literate one. In a sense, almanac makers provided a bridge between the cultures of different economic and social classes by introducing readers from these spheres to reading material they might not ordinarily have encountered. That many almanac makers were successful in attracting such a broad readership is a prime reason for the genre's popularity in the second half of the eighteenth century and the first half of the nineteenth.[21]

Franklin's *Poor Richard* almanac was one of the most successful (and most imitated) of its kind in colonial America, reaching a print run of ten thousand copies annually. But circulation figures for Franklin's almanac paled in comparison with those of the almanac of Nathaniel Ames, father and son, which numbered between fifty and sixty thousand a year.[22] Robert Thomas's *Farmer's Almanack* (its title was later changed to *The Old Farmer's Almanack*) numbered around twenty thousand during the 1790s and early 1800s. The increasing popularity of one late eighteenth-century almanac, Thomas Greenleaf's *New York, Connecticut, and New Jersey Almanack*, is noted in a 1797 advertisement: "This is the eighth successive year that the Editor has printed his Almanack; the first year he ventured only to issue 5,000 copies, the next 7,000; the sale of them increased so rapidly, from year to year, that the last season he was obliged to issue a third edition, completing upwards of 15,000 copies, which were every one sold off. The increased demand is so flattering to him, that he shall, without scruple, issue 20,000 copies this year." Booksellers, printers, storekeepers, merchants, and peddlers assumed brisk sales of almanacs and thus made them a staple of their inventories. For example, Thomas Legate, a storekeeper in Leominster, Massachusetts, was so confident of selling the annual almanacs of Benjamin West and Nathanael Low that he purchased enough copies to supply every household in and around his town.[23]

The public's growing demand for almanacs and the desire by printers to take advantage of this demand led to a proliferation of almanacs from the middle of the eighteenth century to the early decades of the nineteenth, a period that encompassed the golden age of the genre.[24] But as successful as the almanac trade was, it was not immune to pressures from within the publishing community in particular or American society in general. While almanac makers competed with each other, the almanac itself faced increasing competition in the nineteenth century from other forms of popular print, especially the growing numbers of newspapers, magazines, and novels. Moreover, the almanac's traditional role as calendar and, especially, keeper of time was increasingly challenged in the middle decades of the nineteenth century by the emergence—at least in urban areas—of advertising calendars, clocks, and inexpensive wristwatches. Clocks and wristwatches brought a semblance of order to commerce, transportation, and the workplace and thus were embraced by a society that was becoming more and more market oriented.[25]

Demographic changes also affected the almanac trade. As the United States became more industrial and urban, the almanac, directed traditionally to a farming audience, became less relevant to an expanding middle-class readership. Many American printers and publishers began to specialize, concentrating on specific—and timely—topics and targeting specific audiences. The 1820s witnessed the emergence of specialty almanacs. Right up to the Civil War, general almanacs faced competition from others devoted to religion, politics, humor, agriculture, health and medicine, and fraternal organizations and to various causes associated with antebellum reform movements.[26]

THE AMERICAN book trade began to change in the decades following the Revolutionary War. The conflict itself had afforded American printers greater prominence because of the leading roles they played as promoters of and publicists for the American cause.[27] The economic recovery that followed in the Revolution's wake offered new sources of capital for entrepreneurial printers, and the rise of political factions in the 1790s gave an incentive for them to publish newspapers and pamphlets. In 1792, Congress created the first postal system, which gave subsidies to newspaper publishers, and helped lay the groundwork for a new information network.[28] Moreover, the last decades of the eighteenth century and early decades of the nineteenth marked the beginning of what some historians have referred to as a "reading revolution," which was influenced by technological innovations in printing (stereotyping, steam-powered printing, machine papermaking, and the introduction of cloth bindings) and transportation (the coming of the railroad), increasing literacy, and expanding mass education. Literacy rates for white men, for example, were high during the colonial period, especially in New England. Literacy rates for both white men and white women rose steadily during the eighteenth century and through the early decades of the nineteenth; the 1850 census reported a literacy rate of 90 percent among white men and women. As the ability to read among white Americans increased, so, too, did the demand for reading material. Printers who attempted to meet Americans' demand for more books—and who assumed the financial risks involved—became this country's first publishers. By the 1820s printers had lost their place at the top of the American book trade to entrepreneurs—many of whom were former printers who gave up printing completely—who were involved in publishing and book selling. According to one historian, by 1850 some four hundred publishing firms, three thousand booksellers, and over four thousand printing houses were in business in the United States.[29]

As the demand for printed matter grew, so, too, did the ranks of publishers seeking ways to meet that demand. Competition became intense as publishers raced with one another to be the first to issue the same title or several titles on the same subject. Outpacing the demand and thus flooding the market with books, publishers, to survive, were forced to rely on cooperative mechanisms within the trade. Formal and informal arrangements, such as exchange systems and commission sales, enabled publishers to develop a domestic market for their products.[30]

The book trade was as financially unstable as it was intensely competitive. Publishers could neither wait for nor depend on the profits from one book to finance the next one. Yet to embark on several enterprises at a time required capital, a commodity that few publishers possessed. Thus, many publishers manipulated a complex system of debt and credit to finance their publications. This system, wherein publishers extended and received credit based on anticipated profits, was extremely risky. While a state of indebtedness was commonplace, many in the highly competitive and financially unsteady trade faced bankruptcy and insolvency.[31]

Henry H. Porter of Philadelphia was typical of the many ambitious entrepreneurs entering the American book trade in the early decades of the nineteenth century. Between 1829 and 1832 Porter published five journals, six books, and an almanac, many of which emphasized health and hygiene. Porter's first and most successful publishing venture was the *Journal of Health*, a monthly periodical offering health advice to the layperson. The journal's initial success apparently emboldened Porter to borrow funds to finance subsequent publications. Presumably he received credit based on anticipated profits from the *Journal of Health* and another of his periodicals, the *Journal of Law*. When these two publications began to lose money, however, Porter found himself in a desperate financial bind. In March 1832, awash in a sea of debt, Porter declared insolvency. He was never heard from again.[32]

Porter was one of the many casualties of the rough-and-tumble publishing world of antebellum America, even though he issued works that, to a large extent, addressed subjects that were popular with the book-buying public and profitable for many other publishers of the time. In his attempts to reach the expanding population of urban, middle-class readers, Porter published—and planned to publish—several works on self-improvement, particularly in the area of health. The message conveyed through Porter's published works was that the individual, through self-improvement and personal responsibility, could achieve moral perfection, material success, and physical health. With the emergence of the health reform movement in the 1830s, books on personal hygiene became increasingly popular with middle-class consumers.[33]

Whether the cause or the result of a reading revolution, the American book trade underwent a transformation that began in the last quarter of the eighteenth century. Once dominated by religious leaders and highly educated readers, the business of printing and publishing now responded to an expanding audience of ordinary people. Scores of almanacs, broadside ballads, chapbooks, primers and spelling books, and cheap editions of the Bible and hymn books appeared on the market as publishers attempted to meet the demands of a nascent middle-class readership that sought self-improvement, enlightenment, and entertainment. During the early decades of the nineteenth century, when economic mobility was becoming increasingly possible, Americans sought to tailor their social identity to their improved economic status. Publishers rushed to meet this new demand and, as a result, middle-class men and women, as well as rural and urban workers and other Americans who aspired to middle-class respectability, were targeted with an array of advice manuals, domestic economy books, etiquette guides, and health and hygiene advice books.[34]

That health books for the laity were published in early America should not be surprising, since most medical care took place in the home and was administered by a member of the household, a neighbor, or a local practitioner or midwife. Although several lay health publications were printed in America during the last quarter of the seventeenth century, not until the second half of the eighteenth century were such publications issued in this country with any frequency. Many of these were reprints of texts that were originally published in England. Generally, early American lay health publications fell into one of two categories: remedies for various ailments or directions for midwives, and hygiene or regimen advice for healthy living. These two traditional forms of health advice had evolved by the middle of the eighteenth century into two separate types of publication that had been, by and large, directed to two different audiences. A third, and much smaller, category of health text mixed remedy advice with astrology, folklore, magic, and the occult. *Aristotle's Masterpiece* and the *Erra Pater* books are representatives of this genre.[35]

In colonial America and the early republic, a time when trained physicians were few and the boundaries separating lay and professional practice were imperceptible, lay health publications conveyed a message that reinforced the individual's responsibility in matters of health care and, especially, prevention. Physicians tended to support the publication of these texts and in many instances wrote them. Physician writers, to establish their intellectual legitimacy as well as their social authority in the sphere of treatment, attempted to direct lay practice to prevention and encouraged self-treatment only in times when a physician was inaccessible. Physicians continued to write lay health publications throughout the nineteenth century. The trend continues to the present.

As sectarian practitioners, health reform advocates, itinerate healers, and purveyors of various proprietary medicines increasingly challenged the authority and legitimacy of regular physicians in the sphere of treatment, their rationales for writing popular texts became more defensive. Thus, regular physicians who wrote nineteenth-century lay health guides tended to espouse only prevention. During the first half of the nineteenth century the American market for popular health publications was complicated and fragmented, flooded with health books, pamphlets, journals, newspapers, and almanacs that were directed to the layperson and written and edited by regular physicians, botanical doctors, eclectics, homeopaths, hydropaths, and social reformers. These works offered advice and direction on matters concerning self-treatment of disease, diet, exercise, sex, childbirth and birth control, and child rearing.[36]

FROM THE end of the War of 1812 to the eve of the Civil War, the United States underwent profound economic, political, and social changes. The vibrant trade in lay health publications was occurring in an economy that was being transformed from one based on household production to one adapted to the marketplace. The "market revolution," as recent studies have labeled this transformation, spurred the rise of factories and industries, the growth of cities, the development of new modes of communication and transportation, and the expansion of the West. This economic transformation created new opportunities for some and dislocation and disaster for others. Some Americans were deeply troubled by these dramatic changes, which they saw as negative side effects of this rapid transformation. Anxious about the present and uncertain about the future, many Americans decided to take an active role in improving society by participating in the various reform movements of the period.[37]

Influenced by the emergence of the market economy, the rise of large cities, and the revivalist fervor of the Second Great Awakening, the secular reform movements that began in the 1820s were based on the assumption that society can be changed through individual efforts. The

doctrine of perfectionism, espoused by leaders of the Protestant evangelical movement, held that man is a religious free agent, capable of improving himself—as well as saving his soul—through good deeds and moral
behavior. This belief in the perfectibility of man energized and inspired
many Americans to improve themselves and their society. Confident that
they could make a difference in a society undergoing profound economic
and social change, reformers committed themselves to changing a society
that they believed was in turmoil and becoming materialistic, corrupt,
and immoral.

Reformers directed their efforts primarily at this country's young men
and women, a segment of the population thought to be especially vulnerable to the deleterious influences of city life and the dishonest and
dishonorable practices of the marketplace. Promoting character development as essential to protecting young men and women from the temptations posed by commercialism and the luxuries of urban society, religious
and reform organizations issued conduct manuals and advice books that
inculcated frugality, industry, morality, and temperance.[38]

The health reform movement that began in the 1830s was part of
this larger campaign. As Ronald Walters points out in his 1978 study of
antebellum reform movements, many reformers blurred the distinction
between the body and the soul, believing the one was dependent on the
other. He traces the transition from the "spiritual" perfectionism of the
1820s to the "physical" perfectionism of the following decade. Unlike
many seventeenth-century clerics and laypersons who saw physical affliction as divine retribution, a form of punishment from a vindictive
God, health reformers viewed disease as the result of a failure by the
individual to obey the laws of nature created by a merciful God. Living
in accordance with God's laws would restore one's health or keep one
healthy. The responsibility for one's health—like salvation—rested on
the individual. Personal perfection was the first step toward creating a
perfect society.[39]

Combining prevention and piety, physicians, sectarians, and lay reformers embraced various causes, such as temperance, vegetarianism,
physical education, and public health. In the decades leading up to the
Civil War, Americans who sought self-improvement could choose from
a wide array of popular magazines, conduct manuals, advice books, and
domestic economy texts. Directed to an expanding audience of middle-
class readers, these publications often included articles and sections on

personal health and hygiene. Physicians added their voices to the popular health crusade by writing anatomy and physiology textbooks for schools and colleges, books on child care, diet, exercise, and physical education. By prescribing and proscribing certain modes of behavior, these texts provided the reader with directions for achieving personal perfection through perfect health.[40]

WITH THE exception of advice on sex, childbirth, and child rearing, American almanacs offered health information similar to that found in many other genres of popular print, such as newspapers, domestic health guides, regimen texts, domestic economy books, and the numerous publications of medical sects and social reformers. In their attempts to reach the widest possible audience, early American almanac makers not only merged the self-treatment and regimen traditions of health advice, they sometimes provided advice found only in folklore, magic, and occult publications. These understudied artifacts of print culture are indispensable to understanding early American attitudes and practices concerning health and disease and how print shaped and was shaped by these attitudes. Regimen texts and domestic health guides, can, in the words of Charles Rosenberg, "provide clues to practices often so internalized—taken for granted—that they remain invisible in more standard historical sources." The same can certainly be said for almanacs. Yet, unlike the role played by regimen texts and domestic health guides in early American popular medicine, surprisingly little scholarly attention has been paid to the role of the almanac.[41]

Scholarship since the 1970s has added immensely to our knowledge of early American popular medicine and its relationship to the world of print. The works of Rosenberg, Lamar Riley Murphy, and John Blake, to cite but three examples, have been invaluable to scholars and students seeking to understand popular medicine and its literature in America before the Civil War.[42] More work in this area is required, however, especially on long-neglected genres of print, such as almanacs, newspapers, and periodicals. Unlike other popular genres of print that included health advice, with the possible exception of the newspaper, the almanac (specifically the general almanac) interacted to some extent with its audience. We know that almanac readers communicated with almanac makers in various ways, from forwarding remedies to issuing complaints about the omission of the Anatomy to contributing humorous anecdotes. This interaction—or negotiation—between almanac reader and almanac maker demonstrates how the genre both influenced and was influenced by popular health attitudes and practices.

The task of interpreting popular attitudes from early American almanacs—or, for that matter, other genres of print—is complicated by the anecdotal and fragmented evidence provided by the study of these publications. Much of what the historian can determine from their astrological, therapeutic, and regimen advice is inferential. Though many almanac makers pronounced their views on astrology, few expressed their personal thoughts on health and disease. Almanac readers are less visible; they seldom articulated their views on health and disease or left behind evidence confirming or denying that they actually followed an almanac's advice or used its remedies. I am acutely aware, as are historians of the book, that evidence of readers' response is extremely elusive. It is often difficult to adduce how people read and what attitudes they brought to or took away from the reading experience.[43] Nevertheless, the fair amount of interaction that went on between almanac reader and almanac maker provides the historian with enough examples to confirm or disprove what he or she might imply from the scattered evidence. For this study, some of the conclusions are, admittedly, based more on inference than on hard fact. But the conclusions I draw do corroborate—and thus complement—the findings of recent studies of popular medicine in early America, particularly those works encompassing popular print.[44]

THIS BOOK contends that the study of almanacs provides a clearer understanding of popular therapeutic practices and popular attitudes concerning the body, health, and disease, and the behaviors these attitudes informed. This contention is based on the examination of three main categories of health advice offered in the most popular secular publication in America before the 1850s. In conducting this study, I consulted 1,785 almanacs published between 1646 and 1861. A detailed review of the results of my examination of these almanacs is presented in the Appendix.

Chapters 1 through 4 offer snapshots of popular medical attitudes and practices in America before the Civil War, examining how laypersons in early America conceived the body, its composition, and its afflictions within the context of contemporary medical knowledge, and how print shaped and was shaped by these conceptions. In Chapter 1 I argue that the almanac, more than any other genre of popular print, played a leading role in disseminating astrological health information in early America. In Chapter 2, I examine almanac remedies for dropsy, dysentery, and rheumatism, three common afflictions encountered in eighteenth- and early nineteenth-century American almanacs. In Chapter 3, I focus on regimen or hygiene advice. In Chapter 4, I examine health advice contained in the numerous specialty almanacs published between the end of the War of 1812 and the outbreak of the Civil War.

HEAVENLY GUIDANCE

THE INTRODUCTION to the *Methodist Almanac* for 1846, in a brief history of almanacs up to that time, lauds almanacs for disseminating much "useful matter." But the essay also condemns them for conveying "superstitions and injurious trash in the shape of astrological rules."[1] The writer's scornful opinion of astrology was shared by many in the almanac trade, as it had been by many almanac makers of previous generations. Yet astrology, despite the negative views of it held by many almanac makers, had been a staple of American almanacs since the last decade of the seventeenth century. It would continue to be so at least until the Civil War.

Astrology is based on an assumption that the planets and stars influence the human body in particular and human affairs in general and dates to antiquity. Some of astrology's practices were widely accepted in the scientific circles of sixteenth-century England and Europe. Learned men of science and medicine, however, made a clear distinction between the tenets they accepted and those they rejected. While they acknowledged the legitimacy of and even practiced "natural" astrology (used to forecast weather and to treat disease), men of science and medicine vigorously denounced "judicial" astrology, the branch of astrology that involves divination and prognostications of social and political events.[2]

Grounded in the belief that each individual is a microcosm under the sway of the universe in which he or she lives, and that each of the universe's heavenly bodies plays a critical role in determining an individual's health or illness, astrology had been closely linked to medicine. Many trained physicians and learned practitioners consulted the heavens to determine the appropriate times to let blood, perform surgery, and administer medicines. The signs of the zodiac and the location of the moon, for example, played important roles in determining what measures were used to treat illness. The identification of a body part or organ with each sign of the zodiac was based on the concept of shared characteristics or virtues. Thus *Leo* presided over the heart because the strength the lion was located in its heart, and *Scorpio* presided over the genitals because a scorpion's strength was located in its tail.[3]

In England, astrology's popularity, which reached its peak during the second half of the sixteenth century, was not confined to physicians and scientists, for a belief in its influence pervaded all levels of English society. During the seventeenth century astrology gradually—the word *gradually* must be stressed here—lost its standing within scientific and medical circles, as its doctrines were eroded by scientific advances, questioned by growing numbers of critics, and condemned by religious leaders. Yet while astrology slipped in respectability among the learned, it remained popular among ordinary men and women who continued to seek its guidance concerning life's everyday concerns, including health and sickness.[4]

Astrology's popularity flourished with the appearance of various forms of print, particularly at the low end of the market, where almanacs and other cheap publications disseminated astrological advice and other forms of health information to a wider population of readers.[5] For example, one section of *Erra Pater*, a work popular with common readers, deals with the "various and wonderful Operations of the Signs and Planets, and other celestial Constellations, on the Bodies of Men, Women and Children, and the mighty Influences they have upon those that are born under them." Readers of the 1799 Suffield edition were offered a primitive woodcut of the "Zodiac Man" or the "Anatomy" accompanied by a poem explaining the image.[6] Almanacs were enormously popular with common as well as learned readers. Just how popular they were during this period is apparent in the distribution figures which show that during the mid seventeenth century almanac sales averaged about four hundred thousand annually, which, according to Bernard Capp, "suggests that roughly one family in three bought an almanac."[7]

Because astrological medicine was based on the belief that different signs of the zodiac rule over specific parts of the body, readers of almanacs were quite familiar with the image—usually a crude woodcut—of

the "Zodiac Man," the "Man of Signs," or the "Anatomy." The Anatomy depicted the human body—usually a male or an androgynous body,
rarely a female body—surrounded by the twelve signs of the zodiac, and
indicated which parts of the body a particular sign governed as the moon
passed through that sign. The moon's place was critical for determining the best time for bloodletting because it was thought that the moon
controlled the amount of blood in the veins. When the moon was in a
particular sign, the blood in the part governed by that sign would be at
its fullest—the chest area, for example, if the moon were in *Leo*. Thus,
the presence of the moon in a particular sign indicated that it would
be dangerous, perhaps fatal, to bleed the part of the body governed by
that sign. Knowing the moon's place and what that signified helped the
reader determine the appropriate times for administering medicines, let-
ting blood, gathering herbs, and performing surgical procedures. The
Anatomy (see Figs. 1 and 2) became a popular component of English
almanacs as well as their American counterparts.[8]

Harvard almanacs for the most part shunned astrology because their
compilers associated it with paganism. As a result, there were neither
weather predictions nor cuts of the Anatomy in any of these publications. The first American almanac to include a cut of the Anatomy was
John Foster's 1678 annual. A graduate of Harvard, Foster had established the second printing press in Massachusetts (in Boston) and issued
the first almanac to compete with those of the Harvard series. Foster did
not make weather predictions, however.[9]

John Tulley's almanacs diverged more dramatically than did Foster's
from the Harvard series. A teacher of arithmetic, navigation, and astronomy who had taught himself mathematics, Tulley was a forerunner
of the almanac makers of the eighteenth and early nineteenth centuries.
Preparing his almanacs with a broadly diverse audience in mind, Tulley
included cuts of the Anatomy, astrological prognostications, and the first
weather predictions to appear in American almanacs. As a result, his
almanacs elicited harsh criticism from guardians of Puritan doctrine.
When he included a cut of the Anatomy in his 1693 almanac and predicted the death of Louis XIV a year later, Tulley was denounced by
his fellow almanac maker Christian Lodowick for a "sinful love of that
Soul-bewitching Vanity of Star-Prophecy, commonly called Astrology."
Lodowick criticized Tulley for attempting to "withdraw Persons from a
holy Reliance in God's will & Providence" by predicting "Secret things"

Fig. 1. Anatomy, 1797. Title page of *An Astronomical Diary; or Almanack for the Year . . .1797 . . . by Nathanael Low* (Boston: T. and J. Fleet, 1797). (Author's collection)

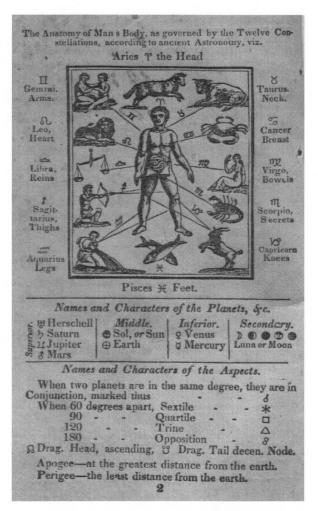

The Anatomy of Man's Body, as governed by the Twelve Constellations, according to ancient Astronomy, viz.

Aries ♈ the Head

♊ Gemini. Arms.

♌ Leo, Heart

♎ Libra, Reins

♐ Sagittarius, Thighs

♒ Aquarius Legs

♉ Taurus. Neck.

♋ Cancer Breast

♍ Virgo, Bowels

♏ Scorpio, Secrets

♑ Capricorn Knees

Pisces ♓ Feet.

Names and Characters of the Planets, &c.

	Middle.	*Inferior.*	*Secondary.*
♅ Herschell	⊕ Sol, *or* Sun	♀ Venus	☽ ◑ ● ◕ ◉
♄ Saturn	⊕ Earth	☿ Mercury	Luna *or* Moon
♃ Jupiter			
♂ Mars			

Names and Characters of the Aspects.

When two planets are in the same degree, they are in Conjunction, marked thus   ·   ·   ☌

When 60 degrees apart,	Sextile	- -	✳
90 - -	Quartile	- -	□
120 - -	Trine	- -	△
180 - -	Opposition	-	☍

☊ Drag. Head, ascending, ☋ Drag. Tail decen. Node.

Apogee—at the greatest distance from the earth.
Perigee—the least distance from the earth.

2

Fig. 2. Anatomy, 1847. *Phinney's Calendar, or Western Almanac . . . 1847* (Cooperstown, N.Y.: H. and E. Phinney, [1846]). (Author's collection)

that only God could know. Tulley's astrological predictions, Lodowick charged, were nothing more than "Heathenish Whimzies and Ridiculous Trifles." [10]

Visions of profits prevailed over threats of damnation, however, and although Tulley, relenting under Lodowick's barrage, ceased his prognostications of royal deaths and pulled the cut of the Anatomy from later almanacs, he continued to publish astrological information. Other almanac makers, too, chose possible financial gain over probable condemnation and included weather predictions and other astrological information in their publications. By the eighteenth century, astrology, including the popular Anatomy, was a common feature of American almanacs. [11]

Along with the Anatomy and weather predictions, almanacs issued from the 1690s through the 1750s offered advice about the appropriate times for gathering herbs, clearing land, and cutting trees and seasonal instructions relating to bleeding and purging. Daniel Leeds's 1694 almanac includes a section titled "Times to gather Herbs, when the Planets that Govern them are signified." His 1695 almanac contains similar advice. [12] Titan Leeds continued his father's practice of offering astrological herbal advice when he began issuing his own almanac in 1714. Under the heading "The most proper time of gathering herbs . . . when the Planet that governs Them is fortified or Strong," his 1715 annual recommends two days in the months of June, July, and August as appropriate times for "Thistles, Barbarries [barberries], Cartlus [carduus?], Garlick, Pepperwort, Nettles, Rubarb [rhubarb], Mustard, Wormwood, Savin [savine], and all Herbs of Mars." Nathaniel Whittemore's almanac of the same year offers his readers advice about when to clear land and when to graft trees. According to Whittemore, the "best times to fell Timber is in the Old of the Moon, in *December*, *January*, and *February*, especially when the Moon is in *Aquar.* or *Pisces*." Timothy Green's 1723 almanac claims that timber cut in the "wane of the Moon, in *February* and *August*" will be "free from Worms." [13]

Benjamin Harris's *Boston Almanack* for 1692 includes advice on the best times to let blood and purge. He believed awareness of the phases of the moon and knowledge of the signs of the Zodiac were essential. Those under the age of fourteen and over the age of fifty-six, he warns, should not be bled at any time. Those above the age of fourteen can be bled "from the Change to the first quarter" of the moon, and those in middle-age "from the first full quarter to the Full." Middle-aged adults can be bled "from the full to the last quarter" while those in their "Old

Age" [over fifty-six], "from the last quarter to Change." On the appropriate times for purging, Harris offers the following advice: "Purge when the Moon is Decreasing in any of these three signs, Cancer, Scorpio, or Pisces, and it will be sure to work the better. For in a moist sign the humours of the Body are stirred up and down, and the better purged out. In this case, it cannot be amiss to prepare humours by something that is Laxitive [*sic*]: Let this be done when the Moon is either in Gemini, Libra or Aquarius. Take a vomit that it may work thoroughly, when the Moon is in Aries, Taurus, or Capricorn."[14]

An article in John Tulley's 1689 almanac entitled "The Nature of the Twelve Signs" informs readers of the importance of understanding the signs of the zodiac and knowing the location of the moon in relation to them. This knowledge was imperative when it came to bleeding. "No man ought to make an incision, nor touch with iron the members governed of any sign the day that the moon is in it," Tulley warns, "for fear of the great effusion of blood that may happen." In the following passage in his 1694 almanac Tulley advises his readers when it is "Good to Purge" and when it is the best time to take other measures:

> With Electuaries, the Moon in *Cancer*.
> With Pills, the Moon in *Pisces*. . . .
> Good to take Vomit, the Moon being in *Taurus*.
> To purge the Head by sneezing, the Moon being in
> *Cancer*, *Leo*, or *Virgo*.
> To make Glysters, the Moon being in *Aries*,
> *Cancer*, or *Virgo*.
> To stop Fluxes and Rheums, the Moon being in
> *Taurus*, *Virgo*, or *Capricorn*.
> To Bath when the Moon is in *Cancer*, *Libra*,
> *Aquarius*, or *Pisces*.
> To cut the Hair of the Head or Beard, when the Moon is in *Libra*,
> *Sagitarius*, *Aquarius*, or *Pisces*.[15]

Daniel Travis's 1709 *Almanack of Coelestial Motions and Aspects* describes the quarters of the year in terms of health, with instructions about how to avoid seasonal illnesses. Like Harris, Tulley, Leeds, and other almanac makers, Travis based his advice on the traditional assumption that the body interacts constantly with its environment, celestial as well as terrestrial. For example, Travis warns that if summer is not, as it should be, hot and dry, it will prove "dangerous to health" and "detrimental to the Husbandman" because the pores of the body, "external and internal," will stand wide open ready to absorb environmental poison. In this situation, Travis advises, one should avoid herbs and medicines that will open the pores even wider.[16] Daniel Fowle warns readers of his 1752 almanac not to bleed or get sick on certain "evil" or "perilous" days, for if a man or a woman "shall be let Blood, they will die within twenty-one Days following, or whose falleth sick on any one of these Days, shall certainly die."[17]

Astrological advice concerning herbs and seasonal recommendations regarding bleeding and purging had, for the most part, disappeared from American almanacs by the time Fowle's 1752 almanac was issued. Over the next hundred years American almanacs confined their astrological information to weather predictions, phases of the moon, and a cut of the Anatomy or a list of the signs of the zodiac linked to a column in the calendar indicating the moon's place for each day. Some almanacs included both the Anatomy and the list. Weather information, of course, was extremely useful to farmers, merchants, seamen, and fishermen, whose livelihoods were affected by climate changes and rough and stormy seas. Information about the phases of the moon served a variety of needs. A segment of almanac readers believed in folk traditions that supported the notion that different phases of the moon dictate appropriate times to geld cattle, shear sheep, graft trees, wean babies, let blood, and administer purges. Finally, the Anatomy or a list of the signs of the zodiac and the corresponding column in the monthly calendar would tell readers which sign the moon was in on a particular day. This information would help readers determine whether bleeding was an appropriate treatment for an ailment. According to this system, when the moon was in the sign governing a particular part of the body, bleeding was prohibited from that part.[18]

Several Philadelphia almanacs issued during the antebellum period countered this minimalist approach by offering astrological advice that was more nuanced than that found in most other almanacs and assumed a higher level of knowledge among its readers. Among these, the *Columbian Almanac* for the years 1833 through 1859, the *Comic Almanac* for 1855, the *Continental Almanac* for 1860, the *Farmer's Almanac* for 1854, the *Farmers and Mechanic's Almanack* for 1833 through 1850, and the *Franklin Almanac* for 1825 all contain a column in the calendar section, "Aspects of Planets and other Miscellanies," where terms are represented by symbols not used in most other almanacs: "Good cupping" (a bleeding cup), "Good bleeding" (a double cross), and "Tolerable good bleeding" (a cross) (see Fig. 3).[19]

The calendar section of the *Columbian Almanac* for 1833 provides several examples of the unique astrological advice offered by this group of almanacs. The first example concerns Wednesday, January 9, 1833. On this day, according to the almanac, the moon was located in the seventh degree of *Virgo.* Although the moon had just entered this sign, most almanacs would have prohibited bleeding from areas proximate to the bowels during this time. Not so the *Columbian Almanac,* which indicates that on this day a reader would find tolerable good bleeding as well as good cupping. According to the calendar, the next day, Thursday the 10th, the moon was located in *Virgo's* twenty-first degree, and bleeding and cupping were prohibited. The second example concerns Monday, January 21, when the moon was in the tenth degree of *Aquarius.* Here again, whereas most almanacs would have proscribed bleeding from the legs on this day, the *Columbian Almanac* states otherwise—good bleeding and cupping. On the next day, the 22nd, the moon was in the twenty-second degree of *Aquarius,* and the almanac prohibits bleeding and cupping.[20]

The *Columbian Almanac* for that same year includes numerous astrological symbols that indicate the moon's location in the heavens and the locations and influences of the planets. Readers needed a high level of astrological knowledge to understand, through the use of these symbols, why bleeding or cupping was prescribed or proscribed. Most almanacs, for example, would have prohibited bleeding from the legs on Monday, January 21, 1833, yet the *Columbian Almanac* did not. Why it did not is explained by a symbol representing the moon accompanied by the phrase "in apo." This meant that the moon was in apogee on that day, that is, that the moon was at its greatest distance from the earth and thus at its weakest in terms of influence.[21]

A century earlier Christopher Sauer, a Pennsylvania German printer, and others like him, issued almanacs that included advice at this same level of sophistication.[22] The most significant link between these eighteenth-century almanacs and the small group of almanacs published in Philadelphia in the nineteenth century is the influence of the local German immigrant community. The *Comic Almanac* for 1855, for example, was published by King and Baird, the proprietors of an "Almanac Warehouse" that issued both English- and German-language almanacs. Moreover, the publishers of both the *Farmers and Mechanic's Almanack*

The twelfth Month, or December—1838,

Week Days.	Remarkable Days.	High Water. R. & S.	Moon rises	Moon's Signs, other Miscellanies.	Aspects of planets and hour, and other Miscellanies.	Sun rises & sets, south.	Moon rises, south.	Nov
Satur	1 Longinus	1 41	rises 42 12	☉ 1st Al. on Me.		7 19 4 41	morn	19
				[8 18]				
						Days' length 9 hours 22 minutes.		
	Advent Sunday.			Matth. 21.				
	48.)							
Sund	2 Candidus	2 42	5 24	☾ runs high		10 7 19 4 41	12 30	20
Mond	3 Cassianus	3 44	6 28			10 7 20 4 40	1 32	21
Tues	4 Barbara	4 44	7 37	Pegasia s. 6 18		10 7 20 4 40	2 32	22
Wed	5 Abigail	5 38	8 45			9 7 21 4 39	3 26	23
Thur	6 Nicholas	6 28	9 43	☾'s lat. 3 d. north		9 7 21 4 39	4 16	24
Frid	7 Agathon	7 18	10 51	Al. on M. 7 52		8 7 22 4 38	5 1	25
Satur	8 Con. V. Mary	7 55	11 55	8th		8 7 22 4 38	5 43	26
				Luke 21.				
	49.) **2d Sunday in Advent.**							
						Days' length 9 hours 14 minutes.		
Sund	9 Joachim	8 35	morn	☾ in Node		7 7 23 4 37	6 23	27
Mond	10 Judith	9 14	12 55	☾ in apo.		7 7 23 4 37	7 2	28
Tues	11 Barsabas	9 53	1 54	✶ s's. 10 22		6 7 24 4 36	7 41	29
Wed	12 Otalia	10 34	2 55	☾ rises 11 32		6 7 24 4 36	8 22	30
Thur	13 Lucy	11 17	3 56	Al. on M. 7 26		5 7 24 4 36	9 5	1
Frid	14 Wash. died	12 3	5 0			5 7 24 4 36	9 51	2
Satur	15 Ignatius	12 31	6 9	eye s. 10 53		5 7 25 4 35	10 43	3
				Matth. 11.				
	50.) **3d Sunday in Advent.**							
						Days' length 9 hours 10 minutes.		
Sund	16 Ananias	1 26	7 18	16th ☾		4 7 25 4 35	11 38	4
Mond	17 Lazarus	2 23	sets	gr. e.		4 7 25 4 35	aft. 35	5
Tues	18 Arnoldus	3 21	6 4	Al. on M. 7 3 ssup		3 7 25 4 35	1 33	6
Wed	19 Emberday	4 17	7 15			3 7 25 4 35	2 29	7
Thur	20 Ammon	5 11	8 30			3 7 25 4 35	3 23	8
Frid	21 St. Thomas	6 2	9 43	☉ enters		2 7 25 4 35	4 14	9
Satur	22 Beata	6 51	10 56	eye s. 9 34 H		1 7 25 4 35	5 3	10
				John 1.				
	51.) **4th Sunday in Advent.**							
						Days' length 9 hours 10 minutes.		
Sund	23 Dagobert	7 38	morn	23d ☾ in node		1 7 25 4 35	5 50	11
Mond	24 Adam, Eve	8 25	12 7	☾ age 8 days		7 25 4 35	6 37	12
Tues	25 Christmas	9 15	1 19	☾ in perigee		7 25 4 35	7 27	13
Wed	26 St. Stephen	10 7	2 34	☿ sta.		1 7 25 4 35	8 19	14
Thur	27 St. John	11 3	3 50	☾'s lat. 4 d. n.		7 25 4 35	9 15	15
Frid	28 Innocents	12 2	5 6	☾'s age 12 days		2 7 25 4 35	10 14	16
Satur	29 Noah	12 26	6 8	eye s. 9 52 r.h.		2 7 25 4 35	11 14	17
				Matth. 1.				
	52.) **1st Sunday after Christmas.**							
						Days' length 9 hours 12 minutes.		
Sund	30 David	1 26	rises	30th ☿ in per.		8 7 24 4 36	morn	18
Mond	31 Silvester	2 27	5 15	Al. on m. 6 6		8 7 24 4 36	12 15	19

Collapse of the Lungs.

Some young children, when they cry, are apt to suffer a collapse of the lungs, or in the language of parents, "hold their breath." This occasions great alarm to parents, and is a real evil, for it is sometimes with difficulty that the breath can be recovered. The following is an easy and certain remedy; close the nostrils of the child with the thumb and finger, then put your mouth to the child's mouth and blow smartly; the lungs will be inflated, and the music will recommence in a moment.

The Croup.

A mother, says the Montreal Transcript, gives as an effectual remedy for the croup—a tea spoon full of the solution of a piece of indigo, about the size of a pea, in a pint tumbler of luke warm water.

To Prevent Burning the Fingers.

If cherry tree gum (gum Arabic has similar powers to the cherry tree gum,) and alum be pounded together, in equal quantities, and the powder mixed with some strong vinegar, which must then be left in a vessel, over hot ashes, for about twenty-four hours, any thing rubbed with this composition, after it has become cold, will not burn.

Linseed Cough Syrup.

Boil an ounce of linseed in a quart of water, till half wasted; then add six ounces of moist sugar, two ounces of sugar candy, half an ounce of Spanish liquorice, and the juice of a large lemon. Let the whole slowly simmer together, till it becomes of a sirupy consistence; when cold, put to it two table-spoonsful of the best old rum.

Cholera.

The following statement, if true, may be invaluable, in the treatment of cholera, and no doubt is the origin of the paragraph that has been making the rounds of the papers. "Two men employed in extracting salt from the lake in the neighbourhood of Salzburgh, were attacked by the disease, and left by their medical attendant as incurable. Their bodies had become completely black, when the overseer of the works undertook to cure them. He heated a quantity of water from one of the salt lakes to a very high degree, and placed one of the dying men in the bath. After being in half an hour, the man recovered his senses, and expressed how delightful were his sensations. Upon this the other sufferer was put into a similar bath. By degrees their bodies turned from black to purple, then to red, and at the end of three hours they assumed their natural colour, and the men were free from disease. It may be believed, that the pores, being opened by the heat, absorbed the saline particles which mingled with the blood and liquified it. This corresponds with the known effects of salt upon coagulated blood.

MOON'S PHASES.

Full Moon the 1st, at 6 o'clock 33 minutes, morning—stormy.

Last quarter the 8th, at 5 o'clock 55 minutes, afternoon—fair.

New Moon the 16th, at 7 o'clock 22 minutes, afternoon—perhaps rain, or snow.

First quarter the 23d, at 10 o'clock 5 minutes, afternoon—perhaps rain, or snow.

Full Moon the 30th, at 7 o'clock 34 minutes, afternoon—perhaps rain, or snow.

REMARKABLE EVENTS.

6 Rhode Island taken 1776
7 Newport taken 76
8 Battle of Great bridge, Virginia 75
14 George Washington died '99
14 Jersey overrun 76
15 Charleston evacuated '83
16 Tea destroyed at Boston '73
26 Hessians taken 76
29 Georgia invaded 78

SUPREME COURT, in Philadelphia 10th, to continue three weeks.

Courts of Quarter Sessions and Court of Common Pleas:

Philadelphia	3		Union	17
Lehigh	3		M'Kean	17
Clearfield	3		Monroe	17
Warren	3		Schuylkill	24
Lycoming	3		Washington	24
Juniata	3		Allegheny	24
Somerset	3		Indiana	24
Bucks	10		Tioga	24
Armstrong	10		Mercer	24
Bradford	10		Potter	24
Butler	10		Cambria	31
Jefferson	10			

...tem in a mortar, and squeeze out the juice, of which give as soon as possible one large spoonful, repeating the dose an hour after, unless the patient is perfectly relieved. If the roots are dried they must be moistened with a little warm water. This remedy is said never to fail.

Fig. 3. Astrological characters "arranged after the system of German Calendars." 1838. *The Franklin Almanac . . . 1838* (Philadelphia: M'Carty and Davis, [1837]).

and the *Franklin Almanac* informed readers that their annuals were arranged "after the systems of the German Calendars." The "systems" to
which they referred were the astrological and astronomical calculations.
Except for those of the *Franklin Almanac*, the calculations for this group
of almanacs were prepared by a Reading, Pennsylvania, "philomath,"
Charles Frederick Eagelmann (sometimes spelled Egelmann). Although
Eagelmann had performed calculations for several Maryland almanacs
and an Ohio almanac that were not based on the German system, he
apparently had strong ties to the German-speaking community.[23] Of
the other Pennsylvania almanacs with which Eagelman was involved,
at least two were issued in German, *Der HOCH-DEUTSCHE Americanische
Calender*, printed in Germantown, and *Der PENNSYLVANISCHE Anti-
Freymaurer Calender*, printed in Reading.

What we can learn from the astrological health advice offered by this
small group of Philadelphia almanacs is that astrology was taken very seriously within the German American community well into the nineteenth
century. Moreover, this small group of almanac makers assumed that
at least some readers outside the German community possessed enough
knowledge of astrology to understand and be interested in receiving the
advice they offered.[24]

Almost 60 percent of the almanacs consulted for this study contain
the Anatomy, while 97 percent list the moon's place in the calendar.[25]
Benjamin Franklin, for example, included the Anatomy in all but one
of his twenty-five *Poor Richard* almanacs. He provided instructions on
how to link the diagram with the calendar: "First find the Day of the
Month, and against the Day you have the Sign or Place of the Moon
in the 5th Column. Then finding the Sign here, it shews the part of the
Body it governs." Many almanacs carried similar directions; some did
not, presumably because their compilers felt their readers' high level of
astrological literacy did not require it, or perhaps because their compilers did not care whether their readers understood the meaning of the
column.[26]

Occasionally, an almanac maker would use a poem to explain the
Anatomy to readers. John Foster printed these lines in his 1678 almanac:

> The *Head* and *Face* the *Ram* doth crave,
> The *Neck* and *Throat*, the Bull will have,
> The loving *Twins* do rule the *Hands*,
> The *Breast* and *Sides* in *Cancer* bands,

The *Heart* and *Back* the *Lyon* [*sic*] claims,
Bowels and *Belly Virgo* gains,
The *Reyns* [*sic*] and *Loyns* [*sic*] are *Libra's* part,
The *Secrets Scorpio's* are by Art,
Thighs to the *Archer* do pertain,
And *Capricorn* the *Knees* doth gain,
Aquarius hath the *Legs* alone,
And *Pisces* must have *Feet*, or none.[27]

Almost a century later, a Virginia almanac offered a similar poem:

The Ram possesseth head and face,
The neck the Bull commands,
The loving Twins, with equal power,
Guide shoulders, arms, and hands.
The breast and stomach Cancer owns,
The heart the Lion claims,
The Virgin loves the belly piece,
To Libra loins and reins.
The Scorpion has the secret part,
The thighs to Sagittarius,
To Capricorn we give the knees,
The legs unto Aquarius.
Now none but Pisces wants a share,
To him we give the feet,
Then Aries head and face again,
And so make both ends meet.[28]

Some almanac makers, through their editorial comments, expressed their faith in the astrological rules (natural astrology) they offered. John Tulley defended himself against Lodowick's blistering attack by observing that he was merely following "several Rules to each [astronomy and astrology or meteorology] of them prescribed by the Authors of these Arts; which Arts for many years have been & still are practiced and followed in *England*."[29] In his *Kalendarium Nov-Anglicanum* for 1706, Samuel Clough argues that astrology is a science based on the observations of "the most celebrated Philosophers and Astronomers from time Immemorial." Clough posed a rhetorical question that if the moon moved the tides, then should not planets move the "thin and tenuous air?"[30] In his 1753 almanac, John Nathan Hutchins defends astrology against "many of our wise Zealots, whose thick Skulls can't penetrate to any Thing above the Earth, or out of the Reach of their Nose, . . . yet are so wise as to call those Arts they know nothing of, sinful, diabolical, whimsical, and what not."[31] Several philomaths (those who sold astrological and astronomical calculations to almanac makers) advertised their astrology skills by promoting themselves, for example, as a "Student in Mathematics and Astrology," "A Student in Astronomy and Astrology," and a "dealer in astrology."[32]

An ardent defender of astrology was Nathaniel Ames Sr., one of the most successful American almanac makers of the eighteenth century. A physician and tavern keeper who was proficient in natural history, astronomy, and mathematics, Ames, in prefatory remarks to his 1764 almanac, confidently asserts that astrology influences human affairs and can, if used with "good Sense and Learning" and "lawful Means," lead men "on to Greatness": "The cealestial [sic] Powers that can and do agitate and move the whole Ocean, have also Force and Ability to change and alter the Fluids and Solids of the humane [sic] Body; and that which can alter and change the Fluids and Solids of the Body, must also greatly affect the Mind: and that which can and does affect the Mind, has a great Share and Influence in the Actions of Men."[33] Keenly aware that astrology had many critics among the learned, who claimed that the practice was based on nothing more than ancient superstition, Ames sought to base his astrology on practical experience. In his 1727 almanac, he offers his readers a Baconian defense of traditional astrological beliefs concerning the weather: "As to what I have predicted of the Weather, it is from Motions & Configurations of heavenly Bodies, which belongs to Astrology: Long Experience testifies that the Sun, Moon and Stars have their Influence on our Atmosphere, for it hath been observed for Seventy Years past, that the Quartile & Opposition of Saturn and Jupiter produce Wet Seasons; and none will deny but the Sun affordeth us his benign Rays & kind influence, and his regular Motion causeth Spring, Summer, Autumn, and Winter."[34]

Ames believed that planetary alignments and changing signs of the zodiac could influence an individual's health. His 1745 almanac, for example, warns readers of potential dangers in the year ahead, predicting the coming of "peripneumonick and pleuritick Fevers, Coughs, Asthmas, and Disorders of the Lungs" in January; and "vernal intermittents" in addition to "nervous slow fevers" and "Stagnation of the Blood" in April.[35] And like many proponents of astrology, Ames was convinced that the moon played a critical role in influencing health and the weather.

According to Ames, one had only to look at the moon's influence on the earth's tides to understand the wide range of subtle effects on the latter's bodies and processes. Yet for all his trust in the moon's power over terrestrial matters, Ames omitted the Anatomy from his post-1734 almanacs. To him, the image represented superstition, and he had included it only to please his readers.

> The Blackmoor may eas'ly change his Skin,
> As Men forsake the ways they'r brought up in;
> Therefore I've set the Old Anatomy,
> Hoping to please my Country men thereby,
> But where's the Man that's born & lives among,
> ——————————— Can please the Fickle throng? [36]

Like Ames, Samuel Clough, who, as quoted earlier, defended astrology in his 1706 almanac, used poetry in his 1703 almanac to ridicule the Anatomy and the readers who believed in it.

> The *Anatomy* must still be in
> Else the *Almanack's* not worth a pin;
> For *Country*-men regard the Sign
> As though 'Twere Oracle Divine
> But do not mind *that* altogether,
> Have some respect to Wind and Weather. [37]

Ames's and Clough's disdain of the Anatomy did not alter their basic commitment to astrology. Their trust in astrology, however, was not shared by many of their peers in the almanac trade. Evidence suggests that the majority of almanac makers, from the seventeenth century through the first half of the nineteenth, held at best skeptical and at worst harsh opinions of astrology.

The Rhode-Island Almanack, first issued in 1728 by James Franklin and continued by his widow, Ann, printed several "predictions" that lampooned astrology. For example, in the 1729 issue Franklin's "Poor Robin" predicts that March will mark an "alteration in the Air" and a change in "Men's Humours and Dispositions." An even temper can be restored, Franklin asserts, with the "best and most approved Remedies," such as "Money, good Clothes, good Eating and Drinking, and above all, a good Conscience." James's brother, Benjamin, continued the family practice of poking fun at astrology when he offered readers of the first issue of his *Poor Richard* almanac a mock prediction of the death of his rival almanac maker, Titan Leeds.[38]

Other almanac makers were more direct in their criticisms of astrology. Thomas Robie, who issued an almanac from 1710 to 1720, had this to say about weather predictions and other astrological prognostications: "I utterly abhor and detest them all, and look upon these to be but the effect of Ignorance and Fancy."[39] Jacob Taylor, compiler of the *Pensilvania* almanac, was equally disdainful, declaring in his 1746 almanac: "Is it not amazing Confidence, in Men destitute of Physical Learning, to persist so boldly in giving their Direction? They could never impose such Fooleries on the World, were not the Writers, and some weak Readers riveted to Superstition, and fastened with Nails of Idolatry."[40] The 1759 *Poor Joseph* almanac claims that astrology is so "foolish and false a Science" that it "ought not to be regarded by any Lovers of Truth." Astrology, the compiler continues, is the "Mother of the greatest Absurdities" and its votaries "the downright Children of Ignorance."[41] "Frank Freeman," compiler of *Freeman's New-York Almanack*, informs readers of his 1767 annual that astrology was no longer relevant in an enlightened age.

> Crafty knaves, who have something more than Vulgar, have often imposed upon *their* Ignorance, by Pretenses to supernatural knowledge, and Powers more than human; whereby they have kept their Inferiors in awe, and made a Property of their Credulity. Thence Astrology took its Rise. . . . But in proportion as learning has become more general, Astrology has lost its credit; and it is now so generally exploded in all Parts of the English Dominions, that hardly any Person can be found so very Ignorant as to not to think it a proper Subject of Ridicule. An Almanack is a conveniency that no family ought to be without, how careful then ought we to be, that it will not be made the means of propagating False Notions?[42]

Almanac-makers' attacks on astrology continued into the nineteenth century. For example, the 1812 edition of *Johnson and Warner's Almanac* carries a scathing rebuke of astrologers, referring to them as "imposters who thrive by the folly of others." "He pretends to foretel [*sic*] events many years before they happen," the editor snorts, "which no man can do, unassisted by revelation." Readers are urged to banish from their minds the "vain" and "sinful curiosity" of predicting the future.[43] And the *Mechanics' Almanac, and Astronomical Ephemeris* for 1825 omitted the Anatomy because, its editors reasoned, "in this present refined state of Science, it is high time that this last relic of Astrology should be expunged from our Almanacs; for however credulous the ignorant and unlearned may be, Astronomers *know*, that the Moon has no more influence over the parts of the human body, than the parts of the human body have over the Moon."[44]

If a majority of early American almanac makers were critical of astrology, why did they allow it to become a staple of their productions? Why did some of astrology's most avowed critics, such as Christian Lodowick, Thomas Robie, and Jacob Taylor, insert astrological material, including weather predictions, phases of the moon, and calendar columns indicating the moon's place, into their almanacs? For answers, one might look to Titan Leeds's poem that accompanies a cut of the Anatomy in his 1725 almanac.

> *Should I omit to place this figure here,*
> *My book would hardly sell another Year.*
> What (*quoth my Country Friend*) d ye think I'll buy
> An Almanack without th' Anatomy?
> *As for its Use, nor he nor I can tell;*
> *However since it pleases all so well,*
> *I've put it in because my Book should sell.*[45]

In this poem, Leeds encapsulates many early American almanac makers' views of astrology. Although he poked fun at the practice and those readers who believed in it, and made light of his own motives for including it, Leeds, one suspects, never considered omitting astrology from his almanac. Almanac makers who dared to omit the Anatomy or astrology altogether courted a reader backlash. Such was the experience of Samuel Clough. After deciding not to include the Anatomy in his 1701 almanac, Clough changed his mind the next year: "I have at the desire of several Country People, added the *Anatomy*, with the *Moons* [*sic*] place, and parts of mans [*sic*] Body she governs, as she passeth through the 12 Signs (a thing omitted the last year) which is of use to them in cutting their Creatures." In the 1704 edition he concedes:

> The *Anatomy's* set here again,
> To know what part the *Sign* is in;
> For if it hath not have his seat;
> The *Almanack* is not compleat.[46]

Like Clough and many other almanac makers of the eighteenth and nineteenth centuries, "Frank Freeman" strongly believed that planetary influences were "altogether imaginary." He saw no reason to include astrology in his first annual, which appeared in 1767. But though he sold three thousand copies that year, he admitted that many potential readers "did refuse to buy because of the omissions."[47] Isaiah Thomas omitted the Anatomy and weather predictions in his 1799 almanac to "make room for more important articles," asserting that the Anatomy and weather predictions "can only be of use to those who deal in the marvelous." That both appeared with regularity in subsequent years suggests that Thomas received an angry response from his readers.[48] The compiler of the 1801 *Virginia & North Carolina Almanack* may have faced the same hostility as Thomas. The former grudgingly admitted that "there are many people, even in this 'enlightened country,' who still believe in this pretended Art, and, with whom, an Almanack is thought to be very imperfect that does not display the influence of the Stars, etc." Likewise, the compiler of *Stoddard's Diary; or, the Columbia Almanack* for 1833 thought that the supposed influence of the moon was "a relic of ancient astrology, which, in this enlightened age, ought to be exploded." Yet astrology was included in the issue "in compliance with the wishes of many of our readers."[49] More than twenty years later, according to the publisher of *Webster's Calendar or the Albany Almanac*, the situation had not changed: "In this country the almanacs have gone no farther than to publish the column of the Moon's influence on the parts of the human body. This has become obnoxious to many, but it affords a very harmless pastime to others; and its omission would be highly resented by a portion of the patrons of this almanac, who think they stand in need of no instruction, and decline to see the force of any argument against the power of the moon."[50]

Do the passages cited above provide an accurate picture of astrological belief and practice in America before the Civil War? Was there, as almanac makers suggest, a vocal constituency of readers who demanded astrology and astrological health advice in their almanacs? If so, what can this tell us about astrology's role in the health beliefs and practices of early Americans? Or had astrological information, including health advice, become essentially irrelevant—"a very harmless pastime"—to readers by the 1850s? Unfortunately, these questions are difficult to answer because of inadequate documentation concerning the state of astrology and astrological medicine in early America.

The first generations of colonists who immigrated to Massachusetts Bay in the seventeenth century would have encountered an environment more hostile to the practice of astrology than the one they left in England. The Puritan ideal of a Christian society free from European traditions of magic and the occult dictated condemnation of a belief in astrology and its practice. Yet as settlements grew and increasingly complex religious configurations took shape, practices that would have been frowned upon by Puritan leaders, such as astrology, fortune telling, and palmistry, emerged among a significant portion of the population. The appearance of astrology in almanacs during the late seventeenth century reflects this trend.[51]

Puritan divines and men of science unanimously condemned judicial astrology as blasphemous. Natural astrology, too, was often criticized, but Puritan leaders were divided in their opinions of this form of the practice. Christian Lodowick's condemnation of his fellow almanac maker John Tulley in his 1695 almanac exemplifies this ambivalence. Either Lodowick did not see or he chose to ignore the apparent contradiction between his words and his actions: the same issue includes weather predictions and a calendar column for the moon's place.[52] Cotton Mather was a leading crusader against all aspects of astrology, yet his depth of knowledge of the subject implies serious study on his part. Some Puritan writers admitted that the heavens influenced—but did not control—earthly events such as the weather. For example, Puritan divine Charles Morton, whose *Compendium Physicae* was used as a natural science text by Harvard students from the 1680s to the 1720s, believed that the stars exerted both a direct and indirect influence over terrestrial bodies.[53]

Further evidence of Puritan ambivalence can be found in the series of Harvard almanacs. Although they omitted weather predictions and images of the Anatomy, almanac compilers inserted such astronomical information as phases of the moon and locations of the planets, knowing that this information could be used by readers to make their own astrological predictions. Moreover, 87 percent of New England almanacs issued between 1646 and 1700 included a column in the calendar section on the moon's place in the zodiac. And when other New England almanac makers began offering astrology, Puritan leaders made no attempts to censure these publications.[54]

Colonial Americans, whether learned or barely literate, would have brought knowledge of astrology with them from their native lands. In

America those from England would have been exposed to astrology through the magic-occult practices of non-English European immigrants, especially those from German-speaking countries, and, of course, print. Texts that contained sections on astrology, such as Culpeper's *English Physician; and Complete Herbal*, William Salmon's *Compendium of Physick, Chirurgery, and Anatomy*, and various editions of *Erra Pater*, circulated widely in early America, especially among the middling to lower orders.[55] Through these publications, readers would have learned (or have had oral traditions reinforced) that the four seasons were related to the four humors: the cold, wet, "watery" winter; the hot, moist, "airy" spring; the hot, dry, "fiery" summer; and the cold, dry, "earthy" winter. Although few readers may have had the knowledge and expertise to predict the course of a disease or ailment, they could easily have learned the effects of planetary alignments on various herbs as well as the influence of the moon's place on various parts of the body. The image of the Anatomy would have helped the barely literate understand which signs governed the various parts of the body. That many of astrology's fundamental principles were widely known and used by many readers of almanacs may explain why almanac makers omitted explanations of the astrological information they presented in their publications.[56]

Even the learned reader would have been exposed to the works of Culpeper and other writers who supported some of the tenets of astrology. Library lists from late seventeenth- and early eighteenth-century Virginia estate inventories, for example, point to widespread ownership of occult and magic books.[57] But eighteenth-century proponents of astrology were not confined to those who wrote cheap books for the less affluent and less educated. The eminent English physician Richard Mead, whose 1704 *Treatise Concerning the Influence of the Sun and Moon Upon Human Bodies, and the Diseases Thereby Produced* appeared in many editions, acknowledged that celestial bodies could affect the weather, health, and the atmosphere. Of the moon's influence over the earth, Mead writes: "This powerful action of the moon is observed not only by philosophers and natural historians, but even by the common people, who have been fully persuaded of it time out of mind. *Pliny* relates, that *Aristotle* laid it down as an aphorism: *that no animal dies but in the ebb of the tide.* And that births and deaths chiefly happen about the new and full-moon, is an axiom even among women. The husbandmen likewise are regulated by the moon in planetary in planting and managing trees, and several other of their occupations. So great is the empire of the moon over the terraqueous globe."[58] Mead's work would have found its way into the libraries of educated Americans. And so, too, would that of the American writer Jared Eliot, whose 1760 work *Essays Upon Field Husbandry in New England* supports accommodating the signs of the zodiac to science: "The Learned know well enough, that the division of the Zodiac into Twelve Signs, and the appropriating these to the several Parts of the animal Body, is not the Work of Nature, but of Art, contrived by Astronomers for Convenience. It is also well known that the Moon's Attraction hath great Influence on all Fluids. It is also well known to Farmers that there are Times when Bushes, if cut at such a Time, will universally die. A Regard to the sign as it serveth to point out and direct the proper Time, so it becomes worthy of Observation."[59]

Though it was attacked by clergymen as the work of the devil, ridiculed by many of the learned as a practice of the ignorant and the superstitious, and even scorned by numerous almanac makers, astrology survived and continued to attract a strong following among ordinary Americans, both white and black, and even elicited some interest (in natural astrology) from the learned.[60] When the first almanacs appeared in colonies outside of New England during the first decades of the eighteenth century, astrology and astrological health advice were regular features. Astrology remained a staple in American almanacs throughout the remainder of the century and into the first half of the nineteenth. But whether its emergence as a staple in American almanacs accurately reflects its popularity and its use in early America is difficult to determine because of the fragmentary, mainly anecdotal, evidence available.

When the Reverend Ezra Stiles of Newport, Rhode Island recorded in his diary the May 1773 death of Joseph Stafford, a noted astrologer and fellow townsman, the clergyman claimed that the deceased and other "Almanack Makers and Fortune Tellers" were the last manifestations of an "antient [sic] System" that was "broken up." Astrology, Stiles believed, was a "Vessel of Sorcery shipwreckt [sic], and only some scattered planks disjoyned [sic] floating and scattered on the Ocean of the human Activity and Bustle."[61] Several modern historians agree with Stiles's assessment. According to this school of thought, a belief in any form of astrology, as a result of scientific advances, ceased among most Americans by the beginning of the nineteenth century. Peter Eisenstadt, for example, has argued that, with the emergence of the science of meteorology, astrology's role in weather prediction declined. Most recently, he asserted that astrology in general barely survived the eighteenth century.[62] Jon Butler and John Brooke contend that although astrology survived well into the nineteenth century, its practice was confined to the poorer, more marginal segments of American society. Herbert Leventhal claims that, although astrology in general suffered a gradual decline in America during the eighteenth century, medical astrology survived—presumably among the groups mentioned by Butler and Brooke—much longer, thanks primarily to the popularity of almanacs.[63]

Leventhal emphasizes the important link between astrology and almanacs. Outside of reprints of much older works of Culpeper, Salmon, and *Erra Pater*, almanacs were the only publications providing astrological health advice before the Civil War. Several astrology texts—learned and popular—were printed in this period. But these publications focused more on fortune telling than the astrology one would encounter in almanacs.[64] Few of the numerous eighteenth- and nineteenth-century popular medical books, except for those referred to earlier, contained astrological health information of any kind.

Astrology enjoyed a revival in England during the first decades of the nineteenth century. James Wilson's *Complete Dictionary of Astrology* (1816) and Robert C. Smith's *Manual of Astrology* (1828) were the leading works of this revival and both circulated widely in the United States. Beginning in the 1840s, the United States witnessed its own boom of sorts, with the appearance of the first American periodicals devoted to astrology, *Hauge's Horoscope* (1840–41) and *Hauge's Horoscope and Scientific and Literary Messenger* (1845–48), both published by the Philadelphia "Astro-Meteorologist" Thomas Hauge. These publications were followed over the next few decades by a number of astrology monographs and periodicals.[65] But, like the fortune-telling texts of the antebellum period, these works were devoted primarily to judicial astrology. The scores of astrology books and magazines found in today's chain bookstores and at supermarket checkout counters that promise success in everything from business to marriage, as well as the daily horoscopes carried by virtually every American newspaper and growing numbers of Internet sites, can be traced to this mid-nineteenth-century revival.

The books and periodicals produced by this revival added very little to the traditional content of medical astrology. Yet the proliferation of these publications, which would have been directed to urban, middle-class readers, suggests that astrology was popular with segments of the American population broader than the marginal groups referred to by John Brooke and Jon Butler. The small boom in astrology that occurred in mid-nineteenth-century America indicates, I believe, a vibrant—but largely undocumented—interest in practices that, like astrology, were considered out of the mainstream or unconventional by the standards of the time.

Evidence concerning a belief in and practice of astrology in nineteenth-century America may be slim, but there are clues, which, if viewed in their totality, provide a glimpse of astrology's popularity. For example, Ward H. Lamon, in his 1872 biography of Abraham Lincoln, attempts to recreate for the reader the rural, backwoods world of early nineteenth-century Indiana in which the future president of the United States spent his youth. In an effort to portray Lincoln's rise from humble beginnings as a great achievement, Lamon describes a primitive environment "filled with superstitions . . . as antiquated as witch burning."

> Every thing must be done at certain "times and seasons," else it would be attended with "bad luck." They must cut trees for rails in the early part of the day, and in "the light of the moon"; otherwise, the fence would sink. Potatoes and other roots were to be planted in the "dark of the moon," but trees, and plants which bore their fruits above ground, must be "put out in the light of the moon." The moon exerted a fearful influence, either kindly or malignant, as the good old rules were observed or not. It was even required to make soap "in the light of the moon," and, moreover, it must be stirred only one way, and by one person. Nothing of importance was to be begun on Friday. All enterprises inaugurated on that day went fatally amiss. A horse-colt could be begotten only "in the dark of the moon," and animals treated otherwise than "according to the signs in the almanac" were nearly sure to die.[66]

While Lamon's glimpse of backwoods Indiana would seem to support the arguments of Brooke and Butler, there is evidence to support the claim that a belief in astrology was not confined solely to the poor and semi-literate. In April 1832, Christopher Columbus Baldwin, the librarian of the American Antiquarian Society, received a visit from Sullivan Sheffield, an astrologist from Hopkinton, Massachusetts. The visit lasted three hours, during which time Sheffield informed Baldwin that he earned about three hundred dollars a year for his astrological services, most frequently rendered in predicting the outcome of lawsuits and other legal matters. The astrologist also mentioned that he helped people find stolen property and locate lost relatives.[67]

Sheffield, like Joseph Stafford, carried out his business in and around

where he lived. Yet, as Peter Benes has shown, there were numerous astrologers, fortune-tellers, "wise-men," and magical healers who traveled
throughout New England during the eighteenth century and the first half
of the nineteenth. According to Benes, these transient or semi-transient
fortune-tellers and healers were consulted primarily by "unmarried
young persons or by adults engaged in high-risk maritime and mercantile
callings, such as fishermen, seamen, merchants, and shipowners," not the
poorer, more marginal segments of society. This trade continued to flour-
ish in the face of continual attacks by clergymen and other civic leaders.
One suspects that other parts of the country had their own cadre of trav-
eling astrologers, cunning men, magic healers, and fortune-tellers.[68]

A belief in and practice of astrology and astrological rules of health persisted throughout nineteenth-century America despite the protests of various religious and civic leaders and the ridicule it received from the learned.
Astrological health advice would have made sense to many Americans,
especially those who were less educated and culturally isolated, because
it would have fit in with their traditional notions of health, disease, and
the body and how the body interacts with its environment. Let us return
again to *Webster's Calendar, or the Albany Almanac*, this time to the 1849
edition. In an editorial titled "Lunar Influence," the compiler cites a recent
article by an eminent British agriculturist who asserted that a belief in the
moon's influence over the weather was one of the most popular errors
of that time. In response, the compiler issued a strong rebuke: " 'Popular
error,' indeed! Popular fiddlestick. . . . It is well that the Moon itself is out
of reach of this sort of fellows, lest they should attempt to pull it down
altogether, with as little ceremony as they would any Yankee nation. Now
we have no trouble about the weather in this region, where the people
enjoy the utmost confidence in the Moon, weaning their children and kill-
ing their pigs under the proper signs, as laid down in this almanac, and
living in peace and plenty." [69] This passage represents one of the few by a
nineteenth-century almanac maker that supports astrology. By the 1850s
most almanac makers or publishers were either critical of or remained
silent about astrology. Yet astrology was just as much an integral part of
their almanacs as it had been of those of their eighteenth-century predecessors. Whether they looked upon astrology or astrological health advice
as superstition or merely outdated and harmless whimsy, they rightly
sensed that it was still relevant to an important segment of their readership—especially those about whom the compiler of *Webster's Calendar*
wrote.

By the 1850s the golden age of almanacs had passed. A genre that once dominated the market of secular print had lost ground to newspapers, magazines, novels, and specialty almanacs. By the middle of the century American almanac makers and publishers were attempting to hold on to a tenuous niche in an increasingly competitive market. Leading cultural mediators in the eighteenth century, almanac makers and publishers were forced to become aggressive entrepreneurs in the nineteenth. They correctly sensed that while astrology was scorned by the educated and worldly, it remained popular with a segment of their traditional core audience of literate and semi-literate artisans, farmers, and laborers who tended to live in a rural environment where they were more culturally isolated than the typical educated urban dweller. Many within this core audience still clung to the rituals and practices of folklore and folk medicine. Despite their own views of astrology, almanac makers knew that to succeed in the market of print they could ill afford to alienate this important constituency. But they also hoped to maintain the respect and retain the patronage of learned readers. Thus, they strove to minimize the amount of astrology they presented, even criticizing it, and offered information that would appeal to a more sophisticated audience—a growing middle-class urban readership—in an effort to attract customers who increasingly looked upon almanacs and the astrology they contained as relics from an earlier age.

This was a risky endeavor, but it seemed to work—at least until the 1850s. Early American almanac makers were not innovators; they eschewed change and novelty and embraced the tried and the true. In short, they gave their readers what they wanted. Unfortunately for almanac makers and publishers, the print world of the 1840s and 1850s in which they toiled had changed dramatically from the golden days of Ames, Franklin, and Robert P. Thomas. In their attempts to please disparate groups, to be all things to all readers, almanac makers and publishers failed to meet the needs of any one group, except, perhaps the remnants of their core readership, a constituency that, by the 1850s, had lost the economic clout it once had to an expanding urban middle-class readership that exerted an increasingly powerful influence on the print market.

THE ALMANAC was one of several genres of popular print in early America that disseminated lay health advice in the form of remedies and regimens. Americans seeking a cure for a particular ailment or advice on how to live a healthy life could consult numerous domestic medical guides, regimen texts, popular health periodicals, newspapers, and domestic economy books. The almanac complemented these publications. But astrology in general and astrological health advice in particular were another matter. Because there were few astrology publications of any kind issued in America before the middle of the nineteenth century, almanacs were the leading source of such information in these early years. Later, almanacs became identified by many as an outdated vehicle for astrology. And eventually this assessment led, for better or worse, to the marginalization of the almanac as a genre of print. Nevertheless, by gradually changing the way they presented astrology, moving from an active, instructional approach to a more ambivalent, passive approach in response to the desires of a key segment of their readership, almanac makers helped astrology survive (if only within certain segments of American society) and thus shaped contemporary and future perceptions of the practice.

ADVICE FOR THE
AFFLICTED

In ADDITION to astrological advice, early American almanacs offered remedies for various ailments and regimen prescriptions for health and long life. This chapter examines remedies or "cures" offered by American almanacs for dropsy, dysentery, and rheumatism, three afflictions that were common among Americans between 1750 and 1860, and presents several examples that demonstrate the similarity between these remedies and those offered by other genres of print and domestic manuscript recipe and remedy books.

The almanac was just one of several sources to which early Americans would have turned for therapeutic advice. What, then, was its role in popular therapeutics? What influence, if any, did it have in shaping popular assumptions concerning the body, health, and disease? What influence did these assumptions have on the almanac?

Of the pre-1860 American general almanacs consulted for this study, less than 30 percent contain therapeutic advice. This figure is misleading, however, when one considers the fact that this type of advice did not begin to appear in almanacs with any regularity until the middle of the eighteenth century. From the 1750s to 1860, the percentages of almanacs that offered therapeutic advice increased to about 40 percent and even higher in the middle-Atlantic and southern parts of the country.[1] This advice covered a variety of afflictions, ranging from common bruises, colds, corns, earaches, headaches, and warts to more serious and potentially life-threatening complaints such as dropsy, whooping cough, consumption, "bloody flux" (dysentery), bladder stones, and various fevers. These remedies tended to emphasize the medicinal properties of plants, herbs, nuts, and barks that were readily available to lay practitioners, though it was not uncommon for a reader to encounter remedies composed of animal substances and a variety of chemical and mineral ingredients. Several almanacs described the medicinal uses of various herbs and plants, but most did not, probably assuming that either their readers already knew this information or they could readily find it elsewhere.[2] While many remedies appear to have been supplied by almanac compilers or printers or borrowed from other published sources, such as newspapers, domestic health guides, and other almanacs, some were contributed by almanac readers.

The remedies found in early American almanacs—like those encountered in other general and health-related publications of the time—were informed by shared assumptions concerning the body, health, and disease that were profoundly influenced by the theory of humoralism. Humoralism, which originated with the Hippocratic School and was later formalized by Galen (129–ca. 210), interpreted health as a natural balance of the body's humors (yellow bile, blood, phlegm, and black bile) and their respective elements or qualities (hot and dry, hot and moist, cold and moist, cold and dry). The body was viewed in holistic terms; all parts were interrelated. Thus, when one part of the body was disrupted by disease, the rest of the body was also affected. The body was also viewed as an equilibrium system that constantly interacted with its environment. This interaction was visible in the body's system of intake and outgo, a process through which the body constantly strove to achieve a harmonious balance of its humors. Illness was the result not of a specific disease but of humoral imbalance.

Humoral imbalance was caused by too much or too little of one or more elements or qualities. For example, an overabundance of heat indicated the presence of fever in the body; conversely, the absence of heat in the body implied the presence of a "cold." Health was restored when balance was restored; prolonged imbalance, however, could lead to death. The primary role of therapeutics, then, was to restore balance by treating the symptoms of imbalance. Treatment meant administering medicines with properties opposite to those associated with the humoral imbalance. Thus a drug exhibiting "hot" properties would have been used to alleviate an overabundance of "cold" in the body. A drug would also be administered to aid in restoring balance. Balance was restored by depleting the system through a variety of measures, such as bleeding, administering cathartics (to induce defecation), diuretics (to induce urination), and emetics (to induce vomiting); or by strengthening the system through the use of restorative measures that included narcotics and tonics. The remedies encountered in early American almanacs comprised plant, vegetable, animal, chemical, and mineral substances that produced a predicted physiological effect, such as sweating, salivation, or evacuation. Most laypersons understood the humoral system, and both almanac makers and almanac readers assumed that, in an age when trained physicians were few and expensive, the maintenance and the restoration of health were, for the most part, the layperson's responsibility.[3]

The humoral tradition that dominated American lay practice well into the nineteenth century differed, however, from that espoused by Galen and his followers. Beginning in the early seventeenth century, humoralism was challenged by several competing systems and, as a result, by the end of the eighteenth century some of its Hippocratic–Galenic trappings had been discarded. Early American lay as well as professional practitioners took a modified humoral, or neohumoral, approach to therapeutics, one that fused elements of two alternate systems—Paracelsian and solidism—with the basic tenets of humoralism.

In contrast to the Galenic system, Paracelsus (1493–1541) and his followers asserted that diseases were not simply the result of humoral imbalance but were specific entities with specific external causes. And because diseases were specific entities (caused by chemical disturbances), they required specific remedies. Paracelsus and adherents of his philosophy, including Nicholas Culpeper, whose works were popular with lay practitioners and readers, recommended various chemical and mineral remedies, such as mercury, antimony, and arsenic for specific disorders. Chemical and mineral remedies, according to the Paracelsians, were closer to the prime matter from which God created the universe—a process that they believed resembled a chemical separation. Although the Paracelsian approach to disease and therapeutics did not replace humoralism, it certainly influenced it. Its impact on American lay and professional practice is clearly evident in the numerous chemical and mineral ingredients (e.g., mercury, cream of tarter or sodium potassium) that appeared in early American pharmacopoeias, professional medical texts, domestic health guides, family recipe books, and, of course, almanacs.[4]

During the eighteenth century humoralism was further modified—at least among learned physicians—by new theories that saw illness as a condition caused by an abnormal tension or laxity in the body's nervous and vascular systems, which could destabilize humoral balance. For example, Friedrich Hoffmann (1660–1742) viewed the body as something akin to a hydraulic machine that ran smoothly when a mysterious fluid circulated through the nervous system and blood vessels ensuring tone to the muscles and an unimpeded motion of the humors. Disease occurred as a result of muscular tension or weakness that impeded the circulation of the fluid, thus causing humoral imbalance. Hermann Boerhaave (1668–1738) developed a system of medicine that fused humoralism with other competing theories, such as Hoffmann's, that emphasized nervous and vascular tension. Boerhaave asserted that the body was made up of two main components, fluids and solids (vessels that carry bodily fluids). The body was in a state of health when these two components freely interacted; disease was the result of defective interaction caused by weak or rigid blood vessels. Boerhaave's student William Cullen (1710–1790), professor of medicine at Edinburgh, posited that disease resulted from a nervous system that was either over-stimulated or excessively weakened. Like the humoral doctrine, the vascular or tension theories—also known as solidism—viewed health as a state of balance and disease as one of imbalance. Similarly, their respective therapies were designed to deplete or strengthen a system to restore balance. Because of their similarities, humoralism and solidism, according to J. Worth Estes, "were not mutually exclusive" in early American medical practice. Both concepts "were used to explain the signs and symptoms of any given disease" and both "were exploited in the design of appropriate therapy, chosen so as to fine-tune all disturbed balances simultaneously."[5]

To the religious or providential explanations of health and disease held by many early Americans, especially seventeenth-century New Englanders, were added the various medical beliefs, traditions, and experiences of Native Americans, as well as those brought to America by European and African immigrants. Despite these different belief systems concerning health and disease that were either imported or developed here, early Americans seemed to agree on the fundamental notions of humoralism. Views of health and disease within African American communities, for example, were influenced heavily by magic and spiritual beliefs, yet their diagnostic and therapeutic systems were based on a balance model. The seventeenth-century New Englanders who held a providential view of disease simultaneously held a mechanistic view. Puritan clergymen who practiced medicine did so within the confines of humoralism.[6]

Almanac remedies for dropsy and dysentery, both potentially fatal, and for rheumatism provide useful examples of therapeutic assumptions and practices among early Americans. Before examining the various almanac "cures" for these ailments, however, it should be noted that to identify the affliction for which a cure was sought, almanac readers would have had to turn to a family member, a neighbor, a local practitioner or mid-wife, or a printed source. Printed sources that included descriptions of diseases, their symptoms, and their treatments became more accessible in the eighteenth and nineteenth centuries as lay health guides were issued in increasing numbers and became more affordable.[7]

Dropsy

The condition once called dropsy is viewed as symptom of congestive heart failure, kidney and liver failure, and malnutrition. In the seventeenth and eighteenth centuries and well into the nineteenth dropsy was considered a specific disease that denoted an abnormal accumulation of fluid in the body.[8] To a layperson of the time, the edema and pain associated with dropsy would have signified a humoral imbalance that was potentially fatal if not rectified soon. The humoral model of disease helped the patient and practitioner make sense of the clinical manifestations of the malady and provided a framework in which to understand and alleviate it.

From the mid-eighteenth century through the first decades of the nineteenth, almanac readers would have encountered numerous remedies for this disease, much like the one offered by the 1787 *Wilmington Almanack*. This particular "Cure for Dropsy," submitted by Jonathan Zane, resulted in depletion, or, to be more precise, urination. At one time much "swelled" with excess water and unable to locate a trained physician or local practitioner who could relieve his distress, Zane eventually discovered an effective remedy that he wanted to share with other almanac readers. After consuming an "ounce of Salt Petre dissolved in a pint of cold water" every morning and evening for five days, Zane explains, his "evacuations of water were increased," and he was "much relieved."[9]

The purpose of Zane's "Cure for Dropsy" was to rid the body of excess water in order to achieve a state of equilibrium. The dropsy remedies that appeared in American almanacs from the eighteenth century through the first half of the nineteenth were consistent in that they comprised ingredients that would result in elimination of excess fluid. *Poor Richard improved* for 1764 offers a dropsy cure that includes artichoke leaves. This same remedy subsequently appeared in the *South-Carolina & Georgia Almanack* for 1767 and the *Poor Will's Almanack* for 1771.[10] A dropsy remedy in the 1766 issue of the *South Carolina & Georgia Almanack* includes dwarf elder, which would have induced vomiting, defecation, and urination.[11] "A Diet Drink for the Dropsy" in the *Burlington Almanack* for 1772 includes several ingredients to promote depletion: "horse radish root two handfuls, cuttings of small branches of grape vine two handfuls, inner bark of elder two handfuls, sassafras root four handfuls, parsley root two handfuls, fennel seed two handfuls, scurvy grass two handfuls, burdoc root four handfuls, nettle roots two handfuls, elecampane roots one handful, garlic one ounce, rusty iron four pounds."[12] The ingredients in "Cure for the Dropsy" in the 1793 issue of *Hutchins Improved* almanac were meant to promote urination: "Take a six quart jug of old hard cyder [*sic*], put therein a pint of mustard-seed, one double handful of parsley-roots, one double-handful of lignum vitae shavings, and one double handful of horse radish root: let them simper [*sic*] together over a slow fire forty-eight hours, when it will be fit for use. Take a tea cup full of this liquor three times a day, and it will work off the disorder by urine, without any trouble to the patient."[13]

Almanacs issued during the first half of the nineteenth century continued to offer dropsy remedies similar to those of the previous century. The *South Carolina & Georgia Almanac* for 1800 contains a cure for dropsy that recommends cream of tartar because "it will bring away a great deal of water, with little or no pain."[14] A cure in *Bioren's Town and Country Almanack* for 1810 includes parsley roots, horse radish, mustard seed, oxymel of squill, and juniper berries. This same remedy later appeared in the *Citizen & Farmer's Almanac* for 1816.[15] The 1824 issue of the *Farmer's Almanac* (New York) offers readers a cure for dropsy that comprises many of the ingredients recommended by *Bioren's Town and Country Almanack* and the *Citizen & Farmer's Almanac* published six years earlier and more than three decades earlier by *Hutchins Improved* almanac. The *Farmer's Almanac's* "recipe" calls for "a double handful of parsley roots . . . a handful of horse radish scraped, two table spoonsful [*sic*] of pounded mustard seed," and "half an ounce of juniper berries." After the water had "passed off," the patient is advised to regain strength by engaging in "moderate exercise," subsisting on "nourishing food" and abstaining from liquor "as much as possible." [16] The 1838 issue of a Pennsylvania agricultural almanac includes a dropsy remedy that had appeared earlier in a Kentucky newspaper. This "recipe" calls for cinder ash mixed with a pint of honey, which causes the patient "to discharge great quantities of water, purgatively and by urine." [17] Two years later the same almanac published another dropsy remedy that recommends broom seed, assuring readers that nothing "can be more gentle and safe than the operation of this remedy" and if dropsy is in the body, this remedy "discharges it by urine [and] . . . if it is between the skin and flesh, it causes blisters." [18]

The components and expected physiological results of eighteenth- and early nineteenth-century almanac remedies for dropsy were similar to those collected and recorded by laypersons in daybooks, recipe books, and family health journals and prescribed by writers of domestic health guides and professional textbooks and treatises. For example, Moses Appleton, a physician who practiced in Waterville, Maine, at the end of the eighteenth century, recorded in his medical recipe book a "Cure for Dropsy" that had been published in the *New York Herald*. The remedy, consisting of parsley roots, horseradish, mustard seeds, juniper berries, and squills, contains many of the ingredients referred to in the seventeenth-century almanac remedies discussed earlier and is essentially the same one that later appeared in *Bioren's Town and Country Almanack* (1810) and the *Citizen & Farmer's Almanac* (1816): "Put into a stone or earthern [sic] jug a gallon of stale, sound Cider, together with a double handfull of Parsly [sic] roots & tops cut fine; an handful of horseradish scraped; two table spoonfuls of bruised Mustard seed, ½ ounce of Oxymel of squills, one ounce of Juniper berries—The Liquor to be kept warm by the fire twenty four hours, to be often agitated then strained for use." [19]

Kay Moss, in her study of early southern folk medicine, consulted several manuscript recipe and commonplace books and found many dropsy remedies that contained juniper berries, broom, horseradish, mustard, and squills. For example, William Lenoir, of North Carolina, began compiling a book of cures during the first decade of the nineteenth century and continued the practice for the next thirty years. Many of his remedies came from friends and neighbors, as well as from almanacs and newspapers. One of his entries, "Cure for Dropsy," was taken from an almanac and is a slightly modified version of the one Moses Appleton copied from the *New York Herald*.[20] Lenoir's version was taken from an almanac (possibly one of those referred to earlier) whose compiler may have copied it from the *New York Herald*, another newspaper, or another printed source or may have received it from a reader. Whatever the details, occurrences like this were common; it was not unusual for the same remedy to circulate among various genres of popular print—an indication that readers, writers, and printers were consulting and sharing, and borrowing from various sources when seeking health advice.

Eighteenth- and early nineteenth-century readers who made use of the various almanac dropsy remedies would have expected a certain physiological result—an evacuation of some kind that would restore the bodily balance necessary to health. Their knowledge of a certain remedy's ingredients and their expectations concerning physiological results would have been learned or reinforced through oral transmission, trial and error, and consultation of the numerous genres of contemporary print. For example, William Buchan, in his widely read work *Domestic Medicine*, recommends a dropsy treatment that is based on the principle of restoring bodily equilibrium. For the young and robust patient, Buchan advocates "strong vomits, brisk purges, and such medicines as promise a discharge of sweat and urine." Between vomits, induced by a half a dram of ipecacuanha and half an ounce of oxymel of squills, the patient is advised to take a purge of jalap, cream of tartar, and calomel. Before retiring for the night, the patient should take a bolus of five grams of camphor, one grain of opium, and "as much syrup of orange peel as is sufficient." The bolus, according to Buchan, would "generally promote a gentle sweat," which should be "encouraged" by occasionally drinking a small cup of wine mixed with a teaspoonful of a diuretic infusion composed of juniper berries, mustard seed, and ashes of broom.[21]

John Gunn of Knoxville, Tennessee, the nineteenth-century author of *Gunn's Domestic Medicine*, was a strong advocate of bleeding in cases of dropsy. "More diseases of dropsy," he asserts, "have been removed by bleeding, and more relief has been obtained from it, than from any other known remedy." In Gunn's remedy, purges of calomel and jalap accompany bleeding. He recommends a drink of cream of tartar in water, because "all articles which increase the flow of urine, or water from the bladder, called by the physician *diuretics*, are very useful in this complaint." The bark of common elder, according to Gunn, is also an effective remedy for dropsy. "I have used it myself, with universal success," he claims, "and its immediate adoption by the afflicted is truly important and deserving attention." Gunn offers his readers several examples of dropsy cures that contain common elder, including one—though he does not acknowledge this—that is a shortened version of a remedy published in an 1829 Pennsylvania agricultural almanac, whose compiler had borrowed it from an 1828 issue of the *Salem Gazette* (an indication that the remedy may have had earlier vernacular roots). The newspaper had received the remedy from a reader: "Take two handfuls of the green or inner bark of the white common elder; steep them in two quarts of Lisbon wine twenty four hours—if the wine cannot be had, Teneriffe or Madeira will answer: take a gill every morning, fasting, or more if it can be borne by the stomach. The bark and leaves of the elder, have long been known as powerful evacuants." [22]

Most of the dropsy remedies in early American almanacs make no reference to the form of the complaint they are supposed to alleviate. Domestic health guides, for the most part, differentiate the various forms of dropsy, such as abdominal, ovarian, and hydrocephalus, but most prescribe general remedies similar to those found in almanacs. Specific treatments for different forms of dropsy do appear, however, in the professional literature of the time. One suspects that few almanac readers would have consulted a professional text. But if they had, they would have encountered remedies for various forms of dropsy that contained ingredients similar to those found in many almanac cures.[23]

With the advent of various medical sects in the first quarter of the nineteenth century, laypersons were offered therapeutic advice different from that promulgated by regular physicians and writers of mainstream domestic health guides. Thomsonians, botanical doctors, and eclectics (followed in the 1840s and 1850s by homeopaths and hydrotherapists) issued books, periodicals, and newspapers promoting therapeutic practices that assisted nature and were more efficacious and safe compared with the harsh, unnatural measures of the regular medical profession. Sectarian books and pamphlets, especially those of Samuel Thomson and the eclectic Wooster Beach, were very popular, appearing in numerous editions.[24]

Thomson and other botanical practitioners based their therapeutic advice on views of health and disease that varied little from those discussed earlier in this chapter. Like members of the regular profession, Thomsonians and other botanical doctors espoused a one-dimensional system that did not recognize specific diseases. Where they diverged from regular physicians and many mainstream authors of domestic health guides, however, was in their views of bodily heat. According to Thomson, heat was the most important of the body's four elements. A variation of humoralism, Thomson's theory of health and disease was based on the centrality of heat to balance. His therapeutic measures therefore sought to restore balance by restoring the body's heat rather than lowering it. This was accomplished through a combination of powerful herb emetics (especially *Lobelia inflata* or, as it was popularly known, Indian tobacco, puke-weed, vomitwort, and gagroot), spicy botanical medicines (cayenne, black pepper, and ginger) that generated heat, and steam treatments.[25]

Wooster Beach, the founder of a movement subsequently known as eclecticism, also espoused botanic remedies—specifically those containing plants indigenous to the United States—while condemning the regular profession's widespread practice of bloodletting and use of mineral drugs. Beach and his followers, as the name of their movement implies, fashioned a therapeutic approach that incorporated aspects of the practices of Thomson, other botanical practitioners, and certain depletive measures (strong vegetable purges and a moderate use of some chemical preparations) used by the regular profession. Eclectics believed that the healer's primary role was, in the words of their founder, "the servant, or handmaid of nature." Disease, Beach argued, was "a healthy effort of nature rather than otherwise, or a restorative process to bring about healthy action." He and his followers thus prescribed remedies that assisted this process of restoration through the use of vegetable purges, plasters, ointments, and stimulants to revive evacuations or to strengthen the system.[26] Although the ingredients of their dropsy remedies may have differed from those prescribed by regular physicians and writers of mainstream domestic health guides, Thomson, other botanical practitioners, and Beach had the same objective in mind—restoring balance by promoting the elimination of excess fluid.

It is unlikely, however, that readers of early nineteenth-century general almanacs would have encountered dropsy remedies similar to those prescribed by Thomson and Beach, for these tended to appear only in special botanical almanacs or other sectarian publications. Yet, if they had consulted—either by chance or by intent—one or more of the many sectarian publications that circulated in early America, they would have understood the intended physiological results of the dropsy remedies espoused by Thomsonians and eclectics. From the mid-eighteenth century through the first half of the nineteenth, almanac dropsy remedies varied little from those found in contemporary manuscript sources, newspapers, domestic health guides, and professional textbooks and treatises. And while almanac dropsy cures included fewer references to bleeding than remedies encountered in domestic health guides and professional texts, they included a much higher percentage of chemical and mineral ingredients found in sectarian publications.[27]

Bloody Flux (Dysentery)

Dysentery is an inflammation of the large intestine characterized by loose stools containing blood and mucus, and by painful and unproductive attempts to defecate (tenesmus). Although diarrhea (marked by the frequent production of watery stools) may have been confused with dysentery during the period covered by this study, early American references to "bloody flux," according to K. David Patterson, usually referred to true dysentery. Dysentery may be caused by an ameba, *Entamoeba histolytica*, or by several species of bacteria, especially in the genus *Shigella*. Patterson states that it is generally impossible to determine from early American accounts whether amebic or bacillary dysentery was involved, since these forms of dysentery were not clearly identified until late in the nineteenth century.

Environmental and sanitary factors undoubtedly were influential in creating the conditions for many outbreaks of the disorder. As Gerald Grob points out in a recent study of disease in America, "the disposal of organic wastes can contaminate water supplies; improperly handled food can encourage microbial replication; and the absence of personal hygiene can create conditions conducive to infection." Dysentery appeared everywhere in early America, but it was more prevalent in densely populated areas and in the southern states where high temperatures and humidity levels aided its spread.[28]

Early Americans "were fearful of such diseases as smallpox, yellow fever, measles, and diphtheria," Grob writes, "if only because of their visibility and dramatic nature of symptoms." Yet, "despite the high toll in lives, . . . these diseases were by no means the most significant determinants of morbidity and mortality." Endemic diseases, such as dysentery and malaria, "took a far higher toll even though their omnipresent nature tended to reduce public fear." Perhaps not as dreaded as smallpox or yellow fever, dysentery, with its symptoms of debilitating diarrhea, severe cramps, and occasional fever, was taken very seriously by early Americans because it was potentially fatal, especially to infants and young children. It is not surprising, then, to encounter many remedies for dysentery or "bloody flux" in early American almanacs.[29]

A twenty-first-century observer looking at early American dysentery remedies might think that, in keeping with the concept of humoral equilibrium, they would have ingredients to strengthen a system depleted or weakened by the loss of fluids. Certainly the dropsy remedies that promoted depletion to reduce the unnatural accumulation of fluid were consistent with humoralism. In fact, however, many eighteenth- and nineteenth-century almanac remedies for dysentery mixed bleeding and purging with restorative, strengthening measures. For example, a remedy "for the Bloody Flux" in the *Pennsylvania Town and Country-man's Almanack* for 1754 includes stimulants and narcotics, such as ginger and nutmeg, along with "a dose or two" of rhubarb, which was commonly used as a cathartic.[30] A dysentery remedy that appeared in the 1767 issue of the *American Calendar* (and three years later in *Poor Richard improved*) calls for bleeding followed by a vomit induced by ipecac (ipecacuanha). The stomach is then warmed and soothed with chamomile tea.[31] *Poor Will's* almanacs for 1771 and 1779 contain dysentery remedies with the same ingredients. The 1771 remedy contains rhubarb, sanders, cinnamon, "crocus martis," and "*Lucatellus's*" balsam, while the 1779 remedy calls for the promotion of sweats, vomiting through the use of ipecac, rhubarb, and chamomile tea.[32]

As the eighteenth century turned into the nineteenth, almanac remedies for the bloody flux remained consistent; they remained so through the 1850s. The 1797 issue of *Poulson's Town and Country Almanac* offers "Useful hints for persons in the country concerning the Bloody Flux," that, for the most part, would result in depletion. The "hints" presented in the almanac consist of two remedies that would produce opposite physiological reactions. The presence or absence of fever determines which remedy is appropriate:

> It sometimes happens that the *Dysentery* or *Bloody Flux*, occurs without much fever. This kind may soon be cured, by taking a table-spoonful of Caster-oil, or an ounce of Glauber's salts every morning, and thirty or forty drops of liquid Landanum [Ladanum] every night, for four or five times successively; but it is most common for this disease to be attended with fever; in this case, besides the above mentioned treatment, it will be necessary to bleed two or three times, and if the disorder does not quickly

yield, ten or twelve grains of Jalap or Rhubarb, and six or eight grains of
Calomel, instead of the oil or salts every day. Blisters must be applied to
the wrists and ancles [*sic*]: Rennet-whey is the most proper drink—Heating
remedies must be avoided, and the patient's bed and room well aired and
often changed—the stools must be removed immediately.[33]

Because many physicians and lay practitioners of the time believed that
fever was present in most cases of dysentery, almanac dysentery remedies
were often made up of ingredients that would reduce the fever as well
as restore natural bodily evacuations disrupted by the fever. The *United
States Almanac* for 1801 provides such an example. "It sometimes hap-
pens that the Dysentery or Bloody Flux occurs without much fever" the
almanac claims, "but it is most common for this disease to be attended
with fever." The latter situation called for a cure consisting of bleeding
and purging with jalap, rhubarb, and calomel.[34] *Smith & Forman's New-
York & New-Jersey Almanac* for 1816 provides a similar example. This
issue includes a "Cure for the Dysentery" that consisted of "1 ounce of
rheubarb [*sic*], 2 drachms of English saffron," and "2 or 1½ drachms
of cardimen [cardamom] seed" mixed with "one pint of good French
Brandy."[35] That same year the *North-Carolina Almanack* offered its
readers "A Receipt for the Flux" that claims to produce similar results:
"Take of Emetic Tartar 10 grains. Epicacuana [ipecacuanha] 20 grains
Jolop [jalap] 40 grains make them into 30 pills with honey & flour, the
dose one pill three times a day. The diet should be chiefly of mutton &
Chicken broth. When the flux attacks violently, a blister aplied [*sic*] over
the pain is often useful and in such cases the use of the above pills should
be preceeded [*sic*] by a gentle purge."[36]

Eighteenth- and early nineteenth-century almanac dysentery remedies,
like those for dropsy, were similar to the remedies encountered in manuscript commonplace books, daybooks, and journals, as well as in domestic health guides, professional manuals, and sectarian publications of the
period. Many included ipecac, rhubarb, cream of tartar, jalap, calomel,
and other ingredients to promote evacuation of one sort or another, a
treatment that might seem inappropriate for a patient already weakened
by dysentery. But because many writers of lay and professional texts believed that dysentery was accompanied by fever, dysentery treatments
that promoted evacuation to reduce fever actually conformed to—while
seeming to contradict—the basic assumptions of humoralism.

According to William Buchan, the symptoms of dysentery include, along with fever, a "flux in the belly attended with violent pain in the bowels, a constant inclination to go to stool, and generally less or more blood in the stools." [37] William Dewees questioned the belief among some physicians that fever does not accompany dysentery by observing, "We have never seen this in genuine dysentery." [38] The treatments espoused by almanacs and lay and professional texts were intended to subdue fever, remove inflammation of the mucus membrane of the large intestine, decrease the pain associated with the complaint, and restore normal evacuations by promoting defecation, urination, and sweating. To make sense of eighteenth- and early nineteenth-century dysentery remedies and to place them in a larger context of medical thinking of the time, a brief review of contemporary views on fever is in order because many physicians and lay practitioners believed that fever invariably accompanied gastrointestinal disorders, such as dysentery. The presence of fever dictated the early stage of the therapeutic regimen for the complaint.

"Hitherto no definition of fever has been given, which is free from all uncertainty, or ambiguity," wrote Dewees in 1830. The doctor's observation concerning a general definition of fever was a mild way of saying that there was much confusion and little agreement within the medical profession about febrile illnesses.[39] From the time of Hippocrates to the beginning of the nineteenth century, much had been written about the cause, nature, and treatment of fever. And while there was no consensus regarding its cause and treatment, most agreed that fever is a natural bodily reaction to the presence of disease.

According to the Hippocratic tradition, an overabundance of one humor marks the appearance of disease within the body. The body, in its attempt to restore natural balance, combats disease through the action of innate heat. Increased bodily heat results in a concoction of the humors that restores them to a natural or healthy state. The body's discharges of excess or morbid humors indicates that the body has won its battle with disease. Hippocratic writings emphasize treatment that complements the body's struggle to rid itself of disease, espousing a strict diet that includes an adequate amount of fluids to reduce morbid humors in the body. Galen, as we have seen, also believed that disease was the result of an overabundance of humors. He, too, saw fever or excessive heat resulting from humoral imbalance. To restore balance, however, Galen did not recommend the treatment advocated by the Hippocratic writings but relied instead on bleeding and cooling drinks.[40]

Galenic theories concerning fever remained dominant until the seventeenth century, when they faced the first of several challenges. Thomas Sydenham (1624–1689), working within the framework of humoralism, claimed that disease is a disorder not of all humors but of one only, blood. Thus, according to the "English Hippocrates," every disease is, in one way or another, a disorder of the blood, and fever denotes the body's attempt to rid the blood of morbid matter through several bodily evacuation processes. To assist the *vis medicatrix naturae* or the natural bodily function of eliminating excess matter, Sydenham cautiously advocated bleeding and mild purging.[41]

Boerhaave and his pupils, most notably Gerhard van Swieten (1700–1772), constructed their own theories of disease that fused humoralism with new discoveries in anatomy and physiology. Boerhaave noted that a rapid pulse is always present in fever, indicating an increased motion of the heart and blood flow. Fever, according to Boerhaave, occurs as a result of increased vascular resistance to the increased circulation of the blood. Boerhaave and van Swieten recommended therapeutic measures, such as bloodletting and purging, that would restore balance by ridding the body of an unnatural substance caused by excessive activity, or restorative measures that would strengthen a system weakened by the complaint. Like Sydenham, Boerhaave and van Swieten advocated moderation in the administration of treatments involving bleeding and purging.[42]

William Cullen claimed that all fevers go through three stages. The first stage consists of the debilitation of nervous power or diminished strength of the arteries. The second stage, marked by irritation or inflammation of the heart and arteries, leads to cold shivering or chills. The third stage witnesses increased body heat resulting from spasms of the arteries reacting to irritation. Arterial spasms, which produce perspiration, are the body's way of restoring the tone of the arteries. When the arteries regain their normal tone, health is restored. Thus, stimulating therapy, consisting of wine, opium, tonics, and cinchona bark, to assist nature's course and combat debility, play a significant role in Cullen's recommendations. While he dismissed the excessive use of the lancet and other depletive measures, Cullen did advocate a moderate recourse to these procedures for certain fevers or at certain stages of fevers, such as the inflammation or spasm stage.

Benjamin Rush (1745–1813), one of Cullen's students and the most influential American physician of his time, modified his teacher's theory and argued that all fevers were preceded by debility, which in turn caused excessive stimulation. Overstimulation, according to the Philadelphia physician, left the body vulnerable to an array of disease-causing agents, which could produce irregular convulsive activity of the blood vessels. Rush, like Cullen, espoused stimulating measures to combat debility caused by excessive stimulation. Breaking with his teacher, however, Rush vigorously advocated depletive measures to address the excessive arterial action caused by debility. His theories were controversial not so much because he advocated depletion—a belief in the efficacy of bleeding and purging in combating fevers was widespread—but because they seemed so excessive. Rush's practice, though challenged vigorously by leading physicians, had many adherents in the American medical profession. His was the predominant view from the 1790s until the 1830s.[43] The strident arguments for and against Rush's controversial therapies reveal that debates among physicians and lay practitioners over the cause and character of fever continued into the early decades of the nineteenth century. Yet, despite these debates, judging by the remedies they espoused, there seems to have been consensus among lay and professional practitioners that fever should be treated with a mix of depletive and stimulating measures.

Lay and professional texts issued in the eighteenth and early nineteenth centuries, in general, advocated similar dysentery remedies. For example, Buchan advised the patient "immediately to take a vomit" at the first appearance of the symptoms of dysentery. A vomit, promotion of sweat, and a "dose or two of rhubarb" would often cure the disease. In most cases, however, more powerful treatments were warranted. "At the beginning . . . it is always necessary to cleanse the first passages. For this purpose a vomit of ipecacuanha must be given, and wrought off with weak camonile [chamomile]-tea . . . a scruple, or at most half a dram of ipecacuahna, is generally sufficient. . . . The day after the vomit, half a dram, or two scruples of rhubarb, must be taken. This dose may be repeated every other day for two or three times. Afterwards small doses of ipecacuanha may be taken for some time. Two or three grains of the powder may be mixed in a table-spoonful of syrup of poppies, and taken three times a day." If these "evacuations," along with a regimen consisting of cleanliness, fresh air, and a bland meatless diet, did not produce a cure, Buchan recommended the use of astringents or other stimulating measures.[44]

Sixty years later John Gunn was advocating a similar therapeutic approach when he advised the "loss of some blood in the *first stage*" of dysentery but only if the "patient is vigorous, hale, and generally healthy" and there is "considerable fever." All sufferers of dysentery, Gunn asserted, should first "cleanse the stomach by an emetic of puke of ipecacuanha" followed by "a purge of calomel." The puke and purge should be complemented by clysters "made of slippery elm." Gunn urged the continuation of these measures until the body's normal evacuations were restored. Once this occurred, Gunn recommended a diet "of the lightest kind" and mild drinks to soothe the stomach and bowels irritated by the purges.[45]

Dysentery remedies encountered in the professional literature of the eighteenth and early nineteenth centuries were similar to those espoused by Buchan and Gunn.[46] Dysentery remedies espoused by botanical and eclectic practitioners, however, differed in their approach to fever. Whereas professional texts and domestic health guides prescribed treatments that reduced heat associated with fever, Thomson and other botanical doctors argued that heat was natural and should be increased because cold was the primary cause of illness. In keeping with the Hippocratic tradition, Thomson asserted that "fever is a friend, and cold the enemy."[47] Both Thomson and Beach deplored the practice of reducing the heat of fever through bleeding and the use of mineral drugs. Yet both advocated remedies that produced virtually the same physiological results as those espoused by the very practitioners they criticized—a restoration of a healthy balance, be it of the humors, solids, or a combination of both.

How Thomson and Beach viewed fever influenced their therapeutic approaches to dysentery. Thomson, for example, asserting that cold and morbid obstruction in the stomach and bowels caused dysentery, prescribed his usual combination of emetics and steam treatments to eradicate the disorder.[48] Beach advocated a three-step process. To correct the "acrimonious state of the fluids" and to "cleanse the alimentary canal," he prescribed a purge consisting of rhubarb, potash, peppermint plant, and cinnamon mixed with brandy. Beach then called for a clyster composed of slippery elm, milk, olive oil, molasses, and salt to calm the stomach and remove inflammation and irritation. The treatment was concluded with a decoction of hops, tansy, horehound, and catnip to relieve the pain.[49]

Recall that the 1797 issue of *Poulson's Town and Country Almanac* cautions readers to treat dysentery patients differently if fever is present. This advice was unusual among almanac dysentery remedies. Most remedy advice assumed readers would know whether the patient had a fever and whether the remedy was appropriate. A lay practitioner—a parent, spouse, neighbor, midwife, or local clergyman well read in medicine—would have had experience with fever and its varied symptoms, such as cold sweats, warm skin, flushed cheeks, and a quick pulse. If the lay practitioner felt that the almanac remedy did not provide all of the information needed, he or she would have turned to another source—a manuscript recipe book, a domestic health guide, or, perhaps, a professional text—to help treat the bloody flux. Because of shared attitudes concerning health and disease, the dysentery remedies the lay practitioner would have encountered in the almanac and other sources, which appear complicated and antihumoral to a modern observer, would have seemed reasonable and appropriate.

Rheumatism

Rheumatism was used in early America as a general term for a condition marked by inflammation and pain in the joints and muscles. In a time before the identification of arthritis, chronic rheumatoid arthritis, and other bone and joint disorders as discreet conditions, rheumatism was a catch-all term that covered many aches, pains, and swellings. The complaint, according to William Buchan, "generally attacks the joints with exquisite pain, and is sometimes attended with inflammation and swelling." He divided rheumatism into two categories, acute and chronic, or "rheumatism with and without fever."[50] Buchan's description mirrors that of most writers of lay and professional texts that were published in the late eighteenth century through the first half of the nineteenth. George Bacon Wood, however, writing in the late 1840s, divided the complaint into four types: acute, subacute, chronic, and nervous. Acute rheumatism was marked by violent local inflammation and fever, subacute by less violent inflammation and little or no fever. Chronic rheumatism was characterized by its long duration and by the absence of fever. In the nervous form of the disorder, neither inflammation nor fever was present; the disease was marked by irritation of the nervous tissue.[51]

Buchan observed that rheumatism "commonly begins with weariness, shivering, a quick pulse, restlessness, thirst, and often symptoms of fever." These signs, he points out in his medical text, are followed by

pains in the joints that are "often affected with swelling and inflammation." The causes of rheumatism, according to Buchan, are "frequently
the same as those of an inflammatory fever; *viz.* an obstructed perspiration, the immoderate use of strong liquors, and the like," as well as
"all quick transitions from heat to cold." Furthermore, "the rheumatism
may likewise be occasioned by excessive evacuations, or the stoppage
of useful discharges."[52] Dewees attributed the onset of rheumatism to
causes similar to those cited by Buchan: "Rapid changes from heat to
cold moisture, perspiration suddenly suppressed, gross living, exertion,
compression." "Everyone agrees," he asserts, "that a sudden application
of cold is the direct cause." The cumulative effect of these causes is pain
throughout the body, especially in the joints, accompanied by swelling
and redness.[53]

Rheumatism remedies that appeared in early American almanacs
rarely specified what form of the disorder (chronic, acute, etc.) they were
supposed to alleviate (see Fig. 4 for almanac remedies, including one for
rheumatism). Moreover, almanac readers would not have encountered
passages that described the causes and symptoms. Almanac makers assumed that readers looking for a cure either already knew the complaint
from which they suffered, or they were seeking remedies to file away or
record into a daybook or journal for later use. An almanac rheumatism
cure that was popular in the second half of the eighteenth century was
one that advocated "Seneca Rattle Snake Root," garlic, and "Gum Ammoniac."[54] A remedy in *Poor Will's Almanack* for 1771 includes senna,
hermodactylus, turpethum, scammony, ginger, zedoary, and cubeba.[55]
The *Burlington Almanack* for 1773 offers a rheumatism cure that calls
for "two ounces of snake root, two handfuls of burdock seed, two
drachms of cochineal, [and] three heads of garlic."[56] Another popular
rheumatism cure appears in the 1804 issue of the *New-England Almanack, or Lady's and Gentleman's Diary*. The remedy, extracted from the
works of the eminent English physician Sir John Pringle, contains gum
guaiacum, a popular component of early American rheumatism cures:
"Take half a drachm of powder of gum guaiacum in a draught of warm
ale going to rest, and be covered with a larger quantity of clothes than
usual; persist in this method a few days, and you will find relief. Bleeding
is of service in phlethoric constitutions."[57]

Almanac rheumatism remedies remained consistent throughout the
first half of the nineteenth century. The *Baltimore Almanac, or Time
Piece* for 1822, for example, offers a rheumatism cure that consists of a

RECEIPTS.

A Cure for Tetters.

The powder of the sharp-pointed Dock-root, with Vinegar, is a certain remedy. Ring-worms, rubbed with Dock Bark, are soon taken off.

For the Itch or Scab.

Take Dock-root (sharp-pointed) either dug up fresh, or dried in the shade; boil it, and wash the hands and feet of such as have the Itch or Scab. Let the Scab be ever so great, scurffy or ugly, ten nights washing in this, and laying on the boiled Dock-root all night, like a poultice, will cure it.

An excellent pain-easing and ripening Poultice.

Take of Elder flowers one ounce; roots of Althea and White Lillies, of each two ounces; leaves of Mallows a handfull; powder of Linseed one ounce; boil them in milk or water to a pulp; add to them an onion roasted under the ashes, ointment of Basilicon half an ounce, oil of Lillies enough to make a poultice, and apply it.

For little Ulcers on the Head.

Wash them with a decoction made of Oak Leaves and the inner Bark of Elders.

A Cure for the Quinsey.

Take of Ivy Leaves two or three handfulls, rough Barley as much, boil both close in water, and pour them out into a pipkin or narrow mouthed deep vessel, to receive the steam into the mouth and throat.

A Cure for the Fever and Ague.

Seventy-five grains of Wormwood Seed mixed with Molasses, and made up into a small pill, taken just before the fit comes on, seldom fails to cure.

For the Cholic.

Ten or twelve berries of the Holly-tree eaten are very good for the Cholic.

A decoction of the prickles of the leaves, in a posset drink of ale and milk, often cures the Cholic, when many other things have been tried in vain.

For the Rheumatism.

A person noted for curing the Rheumatism had no other method or secret, but using the tender buds or young leaves of Holly boiled in water, strained, and the liquor sweetened with molasses. The sick person drank half a pound of this warm, in bed, at each dose, and the pain was removed. It was almost powerful sudorific, and plenty of small liquors were drank to dilute it.

For Burns.

Bruise raw onions, mix them with a little salt, and apply them to fresh Burns, not blistered.—They will quickly draw out the fire, and prevent Blisters.

On

Fig. 4. Almanac remedies, 1794. *Poor Richard improved: Being an Almanack and Ephemeris . . . for the Year . . . 1794* (Philadelphia: Hall and Sellers, [1793]). (Author's collection)

decoction of gum guaiacum and "bark of sassafras root" accompanied by regular bathing of the painful joints.[58] *Phinney's Calendar, or, Western Almanac* for 1826 includes a remedy that calls for the application of "a perfect cabbage leaf" along with a "bandage of flannel" to promote a blister.[59] A remedy in the 1853 issue of the *American Farmer's Almanac* calls for gum guaiacum mixed with honey, cream of tartar, flour of sulfur, Jamaica ginger, and nutmeg.[60] A year later, the *Hagers-Town Town and Country Almanack* printed a rheumatism cure, submitted by a reader, that recommends "half an ounce of pulverized saltpetre, put in a pint of sweet oil," as well as bathing "the parts affected." Once these directions are followed, the letter claims, "a sound cure will speedily be effected."[61]

As with both dropsy and dysentery remedies, eighteenth- and early nineteenth-century almanac cures for rheumatism are similar to those collected and recorded by laypersons in daybooks, family journals, and recipe books and prescribed by writers of professional medical texts and domestic health guides of the same period. Kay Moss discovered that guaiacum, mustard, and sulfur—components cited often in almanac cures—are the most popular ingredients in rheumatism remedies found in southern commonplace and recipe books. For example, Eliza Lucas Pinckney, a resident of South Carolina's low country, started a recipe book in 1756 that includes a remedy—and, in this case, a preventative—for rheumatism: "Take one Ounce of Gum Guiacum [*sic*], powder it very fine, and take as much as will lie on an English Shilling in a glass of Water night and morning. Repeat the same quantity every Spring and Fall, tho' you may be free from pain, it will prevent its returning." An early nineteenth-century commonplace book, also from South Carolina, includes a rheumatism cure composed of mustard as well as gum guaiacum. The caregiver is advised to begin with "a level Teaspoonful of Mustard in a half glass of gin or Whiskey every morning for four days successively—afterwards—20 grains of gum guac powdered in honey or molasses for four mornings—then 1½ Teaspoonful of the Tincture of Gum Guac in a wine glass of water for 4 mornings—Keep the Patient from taking Cold." Dorothea Christina Schmidt, a German immigrant who in the late eighteenth century settled with her family in eastern Georgia, recorded in her cookery and medical receipt book "The famous American Receipt for the Rheumatism," which had appeared in the 1777 issue of the *South Carolina and Georgia Almanack*. This cure combines garlic and gum ammoniac: "Take of Garlic two Cloves, of gum armoniac [*sic*] one Drachm, blend them by bruising them together, make them into two or three bolusses with fair Water and swallow them one at night, and one in the Morning. Drink while taking this Recipe, Sassafras tea, made very strong, so as to have the teapot filled with chips. This is generally found to banish the Rheumatism and even Contractions of the joints in a few times taken." [62]

The writers of domestic health guides and professional textbooks differentiated between acute and chronic forms of rheumatism when referring to treatments. According to Buchan, treatment for acute rheumatism "is nearly the same as in acute or inflammatory fever." If the patient is young and strong, he contends, "bleeding is necessary." Besides bleeding, Buchan advises keeping the stomach "open by emollient clysters, or cool opening liquors," a light diet, a concoction consisting of "wine-whey, a dram of the cream of tartar, and a half a dram of gum guaiacum," and warm bathing "after proper evacuations." Buchan claims that chronic rheumatism differs from the acute form because it is "seldom attended with any considerable degree of fever," it is "generally confined to some particular part of the body," and it is "seldom [accompanied by] any inflammation or swelling." Moreover, people "in the decline of life are most subject" to the chronic form of rheumatism. Despite the differences between the two forms of rheumatism, Buchan recommends a course of treatment that is, except for bleeding, "nearly the same as in the acute." [63]

Decades later, Gunn, too, recommended bleeding during the first stage of acute rheumatism as long as the pulse was full and the patient possessed a robust constitution. Because bleeding should not be allowed to produce debility, in his text Gunn advocates "an active purge of calomel and jalap" after the first bleeding to produce "a gentle sweat or moisture on the skin." For the patient who is suffering from extreme pain, with his or her skin "red, swelled and inflamed," Gunn recommends cupping. Chronic rheumatism, according to Gunn, demands that "the bowels be kept open by the simple laxative of sulphur." "The next object in curing this complaint," he continues, is to "keep up a gentle moisture on the skin [using] . . . one ounce of *gum guaiacum* and two drachms of *saltpetre*," which "acts as a powerful stimulant—produces general sweating, etc." The main objective to be pursued in removing chronic rheumatism was, for Gunn, very simple: "it is either by *moderate* or by *profuse*, which means *large sweats*." [64]

The therapeutic measures prescribed over a sixty-year period, from those of Buchan to those of Gunn, shared a common purpose, to restore balance by reducing fever (in acute rheumatism) or inflammation, to restore normal circulation and bodily evacuations that caused irritation or inflammation, and to alleviate the pain associated with the complaint. Readers would have encountered similar therapies in the professional literature from the middle decades of the nineteenth century. Not so, however, in the early nineteenth-century publications of the sectarians Samuel Thomson, Elias Smith, or Wooster Beach. In these publications early American readers would not have encountered rheumatism cures that included bleeding or, for the most part, mineral drugs. Thomson, who explains that rheumatism is "caused by cold obstructing the natural circulation," advises taking "such medicine as will cause perspiration and remove obstructions." This course would have required his usual treatment of emetics, stimulants, and steam baths to restore balance to the system by restoring heat to the affected parts.[65] Smith, like Thomson, did not differentiate grades or types of rheumatism. He speaks disdainfully of those who do: "The doctors tell us of *acute rheumatism, chronic rheumatism, inflammatory rheumatism,* and *rheumatic fever*; *rheumatism in the head, breast, stomach, bowels, etc etc.*," which only proves that "they are almost entirely ignorant of the nature of it, or at least of the medicine that will cure." Rheumatism, to Smith, was simply "a cold in the joints, muscles, and different parts of the system" and could be cured by restoring heat to these parts by using his vegetable powders and elixir, and by taking hot baths.[66]

Beach separated rheumatism into acute and chronic forms and offered remedies for both. Concerning the former, Beach advocated purgatives to lessen the inflammation and lower the fever, sudorifics to promote perspiration, emetics to remove obstruction, oils and liniments to reduce swelling, and anodynes to reduce pain and to help the patient sleep. For chronic rheumatism Beach recommended an internal remedy consisting of a syrup of guaiacum, sarsaparilla, sassafras bark, and burdock seeds, and an external remedy that included bathing the parts with a tincture of cayenne pepper and alcohol. The purpose of these measures was to "stimulate the cutaneous vessels to a healthy action, and thus restore perspiration."[67]

WHEN EARLY Americans got sick they could seek help from a physician, a local lay practitioner, or a midwife. Many, of course, treated themselves.

Most health care took place in the home and was usually administered by a family member or a neighbor. To attempt a cure, a layperson would have to know what complaint he or she was combating. Knowledge of the disorder's symptoms as well as the appropriate measures to address them was essential. But how would a farmer, a merchant, a laborer, a teacher, a midwife, or any other American untrained in medicine, be they affluent or poor, educated or semi-literate, obtain this knowledge? Most likely they would have obtained at least some from a printed source. But they might also have heard remnants of an oral culture, based on folk traditions and empirical knowledge. But oral and print cultures were not mutually exclusive; medical knowledge conveyed orally migrated directly into print or indirectly through manuscript recipe books and family health journals.

The world of semi-vernacular print to which the layperson could turn was complicated and fragmented, especially in the nineteenth century, when American publishing came into its own and its presses were issuing scores of popular health titles. Thanks to the work of historians of medicine, we are aware of the profound influence of the works of such widely read authors as Nicholas Culpeper, William Buchan, John Gunn, William Alcott, and Sylvester Graham. We know very little, however, about other authors or other genres of print—such as almanacs—consulted by the laity. And we know very little about how these genres were used.

As this study shows, the layperson in pre-1860 America had many genres of print from which to choose therapeutic advice. Besides the household manuscript recipe book, books, pamphlets, and broadsides would have been accessible. The almanac, for a time this country's most popular secular publication, would have been one of the most visible and ubiquitous sources from the mid-eighteenth century through the first half of the nineteenth. I would argue that while some laypersons seeking therapeutic advice may have turned to one familiar text, many would have turned to several, including an almanac. At a time when even the most common malady had the potential to disrupt one's ability to work, to devastate a family's economic prospects, and to threaten the life of a patient, men and women would have recorded or filed away remedies gathered from a variety of sources to treat a variety of ailments. Almanacs circulated widely in early America and would have been an obvious source for lay therapeutic advice. Because readers consulted the genre for therapeutic advice and also contributed therapeutic advice to it, the almanac became something akin to a remedy clearinghouse. One could argue that almanac therapeutic advice carried as much authority as that held by trained physicians.

For more than a century—from the 1750s through the 1850s— almanac remedies for dropsy, dysentery, and rheumatism remained consistent. These remedies seldom, if ever, noted the type or level of the complaint they were intended to alleviate. Only in this respect was there any difference between almanac remedies for these three disorders and those encountered in manuscript recipe books and journals, mainstream domestic health guides, professional medical texts, and even sectarian publications of the same period.

ALMANAC REMEDY advice remained consistent throughout the period covered by this study, reflecting the persistence of traditional therapeutic practices in America. By the 1850s traditional therapeutics had faced decades of challenges from some within the medical profession, especially those who had studied under celebrated French physicians and walked the wards of Paris hospitals. The early decades of the nineteenth century had witnessed the beginnings of a transformation within the American medical profession resulting from the impact of French pathology, surgery, and therapeutics, the growing number of proprietary medical schools, and increasing competition from various medical sects. As the boundaries between lay and professional medical knowledge solidified, assumptions concerning the body, health, and disease that were once shared began to diverge. The self-limiting character of disease and the healing power of nature became fashionable topics of discussion and debate at professional gatherings and in the medical press. Yet, despite this growing emphasis on science over tradition, many in the medical profession, even those physicians schooled in Paris where these concepts were in vogue, had to deal with the realities of patients' assumptions and expectations when it came to treating illness. These assumptions and expectations, as demonstrated by almanac therapeutic advice, had changed little from the previous century. Few physicians could afford to alienate their patients by categorically rejecting traditional therapeutics.[68]

PRESCRIBING PREVENTION

THE PURPOSE of therapeutic or remedy advice was to restore a healthy equilibrium to a body that had fallen out of balance. The purpose of regimen advice, however, was to maintain a healthy balance by espousing a way of life that would protect the body from a variety of potential dangers. Of the general almanacs consulted for this study, 16 percent include regimen advice of one kind or another.[1] During the second half of the eighteenth century, however, regimen advice appeared in 25 percent of the almanacs consulted. Although fewer almanacs included regimen guidance than astrological and therapeutic advice, this does not necessarily mean that almanac makers or almanac readers were less concerned about prevention. When pondering the amount of regimen advice in general almanacs, one must consider accessibility, the objectives of almanac makers, and the expectations of readers.

Regimen guidance that appeared in American almanacs between 1750 and 1860, unlike astrological health advice, was available to American readers in several other genres of popular print, including the specialized almanacs that began appearing in increasing numbers during the antebellum period (see chapter 4). Almanac makers endeavored to attract the widest possible audience. Their core audience, however, was made up of literate and semi-literate artisans, farmers, and laborers who tended to live in a rural environment where they were more culturally isolated than urban dwellers. They would not have had the leisure to contemplate and alter their style of life, preferring health advice that was practical and immediate—remedies that would restore their health so they could resume productive daily lives.

The connection between health and long life, on one hand, and personal behavior, on the other, was an important part of Hippocratic medicine and was later popularized in print by scores of works on proper living, most notably those of Luigi Cornaro and George Cheyne. These publications, which offered advice on the preservation of health but rarely on treatment, emphasized the six Galenic "non-naturals": air, food and drink, sleeping and waking, exercise and rest, the evacuations, and the passions of the mind. Regulation of the non-naturals was essential to living in harmony with the laws of physiology or God's natural laws. Abuse of one or more of the non-naturals could result in humoral imbalance that could cause disease or even death; thus moderation—or temperance, as it was then broadly defined—was requisite to a healthy and long life.[2] These regimen texts were to be read (presumably by affluent readers who had time for contemplating their health) but not actively applied, unlike many of the domestic health guides discussed in the previous chapter.[3] The latter belonged to another traditional category of lay medical publications that evolved in much the same way as regimen texts and almanacs. Domestic medical health guides of the period, such as those of Nicholas Culpeper and John Wesley, contain, for the most part, descriptions of a variety of diseases and directions for treating them. Works in this category were most likely intended for an audience similar to the core readership of general almanacs, individuals who could not afford the services of a physician and for whom an extended illness could spell economic disaster.[4]

The most popular lay health publication in early America was William Buchan's *Domestic Medicine*. The key factor in Buchan's extraordinary success, according to Charles Rosenberg, was that he combined in one book the regimen and longevity tradition with the home treatment tradition. Thus, it is not surprising that several of the most successful almanac makers and publishers of the late eighteenth and early nineteenth centuries, in their attempts to reach a wider audience of readers, offered both categories of health advice—sometimes by providing extracts from Buchan's works. Isaiah Thomas, for example, offered readers therapeutic advice to restore their health as well as regimen guidance to preserve it. His 1781 annual includes an example of the latter, an extract from "an excellent" but unnamed author titled "The Art of Preserving Health," which addresses the critical importance of moderation in maintaining the body's delicate balance: "The whole art of preserving health may be said to consist of filling up what is deficient, and emptying what is redundant, that the body may be kept in its natural state; and therefore all the supplies from eating and drinking, and all the discharges by sweating and other channels of nature, should be regulated, that the body may not be oppressed by repletion, nor wasted by evacuation."[5]

Regimen advice in pre-1860 American almanacs was similar to the advice in other genres of popular print of the same period, such as regimen and hygiene texts, domestic health guides, self-improvement manuals, sectarian medical publications, domestic economy books, periodicals, and an array of publications that grew out of antebellum reform movements. Readers were warned about the constant dangers to health—as well as spiritual salvation—posed by drunkenness, gluttony, indolence, and uncontrolled passions (see Fig. 5). That drunkards, gluttons, the indolent, and the morally deficient, through their irresponsible behavior, predispose themselves to a variety of diseases is a theme that readers encountered frequently throughout the period covered by this study.

Almanac regimen advice was often conveyed through essays, poetry, and maxims or pithy sayings, such as the caution that appeared in one 1754 almanac: "Intemperance is the very fruitful Mother of innumerable Distempers, Ailments and Pains." Nathaniel Ames's 1761 almanac includes the maxim, "Live temperate and defy the Physician." The *New-England Almanack, and Gentleman's and Lady's Diary* for 1784 asserts, "The three doctors, Diet, Quiet, and Temperance, are the best physicians." And the 1812 issue of Nathaniel Low's *Astronomical Diary* contends, "Our best physician is temperance."[6] Nathaniel Ames's son, also named Nathaniel, used verse in his 1767 annual to advance a temperance message:

> 'Tis to thy rules, O' Temperance! We owe
> All pleasures, which from health and strength can flow,
> Vigour of body—purity of mind,
> Unclouded reason—sentiments refin'd,
> Unmix'd, untainted joys—without remorse,
> Th' intemp'rate Sensualist's never-failing curse.[7]

A similar message, also in verse, appears in the *Columbian Calendar, or New-York and Vermont Almanack* for 1817.

> In vain we mourn those transitory days
> Consum'd in riot and licentious ways;
> 'Tis Temperance alone preserves our strength,
> In mind and body to life's utmost length.[8]

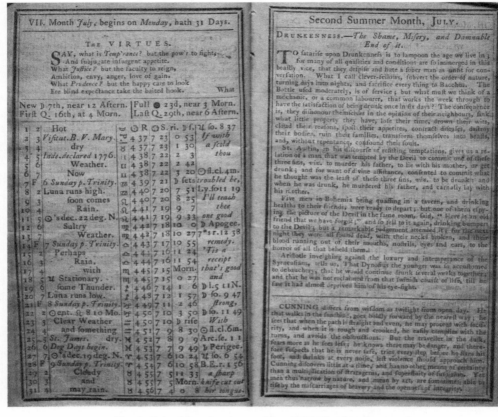

Fig. 5. Calendar and regimen advice, 1793. *Hutchins Improved:*
Being an Almanack and Ephemeris . . . 1793 (New York: H. Gaine, [1792]).
(Author's collection)

Though readers occasionally submitted remedy advice to almanacs, there is no evidence that they did so with regimen advice. Most of the maxims, poems, and essays were either borrowed (usually without attribution) or extracted from other texts (and sometimes from other almanacs) or composed by the almanac maker. A decision to include an original essay or a short passage on regimen provided the almanac maker or printer with an opportunity to display his or her skills—or lack thereof—as a writer.

Benjamin Franklin, admired by many for his facility with words, included "Rules of Health and Long Life" in the 1742 issue of *Poor Richard.* This piece, however, was probably borrowed from another publication. Running to two pages, the rules concentrate on the dangers to health posed by over-

eating and the abuse of ardent spirits. The difficulty with diet, according to
the essay, is "in finding out an exact Measure"; one should "eat for Necessity,
not Pleasure," because "Lust knows not where Necessity ends." A temperate diet protects the body from internal diseases and "arms the body against
all external Accidents"; "a sober Diet . . . preserves the Memory, it helps the
understanding, it allays the Heat of Lust" and "brings a Man to Consideration of his latter End." Finally, the essay reminds readers that a healthy
body also affords spiritual benefits, for temperance makes the body "a fit
Tabernacle for the Lord to dwell in; which makes us happy in this World,
and eternally happy in the World to come." [9] As this chapter shows, regimen
messages linking piety and prevention, morality and moderation, continued
to be disseminated a century after Franklin.

Franklin occasionally conveyed his temperance messages through
biographical sketches of historical figures celebrated for leading lives of
moderation and sobriety. In the 1749 issue of *Poor Richard improved*,
Franklin notes that February 18 is the anniversary of the death of "that
famous reformer" Martin Luther, who died in 1546. Luther, according
to Franklin, "was remarkably *temperate* in meat and drink." Franklin
then extends Cicero's maxim on the value of industriousness: "*Cicero
says, There was never any* great *man who was not an* industrious *man*;
to which may, perhaps, be added, *There was never any* industrious *man
who was not a* temperate *man*: For intemperance in diet, abates the vigour and dulls the action both of mind and body." In the 1756 edition
of his popular annual, Franklin offers his readers a model of living worthy of emulation. He describes the life of Luigi Cornaro, comparing the
Venetian's early life of infirmity with his many later years of continued
health resulting from temperance. Seeking respite from forty years of ill
health, Cornaro devoted himself to the temperate life, and throughout
the next sixty years Cornaro remained, according to Franklin, "so entire
and perfect in his Strength . . . as to be able to walk, ride, hunt, and perform every Office." [10]

Pre-1860 almanac readers learned that the deleterious effects of intemperance—both moral and physical—were many. An 1816 almanac
asserts that intemperance "drives wit out of the head, money out of the
pocket, wine out of the bottle, elbows out of the coat, and health out of
the body." "It is the peculiar characteristic of the vice of intemperance,"
Bennett & Walton's Almanac for 1826 claims, "that it marks for its prey
all that is valuable in man. . . . It enervates the body, palsies the intellect,
and hardens the heart. It blunts the moral and social affections, renders

its victim regardless of reputation, clothes him in the habiliments of poverty, stamps upon every feature the aspect of misery, and having shorn him of present enjoyment and blasted the hope of future bliss, sends him to an untimely death." The temperate life was not an easy one to live. Early Americans were reminded constantly of the evils of excess of one kind or another. Dire warnings that intemperance will inexorably lead to poverty, the ruination of one's career, the destruction of one's family, the loss of one's health, and, eventually, to one's early death, emanated from countless podiums and pulpits, and from the pages of scores of publications. Yet the life of excess, while extremely dangerous, was alluring and seductive, especially to the idle, the unsuspecting, the weak, and particularly vulnerable young men and women. The 1836 issue of one New York almanac warns its readers to brace themselves against intemperance's superficially attractive but ultimately deadly fruits: "Fly from her very first appearance, then: it is not safe to be within the glance of her eye, or sound of her voice; and if you once become familiar with her, you are undone. Let us further add, that she wears a variety of shapes, and all pleasing; all accommodated to flatter our appetite and influence our desire. To the epicure she presents delicious banquets; to the bachanal, store of exquisite wines; to the sensualist, his seraglio of mistresses; to each, the allurement he is most prone to; and to all, a pleasing poison that not only impairs the body, but stupifies the mind, and makes us bankrupts of our lives as well as our credits and estates." [11]

Many passages from the antebellum period encountered in both general and specialty almanacs (as well as scores of conduct books), like this one equating intemperance with an immoral female temptress, appear to have been aimed at young men, particularly artisans, laborers, mechanics, farmhands, as well as at the increasing numbers of single men who were flocking to cities and urban areas in search of employment. [12] For example, an agricultural almanac published in 1854 includes a short essay titled "Temperance is my Physic," promoting the benefits of industry and good habits to its male readers. "Farmers and mechanics, who, generally, are engaged in minding their own business," the writer claims, "mostly steer clear of diseases brought on by a love of lounging" and the "love of grog." The 1843 issue of the *Rhode-Island Almanac* reprinted an article that had appeared thirteen years earlier in Henry H. Porter's *Journal of Health* titled "Hints to Mechanics and Workmen." Drinking nothing more than "pure water," avoiding tobacco, partaking of a plain diet, keeping "regular hours," exercising, and practicing cleanliness, the article asserts, will protect mechanics and workmen from the diseases "which your particular trades and work are liable to produce." [13]

A Tennessee almanac issued in 1839 listed for its readers four secrets of health: "early rising, exercise, personal cleanliness, and the rising from table with the stomach unoppressed." [14] No clergyman, physician, or reformer could have argued with the almanac's "secrets," although each would have volunteered with assurance several additions. The temperance advice in eighteenth- and early nineteenth-century almanacs was similar to that encountered in other genres of popular print. Almanac regimen advice, like regimen advice found in lay health texts, self-improvement guides, and other publications changed little from the eighteenth century through the first half of the nineteenth.

Essays on the specific dangers of too much or too little sleep, too much or too little exercise, and any amount of indolence, and the harmful effects of tobacco appear frequently in early American general almanacs. The evils of drinking and overeating, however, receive the most attention. "Timothy Trueman," in the *Burlington Almanack* for 1772, for example, delivers a strong message against drinking that is echoed in almanacs from throughout the late eighteenth century and the first half of the nineteenth; "Men will indulge a practice by which experience convinces them, they will effectively loose [*sic*] their understanding, and become perfect idiots. What can be conceived more unsuitable to the dignity of human nature, than the Drunkard, with his eyes staring, his tongue stammering, his legs quivering, his hands trembling, his legs tottering, and his stomach heaving. . . . The swine wallowing in the mire is not so loathsome an object as the Drunkard." [15] Verse, used as a mnemonic device, was a favorite medium for almanac antidrinking messages. The cautionary "Jug of Rum" appears in the *New-England Almanack or Lady's and Gentleman's Diary* for 1799:

> Within these earthen walls confin'd
> The ruin lurks of human kind:
> More mischiefs here united dwell,
> And more diseases haunt this cell,
> Than ever plagu'd the Egyptian flocks,
> Or ever curs'd Pandora's box.
> Within these prison walls repose
> The seeds of many a bloody nose,
> The chattering tongue, the horrid oath,
> The fist for fighting nothing loth,

The nose with diamonds glowing red,
The bloated eye, the broken head!
Forever fasten'd be this door.

Confin'd within, a thousand more
Destructive friends of hateful shape
Even now are planning an escape:
Here, only by cork controul'd,
And slender walls of earthen mould,
In all their pomp of death reside
Revenge, that ne'er was satisfied,
The tree that bears the deadly fruit
Of maiming, murder, and dispute,
Assault, that innocence assails,
The images of gloomy goals,
The giddy thought, on mischief bent,
The evening hour in folly spent;
All these within this jug appear,
And Jack, the hangman, in the rear![16]

The 1811 issue of the *Baltimore Almanack, or, Time Piece* contains the poem "The Lovers of Rum" composed by "A Hater of Rum." The final stanza confirms the ultimate fate of those who indulge in the loathsome beverage.

I've seen men, from health, wealth and ease,
Untimely descend to the tomb,
I need not describe their disease,
Because they were lovers of Rum.[17]

In a colorful and dramatic depiction of the moral and physical destructiveness of rum, a poem offered by a Philadelphia almanac in 1836 would have made a strong impression on even rum's most hardened advocates.

Pimple-maker—visage bloater,
Health corrupter—idlers mate:
Mischief-breeder—vice-promoter,
Credit-spoiler—devil's bait.

. . . .

Nerve-infeebler—system-shatterer,
Thirst-increaser—vagrant-thief;
Cough-producer—treach'rous flatterer,
Mud-bedauber—mock-relief

. . . .
Pain-inflicter—eyes inflamer,
Heart-corrupter—folly's nurse;
Secret-babbler—body-maimer,
Thrift-deflater—loathsome curse[18]

Graphic descriptions of drunkards and the malignant effects drinking
has on the body were not confined to poetry, however. Isaiah Thomas
turned to the often-used metaphor of the "Drunkard's Looking Glass"
in his 1799 annual to impart a dramatic antidrinking message. The passage implies that anyone who keeps company with the bottle should
expect to see a hideous reflection when confronted with a mirror:
"Gout-sickness—tremors of the hands in the morning—bloatedness—
inflamed eyes—red nose and face—sore and swelled legs—jaundice-pains
in the limbs, and burning in the hands and feet—dropsy—epilepsy—
melancholy—idiotism—madness—palsy—apoplexy—death." The description in "The Character of a Sot" in an 1805 Baltimore almanac is just as
brutally realistic: "He is terribly afflicted with various distempers; being
frequently seized with the falling sickness at midnight, accompanied
with a dead palsy in his tongue: St. Anthony's fire has visibly settled
in his face, and so terribly does the ague shake his hand that he cannot
lift a glass of a gin to his head. The pawnbroker is his banker, and the
publican his chief creditor. In short, while he is alive he is worth any
person's notice, but after his death there will be no traces found of his
memory, except on a chalked walls of alehouses." The 1825 issue of
Hunt's Almanack carries an equally horrifying picture of the effects of
drunkenness on the abuser's health, reputation, and family: "[Drunken-
ness] expells reason, drowns the memory, distempers the body, defaces
beauty, diminishes strength, inflames the blood, causes internal, external,
and incurable wounds: is a witch to the senses, a devil to the soul, a
thief to the purse, the beggar's woe and children's sorrow: the picture
of a beast, and self-murderer, who drinks to other's good health, and
robs himself of his own." And the portrait of a drunkard sketched in
the 1836 issue of *"Poor Richards'" New Farmer's Almanac* is that of
a repulsive figure who is destined for the gaol and the gallows if not an
early grave: "The Drunkard is a self-condemned convict, destined to be
his own executioner, and, by his daily potations of liquid fires inflicting
on himself a public, disgraceful, lingering, painful death, bearing about
with him, and exhibited to all eyes, the loathsome displays of his doom,

and tokens of his torments, in his carbuncled visage, lack-lustre eye, and bloated hydropsical carcase." [19]

Except for the culturally isolated who lacked access to other forms of print, most eighteenth- and early nineteenth-century almanac readers would have encountered regimen advice in other publications. Regimen guidance permeated several genres of popular print and, thus, almanacs would have reinforced the prescriptive or proscriptive advice with which many readers would have been familiar. Benjamin Franklin, whose popular almanac occasionally included regimen advice of one form or another, issued many of his antidrinking writings in newspapers with which he was associated. In his "Silence Dogood" essays that appeared in the *New England Courant* in the 1720s and in articles he wrote during the following decade for the *Pennsylvania Gazette*, Franklin often expressed his concerns about excessive drinking and its harmful effects on the individual and on society as a whole.[20] The Philadelphia physician Benjamin Rush, a younger colleague of Franklin's as well as a fellow signer of the Declaration of Independence, wrote several essays and pamphlets on the deleterious effects of ardent spirits on the individual and society. His 1784 pamphlet *An Enquiry into the Effects of Spirituous Liquors upon the Human Body, and Their Influence upon the Happiness of Society* was reprinted often, especially by the American Tract Society in the early decades of the nineteenth century.

Several almanacs printed extracts of Rush's pamphlet, as well as his "Moral and Physical Thermometer, or a Scale of the Progress of Temperance and Intemperance," which had appeared in the *Columbian Magazine* in January 1789. The one-page illustration depicts a thermometer with a scale ranging from seventy degrees above zero to seventy degrees below. Temperance encompasses all the beverages above zero (water to "Strong Beer"), while intemperance in varying degrees encompasses all those below zero (punch to rum, gin, brandy, and whiskey). According to Rush's thermometer, those living within the temperate range will enjoy health, wealth, serenity, happiness, cheerfulness, strength, nourishment, and a good reputation. Those on the low end of the scale, however, are in constant danger of assuming the numerous vices and contracting the various diseases—if not suffering the usual tragic demise—of the habitual drinker. One's health—and ultimate fate—are linked to the degree of one's abuse. Whereas the drinking of punch may lead to idleness, gout, and debt, daily consumption of whiskey will surely lead to "SUICIDE[,] DEATH," and the "GALLOWS." [21]

In addition to the regimen texts of Cornaro, Cheyne, and others, almanac readers of the eighteenth and early nineteenth centuries would have encountered hygiene advice in several leading domestic health guides, especially those of William Buchan and John Gunn. In *Domestic Medicine*, Buchan devotes brief chapters to the non-naturals and one on intemperance in general, where he observes, "The danger of intemperance appears from every construction of the human body." Health depends on the normal performance of the fluids and solids, and whatever "disturbs them necessarily impairs health." Intemperance, Buchan argues, "never fails to disorder the whole animal oeconomy," as it "hurts the digestion, relaxes the nerves, renders the different secretions irregular, vitiates the humours, and occasions numberless diseases." [22]

John Gunn's 1830 domestic health guide includes sections on exercise and the various passions and a chapter containing general remarks on intemperance. According to Gunn, intemperance, "in its broadest signification," means "*excess* in the gratification of our *propensities*, *passions*, and even *intellectual pursuits*." "Every capacity or power of the human system, physical and intellectual," he asserts, "when exercised in moderation, and with strict conformity to the laws of nature, is productive of enjoyment and happiness." But when in eating and drinking we "overload and surcharge the stomach," and when in sleeping "take more repose than is required," we habitually become "*gluttons, drunkards* and *sluggards*, and are a disgrace to ourselves and society." [23]

In the second and third decades of the nineteenth century, several lay publications appeared that linked the traditional message concerning the importance of health and personal hygiene to those espoused by emerging reform movements. Henry Porter's *Journal of Health* was one of the first of these American health-oriented periodicals issued for the laity. Begun in 1829 and edited by two Philadelphia physicians, John Bell and D. Francis Condie, it was a precursor of the numerous health reform publications that appeared in the following decades. The *Journal of Health* forcefully emphasized the individual's responsibility for his or her own health. In the first issue, the editors vow that "the value of dietetic rules shall be continuously enforced" and "the blessings of temperance dwelt on." Intemperate behavior, they continue, especially the consumption of ardent spirits, leads to a number of disorders, including insanity: "The bloated face, and trembling hand, indigestion and dropsy, diseased liver and kidneys are the common and acknowledged effects" of excessive use of alcohol. Not only is the drunkard "prone to madness, and of course liable to become an inmate of a hospital or lunatic asylum," but the chance of recovering from an illness "is infinitely less for the drunkard than the sober man." [24]

By the time the *Journal of Health* appeared on the scene, a national temperance movement promoting abstinence of all alcoholic beverages was well under way. And although the journal's editors were staunch supporters of this movement, they, like Benjamin Rush, many of their peers in the medical profession, and many Americans in general, believed that alcohol, if used in moderation, was an effective restorative with nutritional value. In one of the journal's early issues, the editors speak of malt liquor, "when of good quality and drunk in moderation," as an "innocent and wholesome beverage." By 1831, however, their views had narrowed; reflecting the change of thinking that had occurred within in the medical profession and within society in general—that all alcoholic beverages were "poisonous" and water was the most wholesome alternative. Water not only facilitated digestion but also promoted the "free and equable circulation of the blood and the humours through all the vessels of the body, upon which the due performance of every animal function depends." The alcohol abuser, as depicted in the *Journal of Health*, was similar to the depictions advanced in almanacs of the time: a sad and pathetic figure, a self-centered buffoon who was both a curse and an embarrassment to family, community, and society. In one issue the editors compare the drunkard to Shakespeare's Falstaff: "If we examine the character of Falstaff, in whom all the bewitching qualities of a professed drunkard are exhibited, we shall find it such a one as few would willingly desire their own to resemble. He was not only a wit himself, but the cause of it in other men. He manifests much good humour in hearing the railing of others, and great quickness in retorts of his own. . . . Yet the same character is as strongly represented to us, by the inimitable delineation of nature, as a parasite, vulgar and unseasonable joker, a liar, a coward, a beastly and dishonest man." [25]

The journal's call for complete abstention from all alcoholic drinks was echoed and vigorously espoused by physicians, social reformers, and, of course, temperance advocates.[26] Several almanacs reflected this trend by endorsing the use of water instead of alcoholic drinks. The following poem appeared in the 1842 issue of *Poor Will's Almanac*:

> Fill, fill to the brim—fill, fill to the brim,
> Let the flowing crystal kiss the rim:

My hand is steady, my eye is true,
For I, like the flowers, drink nothing but dew.
Oh water, bright water's a mine of wealth,
And the ores it yieldeth are vigour and health;
So water, pure water, for me, for me!
Give wine to the tremulous debauchee.

Fill again to the brim, again to the brim,
For water strengtheneth life and limb;
To the days of the aged it added length,
To the might of the strong it added strength;
It freshens the heart, it brightens the sight,
'Tis like quaffing a goblet of morning light!
So water, I will drink nothing but thee,
Thou parent of health and energy.[27]

The *North American Almanac*, too, promoted the use of water. In an essay included in its 1852 issue, the compiler insists that pure water drinkers enjoy health because water "is a fluid that requires no digestion, for it is not necessary that it should undergo any changes. It is the natural menstrum that holds in solution both what is essential for the healthy functions of the body, and what has become refuse, after serving its destined office and intention in the animal kingdom. Water, therefore, from its congenial qualities, can never much disturb the system; and when it does, it is speedily expelled by its natural outlets, the skin and the kidneys."[28]

A number of early American almanacs were concerned not only with what their readers were drinking but also with what and how much they were eating. As portrayed in several eighteenth- and early nineteenth-century almanacs, the glutton was as repulsive as the habitual drunk. The *United States Almanac* for 1793, for example, labels the glutton "a monster of ugliness" reviled by those who know him because he is nothing but a parasite on society.

His belly is his god, and the cook the saint he prays to; a full table is his blessing, and yet a full table is his curse; by eating a great deal, he eats up himself; for, like an ox, the fatter he grows, the sooner he goes to the slaughter, and shortens his journey to the land of worms. His body is ever as an hospital, full of diseases; his mind is a thick mud, a standing puddle; no woman will ever marry him had he ever so much; if any do, she shall loathe to lie by such a monster of ugliness; his country hates him, because it knows not how to employ him, for he is fit for nothing; . . . he is an idle man, and an idle man is the devil's cushion.[29]

A moderate diet was one's protection against the physical infirmities, the moral decadence, and the social opprobrium that awaited the glutton. "By a moderate diet," one 1797 almanac claims, "the strength of the body is supported, the spirits are more vigorous and active, humours attenuated, crudities and obstructions prevented, many infirmities checked and kept under; the senses preserved in their integrity, the stomach clear, the appetite and digestion good." [30]

The 1798 issue of the *Columbian Almanac* offers dietary advice for preserving health that emphasizes the kinds of food one should consume and the amount: "Keep constantly to a plain diet, [for] those enjoy most health, and live the longest, that avoid curiosity and variety of meats and drinks." After all, the compiler asserts, many diseases "are cured by fasting, or a very spare diet." But when too much food is consumed, which the stomach can not digest, "the body will consequently be disordered and unhealthy." A poem reinforces this dietary doctrine.

> Accustom early in your youth,
> To lay embargo on your mouth;
> And let no rarities invite
> To spell and glut your appetite;
> But check it always and give o'er
> With a desire of eating more;
> It's very good for to abstain,
> That you thereby good health may gain.[31]

A year later, a similar message emanated from Isaiah Thomas's almanac. In an essay entitled "Rules for preserving health in Eating and Drinking," the writer (it is unclear whether Thomas was the author) advocates a spare diet, avowing forcefully, "*The more you fill your bodies, the more you hurt them.*" And however spare one's diet might be, it should also be plain: "The most unhealthy are found among those who feed high upon the most delicious dainties, and drink nothing but the strongest and most spirituous liquors." From plain and spare meals, "the breeding of those humors is prevented, which causes destruction, rheumatism, gouts, dropsies, giddiness, and corruptions in the mouth from the scurvy." [32]

Denunciations of and admonitions against gluttony disseminated by nineteenth-century almanacs were essentially the same, in terms of presentation and content, as those advanced by their eighteenth-century counterparts. "The great eater," *Low's Almanack* for 1822 proclaims, "commits suicide on his own wit and understanding" because "his brains lay in his belly." Whereas wine "hath slain her thousands," good eating has caused the demise of "tens of thousands, placed in the bill of mortality to the account of various diseases" created "directly or indirectly by gluttony."[33] Poetry continued to be a popular medium for regimen advice well into the nineteenth century, as this passage from an 1833 almanac shows:

> Intemp'rance steals, a subtle cheat!
> The best that life can give;
> But while the glutton lives to eat,
> The wise man eats to live.[34]

The 1833 edition of *Poor Robin's Almanack* (published in Philadelphia) and the 1834 version of the *Cumberland Almanac* (published in Nashville) issued the same "Dietetic Maxims." Seventeen in number, these rules address sleeping habits, exercise, temperance, and the kinds of foods one should eat. The first maxim stresses the importance of early rising, regular exercise, a cheerful mind, and abstinence from intoxicating liquors. Other maxims promote the use of bread, "perfectly raised, fully baked, and one day old," as a worthy complement to one's meal, and regular use of water, "a most wholesome drink."[35]

The concerns emanating from nineteenth-century almanacs regarding what and how much people ate and drank, as expressed in the detailed instructions quoted earlier, reflected the issues uppermost in the minds of social reformers as well as regular physicians, sectarian practitioners, and lay writers associated with the nascent health reform movement.[36] Porter's *Journal of Health*, for example, emphasized the critical role of diet in preserving one's health. The physician editors of the journal, like scores of hygiene proponents active during the antebellum period, stressed the necessity of moderation in diet because gluttony, like excessive drinking, retarded the "vital or organic" laws that governed the digestive process. Despite their denunciations of alcohol abuse, the editors were, in fact, more concerned with Americans' eating habits. To them, a bad diet was to be deplored more than drunkenness. "Shall [we] be told that excessive drinking is the much more faulty and reprehensible of the two, because it deranges the mind, and leads more certainly to other irregularities? That, [we] reply, is true, but as some counterbalance to it, excessive eating is the grosser and more bestial. It is further beneath what belongs to humanity, and is, in the same degree, more unworthy of man." The dangers to health posed by overeating were many, the editors claim, including "dyspepsia, hypochondria, gout, rheumatism, dropsy, jaundice, colic, epilepsy, and other convulsive affections, madness, [and] shapeless obesity with an approach to idiocy." [37]

The relationship between diet and the digestive process was not a product of the nineteenth century. Cheyne, Buchan, and other writers of an earlier period, too, addressed this link in their works. Dietary habits and their effects on digestion that are emphasized in the dietary rules encountered in early nineteenth-century almanacs and medical and lay publications, such as the *Journal of Health*, however, reflect the influence of François Broussais (1772–1838), a Parisian physician who declared that virtually every disease stemmed from gastroenteritis or enteric inflammation. Broussais claimed that inflammation of the stomach could affect other organs of the body and, conversely, inflammation of the stomach could be induced by overstimulation of other organs.[38] Moreover, the digestive system, like the body in general, was governed by natural laws. When issuing warnings concerning intemperance in general or gluttony in particular, general almanacs (unlike some specialty almanacs) seldom referred specifically to these laws. But what almanac regimen advice implied was made explicit by many medical and lay health publications. As mentioned in the Introduction, nineteenth-century health reformers viewed disease as the result of a failure by the individual to obey the laws of nature created by a merciful God. Living in accordance with these laws would restore one's health or keep one healthy. Responsibility for one's health—like salvation—resided with the individual.

Almanac regimen advice, like regimen advice encountered in other genres of popular print, required strict discipline by the individual, especially men and women who resided in large cities. A moderate diet and the avoidance of alcohol were to be complemented by regular exercise, adequate rest, fresh air, a contented mind, and a strong moral constitution. Nathaniel Ames, in his 1755 almanac, champions physical work—specifically farming—as providing the same benefits as regular exercise. "The Husbandman who manures the Glebe, and toils in the Dust and Rain," Ames asserts, "is steel'd with Labour;—his Nerves grow firm and strong" and "he walks unhurt, nor fears Rheumatic Pains or Coughs from Eastern Blasts." Whereas the industrious farmer can enjoy "the Balmy Dew of Sleep," and wake up the next morning refreshed, the "inactive Sluggard" is denied the pleasure. The loafer is condemned to countless restless nights, declares Ames, because "his flacid Nerves are unstrung, his nature sinks, his meals oppress, his Sleep is frantic with pale Spectres, coin'd in his delirious Brains; and monstrous Paintings shock his Soul all Night."[39]

An essay in the *New-Jersey Almanac* for 1828 goes so far as to declare that, except for warm clothes, "nothing is more conducive to bodily health, activity, and cheerfulness of the mind, than *regular* and *seasonable exercise*. . . . Taken in a suitable degree and at proper times," exercise "increases the power of digestion, quickens and renders clear the action of the mind, and preserves that just balance between the mental and physical powers which is necessary to health, strength, and happiness." To the compiler of *Phinney's Calendar, or Western Almanac*, exercise was a moral duty. The 1840 issue of this publication states that the "faculties with which our God has endowed us, both physical and intellectual, are so dependent upon exercise for their proper development that action and industry must be regarded among the primary duties of accountable men." The avoidance of exercise, according to the essay's author, is "disgraceful": "We come into the world feeble in body and in mind, but with seeds of improvement in both; and these seeds grow according to the cultivation they receive from exercise. The body grows in stature and in strength, and the mind gradually expands. But exercise is requisite to the development both of our corporeal and mental capacities. . . . Without exercise of body and mind, there can be no happiness."[40]

While exercise afforded many benefits, it could be overdone. Almanac regimen advice warned readers against overworking the body as well as the mind. In keeping with the traditional humoral concept of balance, almanac regimen advice, like that found in other forms of lay health publications of the eighteenth and early nineteenth centuries, advocated a moderate amount of exercise. Horseback-riding and walking were cited often as two examples of healthy activities. "Of all exercises," according to Isaiah Thomas, "walking is the best" because "it is the most natural for men in good health." The Massachusetts printer and almanac maker also advocated horseback-riding as an excellent exercise for aiding the recovery from illness.[41] *Hutchins' Improved Almanac*, in its 1845 issue, promotes walking over riding as "the best possible exercise." "The Europeans," Hutchins points out, "value themselves as having subdued the horse to the use of man, but I doubt whether we have not lost more than we have gained by the use of this animal. No one thing has occasioned so much degeneracy of the human body. An Indian goes on foot nearly as far in a day, for a long journey, as an enfeebled white does on his horse, and he will tire the best horse. A little walk of half an hour in the morning when you first rise, is advisable. It shakes off sleep, and produces other good effects in the animal economy." [42]

While moderate exercise was strongly encouraged, indolence or laziness was widely condemned. Keeping late hours and sleeping late in the morning or during the day were behaviors especially targeted as morally deficient and physically reckless. Comparing the useless idler to the industrious laborer, the *Farmer's Almanack* for 1816 observes that although the former may possess "more luxury," the latter has "more health." [43] John Grigg's 1829 almanac includes an extract from Buchan's *Domestic Medicine* that denounces the vile practice of wasting the morning in bed: "No piece of indolence hurts the health more than the modern custom of lying a-bed." Because the morning is "undoubtedly the best time for exercise" since the "stomach is empty and the body refreshed with sleep," Buchan advises rising at "six or seven" and "spending a couple of hours in walking, riding, or any active diversion without doors." He asserts that this regimen will keep one's "spirits cheerful and serene throughout the day, his appetite keen, and his body braced and strengthened." [44]

In this passage on the deleterious effects of late rising, Buchan observes critically that sleeping late is "the general practice in great towns," whose inhabitants "seldom rise before eight or nine o'clock." [45] Buchan's remarks concerning the indolent habits of town dwellers implied a negative view of the urban resident in particular and of urban life in general. In keeping with the traditional view that the body is affected by its environment, the charge that towns and cities posed a serious risk to one's physical and moral constitution was a message so entrenched by the eighteenth century that it was encountered often in American popular print of the next century, in self-help guides and readers and spellers, and in the writings of health and social reformers. The *Journal of Health*, for example, urged its readers to avoid the noxious atmospheres and idle amusements of large towns and cities. Contending, in one issue, that it is a well-known fact that "residence in a large and overcrowded city is found to shorten considerably the average duration of human life" and "greatly detract from the health of the system," the journal's editors describe cities as "sepulchres of the dead and hospitals of the living." In contrast, they praise the "primitive simplicity" and the salubrious effect of rural life as well as the health and moral soundness of country residents.[46]

The contrast between the healthy benefits of rural life and the unwholesome dangers of urban living was referred to often in almanacs. While acknowledging that country residents possessed a better chance of resisting disease because they followed a disciplined course of adequate rest, a proper diet, and moderate exercise, almanac regimen advice concentrated on the advantages of their healthy work habits. "No working-man, we believe eats bread and butter with better relish than the farmer," an 1833 almanac argues. "He is seldom troubled with the *dyspepsia*" because the "ploughing, and mowing, and raking, and hoeing, are very effectual scarecrows to the disorder." Six years later, the same almanac continued its praise of the hard-working farmer whose simple life compared favorably with that of the nervous, enfeebled city resident: "Who lives more pleasantly and more happily than the husbandman? If it is homely in manner, compared to the city stylish ones, let me tell you, Mr. Sneer, it is free from city vexation. He is never in the fidgets, lest his note should lie over. He is never obliged to take one emetic, because he gobbled too much beef-steak and brandy for supper. Calomel, jalap and Brandreth's pills, he knows nothing about; his medicine is exercise; his amusement his daily labor." *Phinney's Calendar, or Western Almanac* for 1846 asserts that country people are privileged to live "among the fields which are now putting on their green attire," to be cheered by the "minstreley [*sic*] of birds during the day" and soothed "by the plaintive notes of the frog" during the night. The farmer, declares the almanac, should never envy "those who live without labor," because the latter are most likely "to miss the great ends of life; health, peace of mind, and contentment."[47]

This constant linking of peace of mind and contentment to the good health of the country resident emphasizes the close relationship between a healthy body and a "healthy" mind. This relationship of the body and the mind was part of a traditional medical world view that dates to antiquity. Cornaro and Cheyne, to cite two examples, underscored the importance of controlling the passions as a means of ensuring good health. "The influence of the passions on the nerves, and health of our bodies, is so great," Cornaro writes, "that none can possibly be ignorant of it. He therefore who seriously wishes to enjoy good health, must above all things, learn to conquer his passions." Failure to control the passions leaves one vulnerable to wide array of diseases and could lead to "sudden death." Cheyne's words echo Cornaro's sentiments: "All violent and sudden passions, dispose to, or actually throw people into acute diseases; and sometimes the most violent of them bring on sudden death." [48]

Views similar to Cornaro and Cheyne's were encountered in early American almanacs. According to *Father Abraham's Almanack* for 1766, many diseases "may be changed, or even cured, by the Passions; as Surprise, Joy, and Strong Expectations." Unfortunately, according to the compiler, the "ignorant Multitude" gives most of the credit to the medical profession.[49] The *New-York Almanack* for 1780 urges its readers to manage their passions to maintain good health: "Tranquility of mind should be aimed at by all persons . . . [for] sudden gusts of anger and rage have often proved fatal." [50] In a list of "Rules for Preserving Health" offered by the 1795 *South Carolina and Georgia Almanac*, the sections devoted to the passions were borrowed directly from Cheyne's *Essay on Health and Long Life*. One rule links piety with a tranquil mind and, by extension, good health: "The love of God, as it is the sovereign remedy of all miseries, so, in particular, it effectually prevents all the bodily disorders the passions introduce, by keeping the passions themselves within due bounds. And by the unspeakable joy and perfect calm, serenity and tranquility it gives the mind, it becomes the most powerful measure of health and long life." [51] In 1800, a Philadelphia almanac offered readers "Important Observations on Health and Long Life," which highlight the importance to one's health of balancing the six non-naturals. The section devoted to the "Affection of the mind" accentuates the significance of controlling the passions: "The due regulation of the passions perhaps contributes more to health and longevity, than that of any other of the non-naturals. The animating passions, such as joy, hope, love & etc. when kept within proper bounds, gently excite the nervous influence, promote an equable circulation, and are highly conducive to health; while depressing affections, such as fear, grief and despair, produce contrary effect, and lay the foundation of the most formidable diseases." [52]

Losing control of one's passions was just as dangerous to health as fouling one's stomach with rich food and strong drink. In fact, the *Philadelphia Almanack* for 1834 links disordered passions with dyspeptic stomachs, contending that "in nine cases out of ten," the brain is the primary cause of dyspepsia. "Give that delicate organ some rest," the almanac urges its readers. "Leave your business behind you when you go to your home," and do not sit down to dinner "with your brows knit and your mind absorbed in casting up interest accounts." To avoid the complaint of dyspepsia, the almanac advocates keeping a clear conscience and living temperately, keeping regular habits, and maintaining cleanliness. Moreover, one should be "industrious" while cultivating "the social affections," and one should always "banish gloomy and desponding thoughts." *Phinney's Calendar, or Western Almanac* for 1855 also stresses the health benefits of a positive attitude: "Acquire a composure of mind and body. Avoid agitation or hurry of one or the other, especially just before and after meals. To this end govern your temper—endeavor to look at the bright side of things—discard envy, hatred and malice, and lay your head upon your pillow in charity with all mankind." The *Hagerstown Town and Country Almanack* for 1860 advocates musical activities as a sure way to ensure health: "Music, like painting and statuary, refines, elevates and sanctifies." But music is also "physically beneficial" because it "rouses the circulation, works up the bodily energies, and diffuses life and animation around." After all, the writer of the essay notes, one seldom hears a lazy man sing or a "milk-and-water character strike a note." [53]

The connection between body and mind was the basis for numerous strictures against reading novels and wearing fashionable clothing. An 1815 almanac warns, for example: "The indiscriminate reading of Novels and Romances is to young females, of the dangerous tendency and baleful influence . . . generally gives to the minds of young females, a romantic turn, indisposes them for the engagement of whatever is rational and solidly corrupts every good principle, enfeebles fortitude, induces a sickly and disgusting sensibility, destroys all relish for common blessings and enjoyments, converts them into a bundle of acutely feeling nerves, and makes them 'ready to expire of a rose, in aromatic pain.' " [54]

As far as the *Rhode-Island Almanac* for 1849 was concerned, tight corsets and novels were the main causes of bad health in women.

Romance and corsets have done, probably, more to undermine the constitution, and ruin the health and usefulness of girls, than any other pair of maladies known to the physician. One keeps her from sleeping, and the other from exercising her lungs; while both together fill her with chimeras, indigestion, nightmares, and a passionate desire to wed a knight with a satin beaver shirt on, and spangled with glory and doubloons. From the cradle to old age, too many girls read and dress as if they wished to make lunatics of their heads and hour-glasses of their bodies. And too often succeed . . . consequently, the most of them at the age of twenty, become filled with vapors and haunted castles, instead of being qualified for a good wife or a No. 1 nurse. [55]

One New England almanac published a testimony from a doctor about the deleterious effects of reading novels:. "A physician in Massachusetts says, 'I have seen a young lady with her table loaded with volumes of fictitious trash, poring, day after day and night after night, over highly wrought scenes and skillfully portrayed pictures of romance, until her cheeks grew pale, her eyes became wild and restless, and her mind wandered and was lost—the light of intelligence passed behind a cloud and her soul was for ever benighted. She was insane, incurably insane from reading novels.' " [56]

EIGHTEENTH- AND nineteenth-century American almanac makers and publishers attempted to meet the practical needs of their core audience of literate and semi-literate artisans, farmers, and laborers, but they also included material in their almanacs that would appeal to a more affluent and learned readership. Though many general almanacs offered astrological and therapeutic advice (these two categories often overlapped), which would have met the expectations and needs of a core readership, as this chapter shows, fewer general almanacs offered their readers regimen advice. This difference may be attributable to three factors: regimen advice was widely accessible in other genres of popular print, almanac makers chose to concentrate on health advice that would meet the needs of their core readership, and core readers of almanacs may have preferred health advice that was practical and immediate.

If almanac makers and publishers, however, were attempting to reach the broadest audience, why did not more of them offer health advice of interest to readers beyond their core readership? The historian can only speculate. Perhaps the many almanac makers and publishers who chose to omit regimen advice felt that adding this category of guidance to astrological and therapeutic advice would have resulted in too much of an emphasis on health in a publication in which space was extremely limited. It may be more than coincidence that some of the most successful almanac makers and publishers—Benjamin Franklin, Nathaniel Ames, father and son, Isaiah Thomas, and Robert P. Thomas, whose *Old Farmer's Almanac* has survived to the present—were those who offered both regimen and therapeutic advice in their publications.

The regimen advice that appeared in eighteenth- and nineteenth-century American general almanacs was, for the most part, written by the almanac maker or compiler or borrowed from another genre of popular print. And there was more than enough material from which to choose. Regimen guidance in one form or another was pervasive. One would have encountered this advice in reprints of the works of Cornaro and Cheyne; in domestic health texts, especially those of Buchan and Gunn; in sectarian medical publications; in newspapers; in periodicals; in certain religious publications; and in numerous works produced by antebellum health and social reform movements.

FOR MANY almanac readers, the regimen advice they received would have reinforced their views of the body, health, and disease based on the concept of humoral equilibrium. Eighteenth- and early nineteenth-century almanac regimen admonitions conveyed a familiar message that readers would have heard, read, and struggled with constantly. Living in accordance with God's laws would restore one's health or keep one healthy. And the responsibility for one's health—like salvation—rested with the individual.

HEALTH ADVICE WITH
AN AGENDA

"This is decidedly the age of almanacs," Arthur Prynne asserted in 1841. The Albany-based almanac maker marveled at the rapid growth of specialization in the trade: "We have religious almanacs, political almanacs, phrenological almanacs, comic almanacs, farmers' almanacs, ladies' almanacs, pocket almanacs, and temperance almanacs, which last are distributed at our doors without pay, or so much as the requirement of a nod by way of acknowledgment." Prynne's reference to complimentary copies of temperance almanacs revealed his anxiety over the potential impact these and other specialty almanacs would have on his business. "Who then remains to be supplied with *Prynne's Almanac*?" he asked. His reply, "We shall see," was more an appeal than a nonanswer. Prynne was acutely aware that only the continued loyalty of his customers could supply the answer he desired.[1]

The age of almanacs to which Prynne referred was marked by rapid change. The period between the end of the War of 1812 and the Civil War witnessed the appearance of numerous almanacs devoted to specific causes, directed to specific audiences, or focused on specific subjects. Unlike general almanacs, which offered advice, information, and entertainment their compilers believed readers wanted, specialty almanacs provided readers with content their compilers thought they should have. Whereas the purpose of general almanacs was to generate a profit for their printers and publishers, the purpose of many specialty almanacs, several of which were distributed free of charge, was to advance an agenda, to advocate a cause, or to sell a product other than the almanac itself. For some specialty almanacs, profits generated from sales were used to support a cause.

The pre–Civil War emergence of specialty almanacs influenced the health advice offered to antebellum almanac readers. Some specialty almanacs contained no health advice of any kind. Among those that did offer health advice, it was usually based on astrology. Some almanac makers and publishers, however, fashioned their health advice to fit a particular moral agenda, and their advice tended to espouse prevention rather than treatment (see Fig. 6).[2]

Porter's Health Almanac (Philadelphia, 1832–33), *Thomson's Almanac* (Boston, 1840–44), and the *Health Almanac* (New York, 1842–44) are three examples of antebellum medical almanacs that offered health advice similar to that traditionally encountered in general almanacs. *Porter's Health Almanac* was issued by Henry H. Porter, the Philadelphia publisher who sought a niche in the book trade by publishing works on personal health and hygiene and on general self-improvement, the most important of which was the *Journal of Health* (Philadelphia, 1829–33).[3] In the autumn of 1831, Porter, in an attempt to expand his audience, published the first issue of *Porter's Health Almanac*. Co-edited by John Bell and D. Francis Condie, the Philadelphia physicians who also edited the *Journal of Health*, Porter's almanac offered the same health advice as that publication: the value to health of temperance, a proper diet, regular exercise, cleanliness, and control of the passions.

Linking the traditional belief in the importance of personal hygiene to long life with the reform movements of the period, Bell and Condie espoused moderation and morality as the key elements of perfect health. Considering the professional interests of the editors, it is not surprising that Porter's almanac included neither astrological health advice nor home remedies. As members of a profession under attack by competing medical sects, Bell and Condie concerned themselves with establishing the authority of the regular medical profession in the management of disease. By circumscribing the role of the laity in medicine, the co-editors attempted to strengthen the position of the trained physician in the sphere of treatment.[4] Yet the doctors' message of moderation and morality should not be seen merely as an attempt to promote their professional interests. Their message was also shaped by their attitudes concerning the body, health, and disease. The editors' regimen advice implied a conception of the body as a mechanized equilibrium system governed

Fig. 6. A specialty almanac promoting a reform movement, 1837.
The Temperance Almanac . . . 1837 (Philadelphia:
State Temperance Society, [1836]). (Author's collection)

by—and embodying—the laws of nature created by God. Thus, living in accordance with God's laws would keep one healthy or restore one's health. Disease was the result of unnatural behavior, such as overeating, drinking too much, keeping late hours, or otherwise transgressing against the laws of nature.[5]

Samuel Thomson, whose fierce opposition to the therapeutic practices of the regular medical profession ignited a social movement that achieved national prominence during the antebellum period, published an almanac in Boston during the last years of his life. Thomson used his almanac, like his other publications, to castigate the medical profession while espousing self-treatment based on his own medical philosophy. Recall that Thomson asserted that the body was healthy when its four components—earth, water, air, and fire (heat)—were balanced. Disease was the result of imbalance, which according to Thomson, diminished the body's natural heat. The purpose of Thomson's therapeutic regimen, which comprised emetics, purgatives, steam or vapor baths, and herbal medicines, was to cure disease by restoring the body's natural heat.[6]

Thomson preached about the health benefits that would result from cleanliness, appropriate dress, exercise, the avoidance of alcohol and tobacco, and a proper diet. For example, he endorsed moderate exercise as "one of the most sovereign remedies of which we are possessed, either in preserving or restoring health. . . . It increases the natural heat of body, invigorates the heart, and promotes an equal distribution of blood. It assists the excretions of perspiration, urine, and stool; strengthens appetite and digestion; renders the body less liable to the malignant influence of weather, or the attack of disease." Thomson was highly critical of the use of tobacco. "Next to spirituous liquors," tobacco, Thomson claims in his 1843 almanac, is the "most destructive of all pernicious habits, to health and life." To drive home his point he inserted an antismoking anecdote borrowed from the 1826 issue of the *New York Medical Almanac*: " 'What harm is there in a pipe?' says young Puffwell. 'None, that I know of' replied his companion, 'except that smoking induces drinking—drinking induces intoxication—intoxication induces the bile— bile induces the jaundice—jaundice leads to dropsy—and dropsy terminates in death.' Put that in your pipe and smoke it."[7]

Thomson's Almanac for 1842 advises its readers to avoid "regular doctors" and their "depletive and poisoning system" of bloodletting and mineral drugs. In his 1843 annual, Thomson advances concise rules for maintaining and restoring health: "Rise early, eat moderately, live an active and useful life, cultivate all the virtues and avoid the vices of society, and as soon as unwell use the Thomsonian means for cure."[8] The issue includes descriptions (with woodcut illustrations) of various herbs and plants readers might use in following his remedies. Of his four Boston almanacs, only two contain astrological advice, and that is confined to the column in the monthly calendar denoting the moon's place.

The *Health Almanac*, published by John Burdell, a New York dentist and health reformer, promulgated notions of the body, health, and disease similar to those advanced in *Porter's Health Almanac*. Burdell advocated moderation and moral living as fundamental to achieving and maintaining health. His almanac goes much further, however, than either Porter's or Thomson's in its presentation of the body as a machine, providing detailed descriptions of the various organs and systems of the body, particularly those associated with the process of digestion. Many of these descriptions are accompanied by meticulous woodcuts that depict the body's—and, by implication, God's—intricate design. In this approach, Burdell was in tune with the current trend of teaching anatomy and physiology in American common schools (tax-supported, state-regulated public schools that began to appear in the 1830s) and was also taking advantage of improvements in printing technology.[9]

For diet, Burdell championed vegetarianism. Referring to himself as "A Vegetable Eater" in the 1842 issue of his almanac, Burdell argues that man is intended by God to subsist "upon fruit and vegetables, the natural productions of the earth." Man courts debility and disease when he "departs from this great first principle" and "violates the law of nature." Burdell also promoted the teaching of anatomy and physiology in common schools, as well as dress reform. He included the image of the Anatomy and a related column in each month's calendar for the moon's place and parts of the body affected. Burdell did not offer his readers therapeutic advice, however, though he, like Samuel Thomson, was highly critical of the regular medical profession. Burdell vilified regular physicians for what he believed was their growing use of mineral drugs. These drugs, according to Burdell, played no role in the restoration of health but only exacerbated disease. In his 1844 almanac he asserts, "We need not expect to escape the penalty of violated physical law" by resorting to mineral drugs. When we use this type of medication, he warns, "we involve ourselves in deeper transgressions, and thereby incur a heavier punishment in the end."[10] Readers of Burdell's *Health Almanac* were told that health is achieved by living in harmony with the laws of nature that govern the mechanistic body, and that disease is an unnatural state caused by flouting these laws.

Few of the pre-1860 specialty almanacs, other than those devoted to health, offered their readers much, if any, health advice.[11] Comic almanacs, political almanacs, and antislavery almanacs, to cite three examples, seldom offered health advice. If they did, it was astrological and limited to a column in the calendar section listing the moon's place. Although few specialty almanacs included a cut of the Anatomy, many included astrological health information in their calendars. No matter the purpose of a particular almanac, general or specialty, it would have included a calendar. And in most cases, the almanac makers or publishers made the decisions about what information a calendar section contained. This probably was the only section in specialty almanacs in which compilers added information that was dictated by popular taste and reader expectations.

If a reader encountered health advice beyond astrological information, it tended to be regimen or hygiene advice.[12] Religious almanacs, for example, were full of advice on how to live one's life. Part of a large and vigorous religious publishing industry that emerged from the evangelical revival spawned by the Second Great Awakening, religious almanacs represented one of the largest categories of specialty publications. That religious almanacs served regimen advice along with their usual fare of spiritual guidance and pietistic maxims was consistent with the strong belief among reformers, physicians, religious leaders, and the laity that one's spiritual health was linked to one's physical health. A healthy body depended on a healthy mind and soul and vice versa. One attained both spiritual salvation and physical health by obeying the laws of God built into nature.[13]

The regimen advice offered in various religious almanacs was wide-ranging, addressing behaviors relating to the six non-naturals. The importance of balance and moderation in one's habits relating to eating, drinking, and exercise was encountered often, as was advice concerning cleanliness and control of the passions. The American Tract Society published many almanacs from the 1820s through the 1850s. One of these, the *Christian Almanack*, for example, was issued in various cities in the Northeast. An essay in the 1827 version of this almanac promotes the benefits of abstaining from ardent spirits: "Drink not a drop of them, even in the hurrying season of the year, unless advised to do so by your physician. The experience of many proves that men feel stronger, can perform more labour, and endure the heat better, without this sparkling poison, then with it. Instead of it, drink beer, milk, cider, water-gruel, sweetened water. If *you let ardent spirits alone*, you will be more likely to enjoy health—your children will probably be sober, strong and healthy without it—and besides, you will add the weight of your influence to put an end to intemperance, which is now ruining so many both for this world and the next." The *Christian Almanac, for Connecticut*, first published in 1821 and "devoted chiefly to the subject of missions to the Heathen," began later in that decade to "give a prominent place to the subject of Temperance." It, too, warned its readers of the evils of ardent spirits. The 1831 issue includes a "certain cure for drinking Spirituous Liquors": "Take two ounces of the flour of consideration—dissolve it in a pint of the spirit of self-denial; then add one quart of the juice of resolution. Shake it well together, then put it into a golden bowl (memory), if the golden bowl be not broken, then sweeten it with the sugar of high reputation." [14]

"Temperance," the *Illustrated Family Christian Almanac* for 1850 declares, "puts wood on the fire, meal in the barrel, flour in the tub, money in the purse, credit in the country, contentment in the house, . . . vigor in the body, intelligence in the brain, and spirit in the whole constitution." Intemperance, however, exerts a devastating effect not only on the individual transgressor but on his or her family members and descendents. It was commonly known, the article continues, that the families of the intemperate "run out and become extinct in the second and third generation." Even if a family survives beyond that point, the descendents are "in danger of becoming *idiots* or *insane*." Practicing temperance and other wholesome behaviors, according to the almanac, will do more for preserving one's health than any medicine a physician could prescribe: "Medicine will never remedy bad habits. It is ultimately futile to think of living in gluttony, intemperance, and every excess, and keeping the body in health by medicine. Indulgence of the appetite, and indiscriminate dosing and drugging, have ruined the health and destroyed the life of more persons than famine, sword, and pestilence. If you will take advice, become regular in your habits, eat and drink wholesome things, sleep on mattresses, and retire and rise very regularly. Make a free use of water to purify the skin, and when sick, take counsel of the best physic you know, and follow nature." [15]

Several religious almanacs promoted cleanliness for its benefits as both a health preservative and a health restorative. The *Christian Almanac for*

New-York, Connecticut, and New-Jersey for 1837, for example, urges its readers to bathe regularly. After all, the compiler lectures, if students and professional men "would faithfully attend to this item of their *duty*, we should not hear them speaking so often of *bad digestion, ill health,* and unfitness for study." A clean body will save one from "an untimely grave" and ensure one's living to "a good old age, free of those diseases that in a thousand forms prey upon the body." [16] The *Illustrated Family Christian Almanac* took the concept of cleanliness one step further, stating in its 1849 issue that a clean living environment is just as important to one's health—morally and physically—as a clean body.

> A neat clean, fresh-aired, sweet, cheerful, and well-arranged house, exerts a *moral* as well as *physical* influence over its inmates and makes the members of a family peaceable, and considerate of each others' feelings and happiness. The connection is obvious between the state of mind thus produced, and habits of respect for others, and for those higher duties and obligations which no laws can enforce. On the contrary, a filthy, squalid, noxious dwelling, in which not the decencies of life can be observed, contributes to make inhabitants selfish, sensual, and regardless of the feelings of others. And the constant indulgence of such passions renders them reckless and brutal; and the transition is natural to propensities and habits incompatible with a respect for the property of others, or for the laws. [17]

Like the many physicians and social reformers who believed that uncontrolled passions posed a risk to one's health, some religious leaders viewed the reading of fiction as a serious threat to the delicate balance of the passions. This was certainly the attitude of the *Methodist Almanac,* which included in its 1844 issue a familiar diatribe against novel reading: "Novels and light tales which abound in modern periodicals constitute the literature of a large number who look no further than to the gratification of the moment, and who are reluctant to submit to the labour of thinking. The effect of such habits is to dissipate the mind, and to disqualify it for any higher efforts than to which it is thus accustomed. No information is to be obtained, no just sentiment formed, no stores of knowledge laid up for the practical uses of life. Fictitious sympathy may be created, unreal scenes of life familiarized, and the mind encouraged to entertain dreams which can never be realized." [18]

Of the seventeen religious almanac titles consulted, only two offer therapeutic advice. All but three offer astrological health advice, though this tends to be confined to a list of the signs of the zodiac or a column in the calendar section denoting the moon's location in the zodiac and the parts of the body affected. Only one almanac includes a cut of the Anatomy. Two religious almanacs openly criticize the belief in and practice of astrology. One of these, the *Methodist Almanac*, in its 1846 issue, condemns other almanacs for disseminating "much superstition and injurious trash in the shape of astrological rules for various agricultural operations [and] . . . for bleeding, purging, etc., down to cutting the hair, paring the nails, as well as predictions of the weather and of political events." [19] It is interesting to note that the two religious almanacs that disparaged astrology included columns in their calendar sections relating to the moon's place and the parts of the body affected.

Although most religious almanacs listed a sale price (the average price was six cents an issue), many were given away to those who could not afford them. After all, the collective goal of religious publishers was universal circulation of their publications, not financial gain. Because almanacs cost almost nothing to produce and were popular in the marketplace, they were an attractive venue for religious publishing houses. [20]

Purveyors of proprietary medicines did use the popular almanac for financial gain. Almanacs contributed to a product's success not through numbers sold, however, but by providing a platform on which certain proprietary medicines could be advertised and marketed. Of course, it was not uncommon for early American general almanacs—as well as newspapers—to include advertisements for proprietary medicines. Like newspapers, almanacs that advertised nostrums were, in many instances, issued by printers, such as William Bradford and Benjamin Franklin, who also sold medicines along with books and stationery. [21]

The first almanac proprietary medicine advertisement appeared in Samuel Atkins's 1685 *Kalendarium Pennsilvaniense*, the first American almanac issued outside of New England. Printed in Philadelphia by William Bradford, Atkins's annual includes an advertisement for "some experienced Medicines" sold by Bradford, including "Charles Marshall's Spiritus Mundus, being an excellent medicine against all sorts of Fevers and Agues, Surfeits, Gripes, Plurisies, etc." [22] Bradford also printed Daniel Leeds's almanacs and occasionally used this series to promote several proprietary medicines sold at his shop. For example, Leeds's 1698 issue contains an advertisement for a nostrum imported from London, "Lockyers Universal Pill," which was "famous for the Cure of Agues, Feavers [*sic*], Scurvey, Gout, Dropsie, Jaundice, Bloody Flux, Griping of the Guts, Worms of all sorts, the Gravel, Stone, Collick, and many other diseases."[23]

Many of the medicines advertised in seventeenth- and eighteenth-century American almanacs were imported from Great Britain. This began to change around the turn of the nineteenth century, however, with the appearance of American-made proprietary medicines. And as these American nostrums proliferated, innovative advertising methods were devised to market them. By the second half of the nineteenth century, the proprietary medicine trade had irrevocably transformed the American almanac.[24]

Those in the proprietary medicine business used newspapers, broadsides, handbills, circulars, pamphlets, and even books to advertise and sell their nostrums. Because of its popularity with the American public as well as its low production costs, the almanac was an excellent venue for marketing proprietary medicines. It is not surprising, then, to see nineteenth-century proprietary medicine firms turning to the genre to sell their products. It made good business sense to advertise in a publication that had such a wide distribution and catered to such a broad-based audience. By the middle decades of the century, many proprietary medicine firms were publishing their own almanacs.[25]

The 1816 issue of *Beers' Almanac* presents a typical example of early nineteenth-century proprietary medicine advertising in general almanacs. Three of the last five pages are devoted to promoting a nostrum, Rogers Vegetable Pulmonic Detergent "for Coughs, Consumptions & Asthmas," that was sold at the almanac printer's bookstore. The advertisement begins with an announcement addressed "To the Public" by the medicine's producer, Doctor George Rogers, who informs readers that his detergent is the "result of twenty years experience" dealing with pulmonic diseases. "No expense or trouble has been spared in this composition," claims Rogers. Because modesty restrained him from boasting that "no Medicine for Consumption or Asthmatic complaints" has been as successful "as my Vegetable Pulmonic Detergent," Rogers offers readers a selection of testimonials to the medicine's efficacy submitted by "persons of the highest respectability." And Rogers assures readers that not one of the certificates attesting to the nostrum's successful cures "has ever been fabricated" or "obtained from disreputable sources."[26] The use of testimonials, sometimes signed by well-known physicians, noted statesmen, and famous war heroes, but usually submitted by ordinary Americans or fabricated by advertising firms, was a conventional marketing tool used by proprietary medicine companies.[27]

Several issues of *Phinney's Calendar, or, Western Almanac* from the late 1820s through the 1840s demonstrate the increasing presence of advertising, especially for proprietary medicines, in the genre. The 1826 issue, for example, includes a one-page advertisement for Anderson's Cough Drops and Pectoral Powders, a "valuable medicine for Coughs and Consumptions." A paragraph promoting the many virtues of the cough drops, which were sold by the printer of *Phinney's* almanac as well as "by almost every other Druggist in the United States," is followed by two testimonials.[28]

By the 1838 issue, *Phinney's* was carrying three pages of proprietary medicine advertisements promoting Sears' Hygiene Pills and Dr. Brandreth's Vegetable Universal Pills along with Anderson's Cough Drops and Pectoral Powders. The vegetable universal pills, the concoction of a transplanted Englishman, Benjamin Brandreth, soon became a popular evacuant that contributed significantly to its makers' success and wealth.[29] A two-page advertisement promoting Brandreth's Pills lists twenty-five facts proving the nostrum's efficacy.

First. Animal life originates from a fluid.

2nd. By the circulation of a fluid, animal bodies are formed, increased, and supported.

3^{d}. This *life-giving*, *circulating* fluid, is the BLOOD.

4th. An ordinary man contains about three and a half gallons, or twenty-eight pounds of blood.

5th. About two ounces of blood are propelled by the heart at each contraction.

6th. The heart contracts seventy times per minute, therefore all the blood in the body passes through the heart in three minutes.

7th. The body is constantly subject to two distinct processes, viz: decomposition and reorganization.

8th. Reorganization is affected by the blood, which flowing from the heart through the *arteries*, supplies the waste of the system, by restoring decayed parts.

9th. The blood in its return to the heart through the *veins*, brings with it those particles which have become deleterious through decomposition.

10th. The mere fluid of these deleterious particles pass from the body through the skin in the shape of perspiration; but the grosser humors are discharged through the excretions into the bowels.

11th. The want of proper action in these natural drains, is the *primary cause of all disease. . . .*

18th. There is no effectual method of purifying the blood except by the use of vegetable physic.

19th. This vegetable physic must be of such a nature, that it may be taken for any length of time without injury to the digestive organs.

20th. The *only medicine known* to possess these properties, is *Dr. Brandreth's Vegetable Universal Pills. . . .*

24th. The BRANDRETH PILLS possess the *universal* power of completely curing the most inveterate disease; simply because they purify the blood.[30]

The advertisement's purpose was to persuade readers to purchase Brandreth's nostrum by framing its presentation around the familiar concept of humoral balance.

By 1848 *Phinney's* almanac had expanded its advertisement section to eleven pages, with eight pages devoted to proprietary medicines. Besides Sands' Sarsaparilla Pills and Dr. Reynolds' Imperial Health Pills, the almanac included advertisements for the Graefenberg Vegetable Pills, which, according to the manufacturer, sold thirty thousand boxes "each and every week," and for that "Great Consolation to the Afflicted," Dr. McIntosh's Italian Vegetable Pile Electuary, "the most celebrated remedy for piles ever discovered in any age of the world."[31]

Pre-1840 almanac proprietary medicine advertisements were usually nothing more than text. Occasionally a woodcut image of a druggist's shop or a proprietary medicine firm's building would accompany the advertisement. Change came in the 1840s, however, with advances in printing technology and marketing techniques.[32] The makers of Dr. Townsend's Compound Extract of Sarsaparilla, for example, used many illustrations. In advertisements that appear in the 1847 issue of the *Franklin Almanac* and the 1848 issue of the *Family Almanac, and Franklin Calendar*, a woodcut of Townsend's sarsaparilla factory (located in New York City) is accompanied by several woodcuts, prepared by the firm's own artists, showing various complaints cured by the nostrum. Many of the woodcuts were used to dramatize the testimonials, such as that submitted by John McGown of Albany, describing his long-standing—and, thanks to Townsend's Compound, successful—battle with a cancerous growth on his face. McGown's tale is complemented by a graphic woodcut depicting the growth, in the words of the publisher, "as well as our artist was able to give it." The publisher of the almanac assures readers that "the face in reality was much worse than the drawing represents." [33]

The production of almanacs by proprietary medicine firms was looked upon as an investment in advertising and marketing (see Fig. 7). The makers of Dr. S. P. Townsend's Compound Extract of Sarsaparilla provide a useful model of the important role played by printing and publishing in marketing efforts. Like many purveyors of proprietary medicines, the Townsend firm operated its own printing press that produced circulars, handbills, and labels for the firm's medicines, and, of course, its almanac. The Townsend firm, if its promotional material can be believed, spent fifty thousand dollars a year—a huge sum at the time—advertising its compound.[34]

One of the products of Townsend's press was the *People's Illustrated Almanac*. Like many almanacs, both general and specialty, Townsend's contained astronomical and astrological information, weather predictions, a calendar, and miscellaneous facts. It differed from general almanacs, however, because its purpose was to help sell the firm's nostrum. The almanac contained page after page of testimonials promoting the efficacy of Townsend's Compound Extract of Sarsaparilla. The Townsend firm spent twelve hundred dollars on printing two million copies of the 1848 issue, all of which were distributed free of charge. Complimentary copies were given to anyone who purchased Townsend's Compound and were available at the firm's New York City outlet and in drug stores in other cities and towns that were designated Townsend agents.[35]

Like the *People's Illustrated Almanac*, almanacs issued by other proprietary medicine firms included the usual front matter that readers expected to encounter: astronomical and astrological information, weather predictions, and a calendar. Of the seven proprietary almanac titles consulted, four include a cut of the Anatomy and all include astrological health advice in the calendar section. Only one almanac contains therapeutic advice. At least half of each proprietary medicine almanac is devoted to testimonials and advertisements promoting the firm's nostrums. All of these almanacs were distributed free of charge.[36]

By the second half of the nineteenth century the almanac had lost much of the influence it once held before the Civil War. By the 1870s the almanac trade had been dramatically transformed by the proprietary medicine industry. The publication that people had turned to for enlightenment and entertainment less than a century before was now looked upon with derision and ridicule. Recall the sentiments of Samuel Briggs,

Fig. 7. A proprietary medicine firm's almanac, 1860.
Merchant's Gargling Oil Co.'s National Almanac . . . 1860
(Lockport, N.Y.: M. H. Tucker and Co., [1859]). (Author's collection)

who recoiled at the thought of almanacs promoting the "virtues of pills, potions, and plasters."[37] Yet, although proprietary medicine almanacs were produced to sell a product, the content of those issued before 1860 can enlighten the historian about early American attitudes concerning the body, health, and disease.

Although proprietary medicine firms were not seeking financial gain from sales of their almanacs, they wanted people to read them for the testimonials and advertisements they contained. By distributing their almanacs free of charge and filling them with information people expected to find, proprietary medicine firms counted on people's using them as they would use a general almanac. Readers of these almanacs would have been introduced to various nostrums that offered relief for a wide array of complaints. Testimonies from satisfied customers were offered as proof of a nostrum's efficacy. If therapeutic advice was offered in a proprietary medicine almanac, it was predictable, recommending a particular nostrum. Seldom were the ingredients of a particular medicine revealed to the reader beyond the fact that its ingredients were vegetable or chemical.

What readers did learn, however, was why a particular proprietary medicine would be useful for them and for others who suffered from similar afflictions. Nostrum makers based their explanations on common neohumoral assumptions concerning the body, health, and disease. Dr. S. P. Townsend, for example, was convinced that disease "was the result of defective circulation either in quantity or quality." Knowing that "food produced Life—or new Blood—and being aware that the gastric juice or saliva secreted by the glands decomposed or digested food, and thus assisted nature to create fluids in the body," he produced a medicine that, he promised, would "enter into the circulation" and act "as a diffusive stimulant to the circulation and strengthen the stomach, bowels, Urinary organs without disturbing or debilitating the system." Townsend's Compound Extract of Sarsaparilla, in short, would alleviate humoral imbalance by maintaining or restoring a regular circulation, which would, in turn guarantee the body's natural processes of evacuation.[38]

Restoring regularity by removing obstructions and purifying the blood to maintain regularity was a common pitch used by nostrum venders to sell their products. And, as James Whorton has shown, venders had an audience of avid believers that grew as the century progressed.[39] In his 1847 almanac, Dr. William Moffat claims that his Vegetable Life Pills and Phoenix Bitters will "loosen from the coats of the stomach and bowels the various impurities and crudities" found there, and remove "hardened faeces which collect in the convolutions of the small intestines." By cleaning the kidneys and the bladder, "and by this means the liver and the lungs," Moffat continues, "the healthful action of which entirely depends upon the regularity of the urinary organs" is restored. Once regularity is restored, the blood regains its strength and thus "renews every part of the system, and mounts the banner of health in the blooming cheek." [40]

The makers of Wright's Indian Vegetable Pills declared that their nostrum was efficacious because it was "purely vegetable," and, after all, the natural remedies for the diseases of man "are to be found in the vegetable kingdom." Because of their natural ingredients, the pills "cleanse the bowels and purify the blood" and, by removing "all improper accumulations and local irritations," ensure regularity "throughout the frame." [41] Finally, the makers of Dr. Christie's Magnetic Fluid, Galvanic Necklace and Bracelets, and Galvanic Belt, added a novel twist to the traditional humoral approach (see Fig. 8). Asserting that a healthy nervous system is the key to the general health of the body, *Christie's Family Almanac* for 1853 points to the brain as the body's "Galvanic Battery" that keeps all internal systems functioning and thus in balance. When the brain fails to develop "its proper stimulus," the nervous system breaks down, affecting the rest of the body. Only by resorting to Galvanism can the body "recall Nature to her lost or interrupted functions" and thereby regain health. [42]

EPILEPSY OR FALLING SICKNESS.
FITS AND CONVULSIONS.

Of all the sad afflictions to which poor humanity is subject, these are the most dreadful and alarming. In one moment, and without the least warning, the unhappy victim becomes senseless and powerless, and the awful spasms and contractions which generally accompany the attacks, render the picture one of frightful misery. The frequency and intensity of the attacks are very various. In some cases, six to ten cases may occur in a day, and a very short period suffices to permanently impair the vital energies of the entire system. We have no intention here to enter into a full explanation of the causes which lead to these most terrible afflictions. This has already been done by Dr. CHRISTIE in a work which he has recently published, and which may be had gratis of his authorized agents. We merely state here that Fits of every kind are *entirely nervous* in their character—the seat of the disease in all these cases being the Brain and Spinal Nerves. Let the physician be mindful how he tampers with the already prostrated and enfeebled system by the use of Drugs, Stimulants, or Sedatives, in these cases. *They never do any good*, and often the most irreparable injury. The only chance for relief or recovery is the appropriate and judicious use of Galvanism, and we here state boldly that at least nine out of every ten cases of *Epilepsy, or Falling Sickness, Fits, and Convulsions*, may be immediately relieved and with patience entirely cured, by the application of the Galvanic articles. The complete set should be used—the **Galvanic Belt**,

Necklace, Bracelets, and **Magnetic Fluid.** The astonishing cures which have been made in these cases lead us to hope that the human race will gradually become exempt from these most lamentable and dreadful diseases, which have for ages withstood all the resources of science and medicine, while they have desolated and afflicted humanity.

☞ Those who may be subject to Fits, or who have friends or relatives in such lamentable condition, are earnestly requested to examine this matter with candor and not to determine hastily, because they have been deceived or disappointed before, that there is no hope of relief.

The cases which follow are of the most extraordinary and conclusive character, and are earnestly recommended to the attention of the interested. They are from persons whose name and character must give weight to any statements they may make.

FROM DR. FREDERICK HOLLICK,
THE CELEBRATED
AUTHOR, LECTURER, AND PHYSICIAN
NEW YORK, May 5, 1851.

D. C. MOREHEAD, M. D :—

My Dear Sir,—I beg to acknowledge receipt of your favor asking my opinion and the results I have experienced by the application of Galvanism in Epileptic Fits and Convulsions generally. In reply I would say that I regard the judicious use of Galvanism as the only reli-

Fig. 8. Remedy for Falling Sickness, 1853. *Christies' Family Almanac for the Year 1853* (New York: D. C. Morehead, M.D., [1852]). (Author's collection)

EPILOGUE

THIS STUDY examines the dynamic relationship between popular print and popular medicine in pre–Civil War America. This relationship, of course, did not begin with the founding of the American colonies nor was it derailed by the carnage and economic disruption brought about by the Civil War. The tradition that dates to the invention of the printing press is as vibrant today as it was during the period covered here. Scores of health publications for the laity—many in multiple editions—continued to be published in the United States in great numbers during the second half of the nineteenth century, and the trend continues to the present.

In pre–Civil War America, most health care took place in the home. Today, doctors' offices, outpatient clinics, and hospitals play central roles in the management and treatment of illness. Yet, despite the many advances in medicine and the evolution of hospitals into mega-complexes that treat every disease and engage in cutting-edge research, the desire of twenty-first-century Americans to participate in their own health care is as strong as it was among their seventeenth- and eighteenth-century counterparts. The latter, living in a time when trained physicians were financially inaccessible or geographically unavailable, had few choices in the treatment of illness. If they did not treat themselves, they turned to other family members, neighbors, or a local midwife. And the lay practitioner, whoever it might be, would have possessed as much authority in the eyes of the patient as a trained physician. The medical knowledge they brought to the patient's bedside would have been derived from several sources: oral culture, folk tradition, and print. Moreover, this medical knowledge would have been based on the same assumptions concerning the body, health, and disease held by trained physicians.

Advances in medical science, medical education, and health care in the late nineteenth century, however, began to create a divide between the laity and the profession that has continued to expand, leaving twenty-first-century Americans with a bewildering array of choices regarding health care and often little understanding of a health care system that has become extremely expensive, bureaucratic, and complex. Navigating this complicated system of primary care physicians, specialists, insurance companies, HMOs, and drug companies can be formidable even for the most sophisticated patient. Today, scores of publications are available to help Americans navigate the system, seek alternative care, or treat themselves. The tradition of popular health publications is as strong as it was during the period covered by this book, but now print sources are complemented, as well as threatened, by television infomercials and an ever-growing number of Internet sites.[1]

Except for their role as outlets for the growing proprietary medicine industry, almanacs exerted little influence in the expanding post–Civil War market in popular health publications. The "age of almanacs" cited by Arthur Prynne had passed. The almanac, once the leading secular publication in America, was, by the outbreak of that war, one among many genres vying for the attention of a rapidly expanding population of readers. As the American book trade became increasingly competitive and diverse, the Poor Richards, Poor Robins, and Poor Wills of the almanac trade—once honored guests at every fireside—were replaced by publishers and entrepreneurs who seemed less interested in forging a relationship with their readers. By the late nineteenth century the almanac had drifted to the margins of the American book trade, its image tarnished by the perception among many that it had become a handmaiden of the proprietary medicine industry and that its readership was made up primarily of the gullible and the ignorant. In his 1878 study of American literature, Moses Coit Tyler sums up the current opinion of the genre by referring to the almanac as the "very quack, clown, pack-horse, and pariah of modern literature."[2]

Almanacs, of course, did not completely disappear by the mid-nineteenth century. The genre persisted and has survived to this day, as any reader of the *Old Farmer's Almanac* can attest or a visit to a reference section of a modern chain bookstore will confirm. Political almanacs and sports almanacs are just two categories that come readily to mind in a genre that covers a plethora of subjects. Persistence, however, has brought significant change. This change is strikingly evident as one compares the content of today's almanacs with that of their popular forerunners. Except for the *Old Farmer's Almanac* and several astrology almanacs, few modern almanacs contain monthly calendars, weather predictions, or any of the other categories of information, advice, and entertainment that an eighteenth- or early nineteenth-century reader would have encountered.

One might say that the almanac was, to some extent, a victim of its own success. Many eighteenth- and early nineteenth-century almanac makers were successful because they were providing readers with content that was, for the time, both extremely useful and uniquely entertaining. Facing little competition in the marketplace and available for a price that many Americans could afford, almanacs became the dominant secular publication in America from the early eighteenth century through the early decades of the nineteenth. Having found a recipe for success and a comfortable niche within the marketplace, many almanac makers resisted making adjustments that were required to adapt to dramatic changes occurring within American society in general and within the publishing industry in particular. It is not that the contents of almanacs ceased to be of interest to American readers, rather it was that their contents, including health advice, were integrated into other genres of popular print. By 1860 almanac makers were no longer the cultural mediators that their eighteenth-century predecessors had been. Moreover, almanacs were no longer leading sources of health information. Having lost their relevance by the second half of the nineteenth century, almanacs gradually evolved into a variety of formats, such as ready reference guides, compendiums of facts as well as handy sources for miscellaneous data and trivia, such as population statistics, batting averages, famous firsts, and lists of one sort or another.

THE ALMANAC was a basic component of a complicated, fragmented, semi-vernacular health literature published in America to 1860. For most of the century from the 1750s through the 1850s it served the laity as a leading source of health information. That advice was based on a notion of the body that was familiar to and understood by readers. The body was seen as a microcosm of the universe, a delicate and permeable equilibrium system constantly interacting with and shaped by its environment, both celestial and terrestrial. This conception was part of a worldview that had changed little from its Hippocratic–Galenic origins. The interaction between body and environment was visible in the bodily processes of intake and outgo, operations through which the body constantly struggled to achieve a harmonious balance of its humors.

Among some almanac makers a mechanistic view of the body complemented their neohumoral notions. This materialistic view surfaced in American almanacs by the middle of the eighteenth century. Nathaniel Ames, in the 1752 edition of his almanac, refers to the body as "a well regulated clock," a delicate machine that consists of "an infinite variety of branching and winding channels, thro' whose cylindrical and conic tubes of Blood, a fluid whose momentum of the Heart, like the main spring of a watch, is perpetually propell'd forward in a unwearied circulation."[3] Clearly Ames did not see this Newtonian, scientific-based model as in any way clashing with his older, traditional humoral view. Three decades later Isaiah Thomas, too, assigned a mechanistic interpretation to the body, calling it "a system of pipes, through which the fluids circulate."[4] Two 1830 almanacs published by the American Tract Society extracted an article from the *Medical Advertiser* that compares the human body to a watch: "The human frame may be compared to a watch, of which the heart is the main-spring, the stomach the regulator, and what we put into it the key by which the machine is wound up. According to the quantity, quality, and proper digestion of what we eat and drink, will be the pace of the pulse, and the action of the system in general. When we observe a due proportion between the quantum of exercise and that of excitement, all goes on well. If the machine be disordered, the same expedients are employed for it—adjustments as are used by a watchmaker: it must be carefully cleaned and judiciously pilled."[5] *Peter Parley's Almanac* for 1836 uses the same analogy, referring to the human body as "a piece of a very delicate mechanism; more nice and complicated than the finest watch."[6]

This mechanistic view of the body, too, implies a holistic way of thinking about the human system. One bad part can disrupt the whole delicate mechanism. Charles Rosenberg, in his examination of American physiology schoolbooks issued in the decades preceding the Civil War, has underlined the pervasiveness of this mechanistic interpretation. And, as the views of Ames, John Burdell, and Drs. John Bell and D. Francis Condie presented in previous chapters reveal, it was a notion that in no way rejected or replaced more traditional humoral assumptions. As Rosenberg aptly states, the humoral concern with balance and fluids remained in some form or another, "a fundamental building block in both medical and lay conceptions of health and disease."[7] The physiology texts Rosenberg describes, however, present a body that is more than a mere machine and its interrelated parts. There was an invisible force directing the body's functions. The machine and its processes were guided and animated, in the words of Rosenberg, "by an immanent spiritual gyroscope."[8] Almanacs, too, primarily through the regimen advice they offered, presented a notion of the body that merged the materialistic and the spiritual—a system that was governed by and embodied the laws of nature created by God.

Popular conceptions of the body, health, and disease that can be derived from almanacs provide an explanation of early American lay medical beliefs and practices. Popular notions of the body, for example, dictated and informed therapeutic and behavioral advice offered by almanacs as well as by other genres of print. Conclusions advanced in this study concerning almanac therapeutic advice are based on evidence that comes, in part, directly from almanac readers.

The main purpose of this study is to provide a clearer understanding of popular medical attitudes and practices in America before the Civil War and how these attitudes shaped and were shaped by print. But I do not contend that the views discussed in this work are the only ways in which early Americans conceptualized their bodies or envisioned health and disease. Recent works in cultural history and in the history of medicine, for example, have shown that the body held multiple meanings for early Americans, shaped by ethnicity, gender, race, religious beliefs, and ideas of selfhood.[9] Historians have also shown that one's gender, religious beliefs, and social and economic status influenced the way one thought about health and disease.[10] This work in no way attempts to contradict these recent studies but seeks to complement them.

Because of the narrow focus of this study, the medical beliefs and practices presented herein are not representative of those of all early Americans. Almanac makers and almanac readers were overwhelmingly white and predominantly Christian, thus the views of the body, health, and disease—and the behaviors and practices they informed—discussed in this work were not necessarily those shared by Native Americans or African Americans. Yet, as I state in Chapter 2, although various groups of early Americans came from or developed different belief systems regarding the body, health, and disease, they seemed to agree on fundamental notions of humoralism. For example, conceptions of health and disease within African American slave communities were influenced heavily by spiritual and magical beliefs, yet their diagnostic and therapeutic systems were based on a balance model. Moreover, interactions between white planters and enslaved populations resulted in the sharing of medicines and medical lore, resulting in a fusion of the traditional beliefs and practices of both groups.[11]

I contend in this study that pre-1860 American almanacs were an integral component of a complicated, fragmented, semi-vernacular health literature and, thus, that almanacs had an important impact on popular medicine in early America, especially in disseminating astrological health information. Almanac makers correctly sensed that while astrology was scorned by the educated and worldly, it remained popular with a prominent segment of their readers. Despite their often critical personal views of the practice, and their attempts to minimize the amount of astrology in their publications, almanac makers realized that they could ill afford to alienate an important constituency. In responding to a key segment of their audience, almanac makers and publishers helped astrology survive (if only within certain segments of American society) while shaping contemporary and future perceptions of the practice.

THE ALMANAC was one of several genres of print through which lay therapeutic and regimen advice was disseminated in early America. One seeking a cure for a particular ailment or advice on how to live a healthy life could consult numerous domestic health guides, regimen or hygiene texts, popular health periodicals, newspapers, domestic or household economy books, publications of various medical sects, as well as almanacs. An almanac's therapeutic and regimen advice may have been collected in a family recipe book or a commonplace book, or inserted into a domestic health guide, such as those of Moses Appleton, William Lenoir, and Eliza Lucas Pinckney. An almanac's remedies also may have been memorized or recorded in a family journal for later use. Since early American print culture offered a diverse array of sources of health information for the laity, the almanac may not have been the first place a person would have looked for health advice. Rather, the remedies and regimen advice contained in almanacs would have both reinforced and shaped readers' assumptions about the body, health, and disease and the behaviors and practices these assumptions informed.

APPENDIX

General Almanacs

This study is based on an examination of 1,785 almanacs (1,533 general almanacs and 252 specialty almanacs) published in America between 1646 and 1861 (approximately two-thirds were published between 1750 and 1850). Of the 1,533 general almanacs consulted, 1,493 (97 percent) contain some form of astrological guidance, 441 (29 percent) contain remedy advice, and 240 (16 percent) contain regimen advice. (These percentages differ significantly from those appearing in my 2003 essay "Rules, Remedies, and Regimens." There my conclusions are based on the consultation of 861 almanacs, slightly less than half the sample size used in this work.) These figures, particularly those relating to remedy and regimen advice are profoundly misleading, for two main reasons. Most almanacs published before 1750 do not offer remedy and regimen advice, and the figures do not reflect regional differences. An examination of almanacs by region and date issued, however, reveals that regimen advice and, especially, remedy advice appears more frequently in almanacs published between 1750 and 1860 and in almanacs issued in the middle-Atlantic region and in the South. For example, an analysis of almanacs published in the middle-Atlantic between 1646 and 1861 (see table 1), reveals that remedy advice appears in 33 percent (251 out of 748). The percentage is higher for the same period in the South, where 44 percent (76 out of 173) of the almanacs issued contain remedy advice. When one looks at remedy advice in almanacs published in these two regions from 1750 to 1860, the percentage remains virtually unchanged for southern almanacs (45 percent) but becomes significantly higher in almanacs published in middle-Atlantic region (41 percent). Throughout the period covered by this work, almanacs that were issued in the middle-Atlantic, southern, and western regions of the country were more likely to contain images of the Anatomy and health and regimen advice than those issued in New England, which tended to adhere to a more narrow focus.

My conclusions are based on consulting at least 35 percent of all almanacs issued in America before 1801 and approximately 12 percent of all almanacs issued before 1861. (These percentage figures are based on Shipton and Mooney, *National Index of American Imprints through 1800*, and Drake, *Almanacs of the United States*.) I have consulted virtually all of the leading almanac titles of the eighteenth and nineteenth centuries, as well as long runs of almanacs that I consider to be representative of different regions of the country.

Table 1

General Almanacs by Date and Region

	New England	Middle Atlantic	South	West	Total
		1646–1700			
Almanacs	63	12	—	—	75
Content					
Anatomy	6 (9%)	0	—	—	6 (8%)
List of signs	5 (8%)	8 (67%)	—	—	13 (17%)
Moon's place	55 (87%)	10 (83%)	—	—	65 (87%)
Gen'l. astrology	4 (6%)	9 (75%)	—	—	13 (17%)
Remedy advice	1 (2%)	0	—	—	1 (1%)
Remedies[1]	12	0	—	—	12
Avg. # of remedies	12	0	—	—	12
Regimen advice	0	2 (17%)	—	—	2 (3%)
		1701–1750			
Almanacs	132	160	5	—	297
Content					
Anatomy	66 (50%)	96 (60%)	4 (80%)	—	166 (56%)
List of signs	25 (19%)	55 (34%)	2 (40%)	—	82 (28%)
Moon's place	128 (97%)	160 (100%)	5 (100%)	—	293 (99%)
Gen'l. astrology	19 (14%)	20 (13%)	0	—	39 (13%)
Remedy advice	4 (3%)	9 (6%)	0	—	13 (4%)
Remedies	12	28	0	—	40
Avg. # of remedies	3	3	—	—	3
Regimen advice	3 (2%)	6 (4%)	0	—	9 (3%)
		1751–1800			
Almanacs	209	284	85	—	578
Content					
Anatomy	51 (24%)	235 (83%)	62 (73%)	—	348 (60%)
List of signs	67 (32%)	49 (17%)	27 (32%)	—	143 (25%)
Moon's place	207 (99%)	279 (98%)	85 (100%)	—	571 (99%)
Gen'l. astrology	1 (>1%)	2 (>1%)	1 (>1%)	—	4 (>1%)
Remedy advice	61 (29%)	131 (46%)	43 (51%)	—	235 (41%)
Remedies	247	639	299	—	915
Avg. # of remedies	4	5	7	—	4
Regimen advice	43 (20%)	85 (30%)	19 (22%)	—	147 (25%)
		1801–1861			
Almanacs	167	292	83	41	583
Content					
Anatomy	29 (17%)	242 (83%)	65 (78%)	32 (78%)	368 (63%)
List of signs	91 (54%)	175 (60%)	34 (41%)	34 (83%)	364 (63%)
Moon's place	150 (90%)	290 (99%)	83 (100%)	41 (100%)	564 (97%)
Gen'l. astrology	1 (>1%)	0	0	0	1 (>1%)

Table 1 *(continued)*

Remedy advice	45 (27%)	106 (36%)	33 (40%)	5 (12%)	189 (32%)
Remedies	112	343	105	16	576
Avg. # of remedies	2	3	3	3	3
Regimen advice	25 (15%)	47 (16%)	9 (11%)	3 (7%)	84 (14%)

	1646–1861				
	New England	Middle Atlantic	South	West	Total
Almanacs	571	748	173	41	1,533
Content					
Anatomy	152 (27%)	573 (77%)	131 (76%)	32 (78%)	888 (58%)
List of signs	188 (33%)	287 (38%)	93 (54%)	31 (76%)	599 (39%)
Moon's place	540 (95%)	739 (99%)	173 (100%)	41 (100%)	1,493 (97%)
Gen'l. astrology	25 (4%)	31 (4%)	1 (<1%)	0	57 (4%)
Remedy advice	111 (19%)	251 (34%)	76 (44%)	3 (7%)	441 (29%)
Remedies	383	1,010	404	16	1,813
Avg. # of remedies	3	4	5	5	4
Regimen advice	69 (12%)	140 (19%)	28 (16%)	3 (7%)	240 (16%)

1. *Remedies* refers to the number of remedies that appeared in all almanacs during a given period of time. *Avg. # of remedies* refers to the average number of remedies that appeared in those almanacs that contained remedy advice.

Specialty Almanacs

Of the 252 specialty almanacs consulted, 196 (78 percent) contain some form of astrological health guidance, 38 (15 percent) contain remedy advice, and 45 (18 percent) offer regimen advice (see table 2). Clearly, specialty-almanac makers were less interested in providing their readers with astrological or remedy advice than were their counterparts in the general almanac trade. Conversely, regimen advice appears with about the same frequency in specialty almanacs (18 percent) as in general almanacs (16 percent). Specialty almanacs published by health reformers and religious groups, however, tended to offer readers significantly more regimen advice than did their competitors in both the general and overall specialty trades.

Table 2
Specialty Almanacs by Content, 1646–1861

Type	#	Anatomy	List of signs	Moon's place	Remedy advice	Remedies	Regimen advice
Temperance	12	0	3 (25%)	6 (50%)	0	—	2 (17%)
Agriculture	124	49 (39%)	99 (78%)	121 (97%)	26 (21%)	84	15 (12%)
Religion	37	1 (2%)	29 (78%)	31 (84%)	3 (8%)	10	14 (38%)
Education	2	0	1 (50%)	1 (50%)	0	—	0
Prop. med.[1]	10	5 (50%)	0	10 (100%)	0	—	0
Medical	28	6 (21%)	15 (53%)	18 (64%)	9 (32%)	23	14 (50%)

Table 2 *(continued)*

Type	#	Anatomy	List of signs	Moon's place	Remedy advice	Remedies	Regimen advice
Juvenile	1	0	1 (100%)	0	0	—	0
Political	34	2 (6%)	6 (18%)	11 (32%)	0	—	0
Fraternal	1	0	1 (100%)	1 (100%)	0	—	0
Comic	3	2 (67%)	1 (33%)	3 (100%)	0	—	0
Total	252	65 (26%)	156 (62%)	196 (78%)	38 (15%)	117	45 (18%)

The categories *Gen'l Astrology* and *Avg. # of remedies* are omitted here; none of the specialty almanacs consulted includes general astrology advice, and few include remedy advice.

1. *Prop. Med* refers to almanacs published by proprietary medicine firms, primarily as a means of marketing their products.

General and Specialty Almanacs

MDCXLVII. An Almanack for the Year . . . 1647. Cambridge: Matthew Day, 1647.

MDCXLVIII. An Almanack for the Year . . . 1648. Cambridge: [Matthew Day], 1648.

MDCXLIX. An Almanack for the Year . . . 1649. Cambridge: [Samuel Green], 1649.

MDCL. An Almanack for the Year . . . 1650. Cambridge: [Samuel Green], 1650.

MDCLVI. An Almanack for the Year . . . 1656. Cambridge: Samuel Green, 1656.

MDCLX. An Almanack for the Year . . . 1660. Cambridge: Samuel Green, 1660.

MDCLXI. An Almanack for the Year . . . 1661. Cambridge: Samuel Green and Marmaduke Johnson, 1661.

MDCLXIII. An Almanack of the Coelestial Motions . . . 1663. Cambridge: Samuel Green, 1663.

MDCLXIV. An Almanack of the Coelestial Motions . . . 1664. Cambridge: Samuel Green and Marmaduke Johnson, 1664.

MDCLXV. An Almanack of Coelestial Motions . . . 1665. Cambridge: Samuel Green, 1665.

MDCLXVIII. An Almanack of Coelestial Motions . . . 1668. Cambridge: Samuel Green, 1668.

MDCLXXIX. An Almanack of Coelestial Motions . . . 1679. Boston: John Foster, 1679.

MDCLXXX. An Almanack of Coelestial Motions . . . 1680. Boston: John Foster, 1680.

MDCLXXXI. An Almanack of Coelestial Motions . . . 1681. Boston: John Foster, 1681.

MDCLXXXIII. The Boston Ephemeris. An Almanack for . . . MDCLXXXIII. Boston: Samuel Green, 1683.

MDCLXXXIIII. Cambridge Ephemeris. An Almanack of Coelestial Motions . . . for the Year . . . 1684. Cambridge: Samuel Green, 1684.

MDCLXXXV. Cambridge Ephemeris. An Almanack of the Coelestial Motions, for the Year . . . 1685. Cambridge: Samuel Green, 1685.

MDCLXXXVII. Cambridge Ephemeris. An Almanack of Coelestial Motions . . . for the Year 1687. Cambridge: Samuel Green, 1687.

MDCCVII. An Almanack of the Coelestial Motions . . . 1707. Boston: Bartholomew Green, 1707.

MDCCIX. An Almanack of Coelestial Motions . . . 1709. Boston, 1709.

MDCCIX. An Ephemeris of the Coelestial Motions . . . 1709. Boston: Bartholomew Green, 1709.

MDCCX. An Almanack of Coelestial Motions . . . 1710. [New York: William Bradford], 1710.

MDCCXI. An Almanack of the Coelestial Motions . . . 1711. Boston: Bartholomew Green, 1711.

MDCCXII. An Almanack of the Coelestial Motions . . . 1712. [Edward Holyoke]. Boston: Bartholomew Green, 1712.

MDCCXII. An Almanack of the Coelestial Motions . . . 1712. [Daniel Travis]. Boston: Bartholomew Green, 1712.

MDCCXII. An Almanack of the Coelestial Motions . . . 1712. [Thomas Robie]. Boston: Bartholomew Green, 1712.

MDCCXIII. An Almanack of the Coelestial Motions . . . 1713. [Edward Holyoke]. Boston: Bartholomew Green, 1713.

MDCCXIII. An Almanack of the Coelestial Motions . . . 1713. [Daniel Travis]. Boston: Bartholomew Green, 1713.

MDCCXIV. An Almanack of the Coelestial Motions . . . 1714. [Thomas Robie]. Boston: Bartholomew Green, 1714.

MDCCXV. An Almanack of the Coelestial Motions . . . 1715. [Edward Holyoke]. Boston: Bartholomew Green, 1715.

MDCCXV. The Loyal American's Almanack for the Year . . . 1715. Boston, 1715.

MDCCXV. The Young American Ephemeris for the Year . . . 1715. Boston, 1715.

MDCCXV. An Almanack for the Year . . . 1715. Boston, 1715.

MDCCXVI. An Almanack of the Coelestial Motions . . . 1716. [Daniel Travis]. New London, 1716.

MDCCXVI. An Almanack of the Coelestial Motions . . . 1716. [Thomas Robie]. Boston: Thomas Fleet and Thomas Crump, 1716.

MDCCXVI. An Almanack for the Year . . . 1716. Boston, 1716.

MDCCXVII. An Almanack of the Coelestial Motions . . . 1717. [Thomas Robie]. Boston: Thomas Fleet and Thomas Crump, 1717.

MDCCXVII. An Almanack of Coelestial Motions . . . for the Dionysian Year . . . 1717. [Daniel Travis]. Boston: Bartholomew Green, 1717.

MDCCXVII. An Almanack for the Year . . . 1717. [Boston: Thomas Fleet, 1717].

MDCCXVIII. An Almanack of Coelestial Motions . . . 1718. [Thomas Paine]. Boston: Thomas Crump, 1718.

MDCCXVIII. An Almanack of the Coelestial Motions . . . 1718. [Thomas Robie]. Boston: Thomas Fleet and Thomas Crump, [1717].

MDCCXVIII. An Almanack of Coelestial Motions . . . 1718. [Daniel Travis]. Boston: Bartholomew Green, 1718.

MDCCXVIII. An Almanack for the Year . . . 1718. [Boston: Thomas Fleet, 1717].

MDCCXIX. An Almanack of the Coelestial Motions . . . 1719. [Thomas Paine]. Boston: Thomas Fleet, 1719.

MDCCXIX. An Almanack of Coelestial Motions . . . 1719. [Daniel Travis]. Boston: Bartholomew Green, 1719.

MDCCXIX. An Almanack for the Year . . . 1719. Boston: Thomas Fleet, 1719.

MDCCXX. An Almanack of the Coelestial Motions . . . 1720. Boston: Thomas Fleet, 1720.

MDCCXX. An Almanack of the Coelestial Motions . . . 1720. [Thomas Robie]. Boston: Thomas Fleet, 1720.

MDCCXX. An Almanack of the Coelestial Motions . . . for the Dionysian Year . . . 1720. [Daniel Travis]. Boston: Bartholomew Green, 1720.

MDCCXX. An Almanack for the Year . . . 1720. Boston: Thomas Fleet, 1720.

MDCCXXI. An Almanack of the Coelestial Motions . . . 1721. Boston, 1721.

MDCCXXI. An Almanack of Coelestial Motions . . . for the (Dionysian) Year . . . 1721. [Daniel Travis]. Boston: Bartholomew Green, 1721.

MDCCXXII. An Almanack of Coelestial Motions . . . for the (Dionysian) Year . . . 1722. [Daniel Travis]. Boston: Bartholomew Green, 1722.

MDCCXXII. An Almanack for the Year . . . 1722. Boston: Bartholomew Green, 1722.

MDCCXXII. The New-England Diary, or, Almanack for the Year . . . 1722. Boston, 1722.

MDCCXXIII. An Almanack of the Coelestial Motions . . . 1723. [Robert Treat]. New London: Timothy Green, 1723.

MDCCXXIII. An Almanack of Coelestial Motions . . . for the (Dionysian) Year . . . 1723. [Daniel Travis]. Boston: Thomas Fleet, 1723.

MDCCXXIII. The New-England Diary, or, Almanack for the Year . . . 1723. Boston: Bartholomew Green, 1723.

MDCCXXIV. The New-England Diary, or, Almanack for the Year . . . 1724. Boston: Bartholomew Green, 1724.

MDCCXXV. An Almanack of the Coelestial Motions . . . 1725. [Robert Treat]. New London: Timothy Green, 1725.

MDCCXXV. The New-England Diary, or, Almanack for the Year . . . 1725. [Nathan Bowen]. Boston: Bartholomew Green, 1725.

MDCCXXV. The New-England Diary, or Almanack for the Year . . . 1725. [Nathaniel Whittemore]. Boston: James Franklin, 1725.

MDCCXXVI. The New-England Diary, or, Almanack, for the Year . . . 1726. [Nathan Bowen]. Boston: Bartholomew Green, 1726.

MDCCXXVII. An Almanack of Coelestial Motions . . . 1727. [Robert Treat]. New London: Timothy Green, 1727.

MDCCXXVII. The New-England Diary, or, Almanack, for the Year . . . 1727. [Nathan Bowen]. Boston: Bartholomew Green, 1727.

MDCCXXVIII. The New-England Diary, or, Almanack for the Year . . . 1728. [Nathan Bowen]. Boston: Bartholomew Green, 1728.

MDCCXXVIII. The Rhode-Island Almanack . . . 1728. Newport: James Franklin, 1728.

MDCCXXIX. The New-England Diary, or, Almanack for the Year . . . 1729. [Nathan Bowen]. Boston: Bartholomew Green, 1729.

MDCCXXIX. The Rhode-Island Almanack . . . 1729. Newport: James Franklin, 1729.

MDCCXXX. An Almanack for the Year . . . 1730. [Nathan Bowen]. Boston: Bartholomew Green, 1730.

MDCCXXX. The Rhode-Island Almanack . . . 1730. Newport: James Franklin, 1730.

MDCCXXXI. The New-England Diary: or, Almanack for the Year . . . 1731. [Nathan Bowen]. Boston: Bartholomew Green, 1731.

MDCCXXXII. The New-England Diary, or, Almanack for the Year . . . 1732. [Nathan Bowen]. Bartholomew Green, 1732.

MDCCXXXII. The Rhode-Island Almanack . . . 1732. Newport: James Franklin, 1732.

MDCCXXXIII. The New-England Diary, or, Almanack for the Year . . . 1733. [Nathan Bowen]. Boston: Bartholomew Green, 1733.

MDCCXXXIII. The Rhode-Island Almanack . . . 1733. Newport: James Franklin, 1733.

MDCCXXXIV. The New-England Diary, or, Almanack for the Year . . . 1734. [Nathan Bowen]. Boston, 1734.

MDCCXXXIV. The Rhode-Island Almanack . . . 1734. Newport: James Franklin, 1734.

MDCCXXXV. The New-England Diary: or, Almanack for the Year . . . 1735. [Nathan Bowen]. Boston: Thomas Fleet, 1735.

MDCCXXXV. The Rhode-Island Almanack . . . 1735. Newport: James Franklin, 1735.

MDCCXXXVI. The New-England Diary: or, Almanack for the Year . . . 1736. [Nathan Bowen]. Boston: Thomas Fleet, [1735].

MDCCXXXVII. The New-England Diary: or, Almanack for the Year . . . 1737. [Nathan Bowen]. Boston: Thomas Fleet, 1737.

MDCCXXXVII. The Rhode-Island Almanack . . . 1737. Newport: Ann Franklin, 1737.

MDCCXXXVIII. The Rhode-Island Almanack . . . 1738. Newport: Ann Franklin, 1738.

MDCCXXXIX. The Rhode-Island Almanack . . . 1739. Newport: Ann Franklin, 1739.

MDCCXL. The Rhode-Island Almanack . . . 1740. Newport: Ann Franklin, 1740.

MDCCXLI. The Rhode-Island Almanack . . . 1741. Newport: Ann Franklin, 1741.

1666. An Almanack or, Astronomical Calculations . . . 1666. Cambridge: Samuel Green, 1666.

1667. An Almanack for the Year . . . 1667. Cambridge: Samuel Green, 1667.

1669. An Almanack of Coelestial Motions for the Year . . . 1669. Cambridge: Samuel Green, 1669.

1670. An Almanack of Coelestial Motions for the Year . . . 1670. Cambridge: Samuel Green and Marmaduke Johnson, 1670.

1671. An Almanack of Coelestial Motions for the Year . . . 1671. Cambridge: Samuel Green and Marmaduke Johnson, 1671.

1673. An Almanack of Coelestial Motions for the Year . . . 1673. Cambridge: Samuel Green, 1673.

1674. An Almanack of Coelestial Motions . . . for the Year . . . 1674. Cambridge: Samuel Green, 1674.

1675. An Almanack of Coelestial Motions for the Year . . . 1675. Cambridge: Samuel Green, 1675.

1676. An Almanack of Coelestial Motions for the Year . . . 1676. Boston: John Foster, [1675].

1676. An Almanack of Coelestial Motions . . . for the Year . . . 1676. Cambridge: Samuel Green, 1676.

1677. An Almanack of Coelestial Motions . . . for the Year . . . 1677. Cambridge: Samuel Green, 1677.

1678. An Almanack of Coelestial Motions for the Year . . . 1678. Boston: John. Foster, 1678.

1678. An Almanack of Coelestial Motions . . . for the Year . . . 1678. Cambridge: Samuel Green, 1678.

1684. The Boston Ephemeris. An Almanack for . . . MDCLXXXIV. Boston: Samuel Green, 1684.

1685. The Boston Ephemeris. An Almanack of Coelestial Motions . . . MDCLXXXV. Boston: Samuel Green, 1685.

1686. The Boston Ephemeris. An Almanack of Coelestial Motions . . . MDCLXXXVI. Boston: Samuel Green, 1686.

1694. An Almanack of the Coelestial Motions . . . MDCXCIV. Boston: Bartholomew Green, 1694.

1695. The New England Almanack for . . . MDCXCV. Boston: Bartholomew Green, 1695.

1705. An Almanack for the Year MDCCV. Boston: Bartholomew Green, 1705.

1706. An Almanack for the Year . . . MDCCVI. Boston: Bartholomew Green, 1706.

1708. An Almanack for the Year . . . 1708. Boston: Bartholomew Green, 1707.

1713. An Almanack for the Year . . . 1713. [Boston: Bartholomew Green?], 1713.

Agricultural Almanac, for the Year . . . [1829, 1832, 1838, 1840, 1846, 1848, 1850, 1852]. Lancaster, Pa.: John Baer, [1828, 1831, 1837, 1839, 1845, 1847, 1849, 1851].

An Agricultural and Economical Almanack . . . 1816. New Haven: J. Barber, [1815].

Agricultural and Family Almanac . . . for the Year . . . [1847, 1848]. New York: William B. Moffat, [1846, 1847].

Allen's New-England Almanack . . . 1807. Hartford: Lincoln and Gleason, [1806].

Allen's New-England Almanack . . . 1810. Hartford: Peter B. Gleason, [1809].

Allen's New-England Almanack . . . [1815, 1816, 1819]. Hartford: Peter B. Gleason and Co., [1814, 1815, 1818].

Almanac for the Year . . . 1816. Hamilton, Ohio: Intellegencer Office, [1815].

Almanac of the American Temperance Union, for [1843, 1846]. New York: American Temperance Union, [1842, 1845].

An Almanack and Ephemerides for the Year . . . 1693. Philadelphia: William Bradford, 1693.

An Almanack and Ephemeris, for the Year . . . 1776. Newport: Solomon Southwick, [1775].

[An Almanack for the Year . . . 1646]. [Cambridge: Stephen Daye, 1645?].

An Almanack for the Year . . . [1657, 1662]. Cambridge: Samuel Green, 1657, 1662.

An Almanack for the Year . . . 1687. Philadelphia: William Bradford, 1687. [Broadside]

An Almanack for the Year . . . [1694–1700]. New York: William Bradford, 1694–1700.

An Almanack for the Year . . . [1709, 1711, 1712, 1719, 1720]. Philadelphia, 1709, 1711, 1712, 1719, 1720.

An Almanack for the Year . . . 1721. Boston: Thomas Fleet, 1721.

An Almanack for the Year, [1723, 1725, 1727, 1729]. [John Jerman]. Philadelphia: Andrew Bradford, [1722, 1724, 1726, 1728].

An Almanack for the Year . . . [1723, 1726, 1728]. [Nathaniel Whittemore]. Boston: Thomas Fleet, 1723, 1726, 1728.

An Almanack for the Year . . . 1724. [Nathaniel Whittemore]. Boston: Bartholomew Green, 1724.

An Almanack for the Year . . . 1725. [Nathaniel Whittemore]. Boston, 1725.

An Almanack for the Year . . . 1727. Philadelphia: Samuel Keimer, 1727.

An Almanack for the Year . . . 1727. [John Hughes]. Philadelphia: Andrew Bradford, [1726].

An Almanack for the Year . . . 1730. [William Birkett]. Philadelphia: Andrew Bradford, [1729].

An Almanack for the Year . . . [1739, 1740]. [Joseph Stafford]. Boston: Thomas Fleet, 1739, 1740.

An Almanack for the Year . . . 1744. [Joseph Stafford]. Boston: Allen, Bushell, Green, 1744.

An Almanack, for the Year . . . 1749. [John Nathan]. New York: Catharine Zenger, [1748].

An Almanack for the Year . . . 1753. [John Nathan Hutchins]. New York: Hugh Gaine, [1752].

An Almanack for the Year . . . 1761. [Roger Sherman]. Boston: Daniel Kneeland and John Kneeland, [1760].

An Almanack, for the Year . . . 1763. [Benjamin West]. Providence: William Goddard, [1762].

An Almanack . . . for the Year . . . [1768, 1769]. [William Ball]. Charleston, S.C.: Charles Crouch, [1767, 1768].

An Almanack, for the Year . . . 1777. [Daniel George]. Boston: Draper and Phillips, [1776].

An Almanack, for the Year . . . [1778, 1780] . [Daniel George]. Newburyport, Mass.: John Mycall, [1777, 1779].

An Almanack for the Year . . . 1779. [Daniel George]. Boston: Draper and Folson, [1778].

An Almanack for the Year . . . 1786. [Daniel George]. Boston: Adams and Nouse, [1785].

An Almanack, for the Year 1799. Litchfield, Conn.: T. Collier, [1798].

An Almanack, for the Year . . . 1801. [Joseph Osgood]. Boston: Joseph White, [1800].

An Almanack for the Year 1705. An Ephemeris of the Motions and Aspects of the Planets. Philadelphia: Tiberius Johnson, [1704].

An Almanack of the Coelestial Motions for . . . 1659. Cambridge: Samuel Green, 1659.

[An Almanack of the Coelestial Motions . . . for the Year . . . 1715. Boston, 1714].

An Almanack or Diary, for the Year . . . 1729. Boston, 1729.

An Almanack or Register of Coelestial Configurations . . . 1679. Cambridge: Samuel Green, 1679.

The American Agriculturist Almanac, for 1845. New York: Saxton and Miles; Boston: Saxton, Pierce and Co.; Philadelphia: Thomas Cowperthwait and Co., [1844].

The American Agriculturist Almanac, for 1846. New York: Samuel S. and William Wood, [1845].

The American Almanac for the Year . . . 1715. New York: William Bradford, [1714].

The American Almanac. For the Year . . . 1760. Philadelphia: William Dunlap, [1759].

The American Almanac, for the Year . . . 1762. [John Jerman]. Philadelphia: William Dunlap, [1761].

The American Almanac, for the Year . . . 1801. New Brunswick, N.J.: Abraham Blauvelt, [1800].

The American Almanac for 1845. Philadelphia: Griffith and Simon, [1844].

The American Almanac and Repository of Useful Knowledge . . . 1844. Boston: David H. Williams, [1843].

The American Almanack for the Year . . . [1728, 1729]. Philadelphia: Samuel Keimer, [1727, 1728].

The American Almanack for the Year . . . 1730. [Felix Leeds]. New York: William Bradford, [1729].

The American Almanack for the Year . . . 1730. [Titan Leeds]. Philadelphia, [1729].

The American Almanack for the Year . . . [1731, 1735, 1736, 1741, 1748, 1751].

[John Jerman]. Philadelphia: Benjamin Franklin, [1730, 1734, 1735, 1740, 1747, 1750].

The American Almanack, for the Year . . . 1737. [William Birkett]. Philadelphia: Andrew Bradford, [1736].

The American Almanack for the Year . . . [1737, 1739]. [Titan Leeds]. New York: William Bradford, 1737, 1739.

The American Almanack, for the Year . . . [1739, 1740]. [John Jerman]. Philadelphia: Andrew Bradford, [1738, 1739].

The American Almanack for the Year . . . [1741, 1742]. [Titan Leeds]. Philadelphia: Andrew Bradford, [1740, 1741].

The American Almanack for the Year . . . 1743. [John Jerman]. Philadelphia: William Bradford, [1742].

The American Almanack for the Year . . . 1745. [Titan Leeds]. Philadelphia: Cornelia Bradford, [1744].

The American Almanack for the Year . . . 1745. [John Jerman]. Philadelphia: Isaiah Warner and Cornelia Bradford, [1744].

The American Almanack, for the Year . . . 1746. [John Jerman]. Philadelphia: Cornelia Bradford, [1745].

The American Almanack, for the Year . . . 1747. [John Jerman]. Germantown, Pa.: Christopher Sauer, [1746].

The American Almanack. For the Year . . . 1750. [W. Jones]. New York: Henry De Foreest, [1749].

The American Almanack for the Year . . . [1752–1756]. [John Jerman]. Philadelphia: B. Franklin and D. Hall, [1751–55].

The American Almanack for the Year . . . 1758. [John Jerman]. Philadelphia: Anthony Armbruster, [1757].

The American Baptist Almanac for the Year . . . 1860. Philadelphia: American Baptist Publication Society, [1859].

The American Calendar; or an Almanack . . . 1764. Philadelphia: William Bradford, [1763].

The American Calendar; or an Almanack . . . [1767, 1768, 1771–1773]. Philadelphia: William and Thomas Bradford, [1766, 1767, 1770–72].

The American Country Almanack, for the Year . . . [1746, 1748–1753]. New York: James Parker, [1745, 1747–52].

The American Country Almanack, for the Year . . . 1754. New York: James Parker and William Weyman, [1753].

The American Country Almanack, for the Year . . . 1755. Philadelphia: B. Franklin and D. Hall, [1754].

The American Ephemeris; or, an Almanack . . . 1757. New York: James Parker and William Weyman, [1756].

The American Ephemeris, or, an Almanack . . . 1759. New Haven: James Parker and Co., [1758].

American Farmer's Almanac. For 1852. Auburn, N.Y.: Henry Oliphant, [1851].

The American Farmers' Almanac . . . 1815. Lexington, Ky.: W. Essex and Son and H. C. Sleeght, [1814].

The American Farmers' Almanac, for the Year 1847. New York: Saxton and Miles, [1846].

The American Farmer's Almanac 1853. New York: Huestis and Cozons, [1852].

The American Farmers' Almanac [1854, 1858]. Philadelphia: Fisher and Brother, [1853, 1857].

The American Ladies Pocket Book, for the Year 1799. Philadelphia: William Y. Birch, [1798].

The American Medical Almanac, for 1840 . . . Being also a Pocket Memorandum and Account Book and General Medical Directory of the United States, and the British Provinces. Boston: Marsh, Capen, Lyon and Webb, 1840.

The American Medical Almanac, for 1841 . . . Being also a Pocket Memorandum and Account Book and General Medical Directory of the United States and the British Provinces. Boston: Otis, Broaders and Co., 1841.

Ames's Almanack 1759. Boston: Draper, Green and Russell and Fleet, [1758].

Anderson improved: Being an Almanack . . . for . . . [1773–1775]. Newport: Soloman Southwick, [1772–74].

Anderson Revived: The North-American Calendar, or, an Almanack, for the Year . . . 1780. Providence: Bennett Wheeler, [1779].

The Annual Visitor or Almanac . . . 1781. Baltimore: Thomas, Andrews, and Butler, [1780].

The Annual Visitor, or Almanac . . . 1805. Baltimore: John West Butler, [1804].

The Annual Visitor and Citizen and Farmer's Almanac . . . [1810, 1815]. Wilmington, Del.: James Wilson, [1809, 1814].

The Anti-Masonic Sun Almanac for the Year . . . 1832. Philadelphia: J. Clarke, [1831].

An Astronomical Diary, or an Almanack for the Year . . . 1723. New York and Philadelphia: William Bradford, [1722].

An Astronomical Diary, or, an Almanack for the Year . . . [1726–1733] . . . by Nathaniel Ames. Boston: B. Green, 1726–33.

An Astronomical Diary, or, an Almanack, for the Year . . . [1734, 1735] . . . by Nathaniel Ames. Boston: Printed by the Booksellers, 1734, 1735.

An Astronomical Diary, or, an Almanack for the Year . . . [1736–1746, 1747–1760, 1762, 1763] . . . by Nathaniel Ames. Boston: John Draper, 1736–46, [1746–59, 1761, 1762].

An Astronomical Diary, or, an Almanack for the Year . . . [1750, 1751] . . . by Roger Sherman. Boston: John Draper, [1749, 1750].

An Astronomical Diary, or, an Almanack for the Year . . . [1752, 1753] . . . by Roger Sherman. New York: Henry De Foreest, [1751, 1752].

An Astronomical Diary: or, an Almanack for the Year . . . [1752, 1754, 1755] . . . by George Wheten. Boston: Daniel Fowle, [1751, 1753, 1754].

An Astronomical Diary, or, an Almanack for the Year . . . 1754 . . . by Roger Sherman. New London: Timothy Green, [1753].

An Astronomical Diary: or, an Almanack for the Year . . . 1755 . . . by Nathaniel Ames. Boston: John Draper, [1754].

An Astronomical Diary: or, an Almanack, for the Year . . . 1755 . . . by Roger Sherman. Boston: Daniel Fowle, [1754].

An Astronomical Diary; or, an Almanack for the Year . . . 1757 . . . by George Wheten. Boston: Benjamin Edes and John Gill, [1756].

An Astronomical Diary: or, an Almanack for the Year . . . 1758 . . . by James Davis. Boston: Benjamin Edes and John Gill, [1757].

An Astronomical Diary: or, an Almanack for . . . 1758 . . . by David Sewall. Portsmouth, N.H.: Daniel Fowle, [1757].

An Astronomical Diary: or, an Almanack for the Year . . . 1759 . . . by John Eddy. Boston: Benjamin Edes and John Gill, [1758].

An Astronomical Diary, or an Almanack for the Year . . . 1760 . . . by Roger Sherman. Boston, [1759].

An Astronomical Diary, or an Almanack for the Year . . . 1761 . . . by Nathaniel Ames. Boston: Daniel and John Kneeland, etc., [1760].

An Astronomical Diary, or, an Almanack for the Year . . . [1762–1765] . . . by Nathanael Low. Boston: Daniel Kneeland and John Kneeland, [1761–64].

An Astronomical Diary: or, an Almanack for the Year . . . [1764–1766] . . . by Nathaniel Ames. Boston: R. and S. Draper, [1763–65].

An Astronomical Diary, or Almanack, for the Year . . . [1766, 1767, 1769] . . . by Samuel Ellsworth. Hartford: Thomas Green, [1765, 1766, 1768].

An Astronomical Diary; or, Almanack, for the Year . . . 1767. Portsmouth, N.H.: Daniel and Robert Fowle, [1766].

An Astronomical Diary; or, an Almanack for the Year . . . [1767–1771] . . . by Nathaniel Ames. Boston: Printers and Booksellers, [1766–70].

An Astronomical Diary; or Almanack for the Year . . . 1767 . . . by Nathanael Low. Boston: Daniel Kneeland, [1766].

An Astronomical Diary; or Almanack for the Year . . . [1768–1772] . . . by Nathanael Low. Boston: Kneeland and Adams, [1767–71].

An Astronomical Diary; or Almanack, for the Year . . . [1772–1775] . . . by Joseph Perry. New Haven: Thomas and Samuel Green, [1771–74].

An Astronomical Diary; or Almanack for the Year . . . 1772 . . . by Nathaniel Ames. Boston: Ezekiel Russell, [1771].

An Astronomical Diary; or, an Almanack for the Year . . . [1773, 1774] . . . by Nathaniel Ames. Boston: Draper, Edes and Gill, and T. and J. Fleet, [1772, 1773].

An Astronomical Diary; or, Almanack for the Year . . . [1773–1775] . . . by Nathanael Low. Boston: John Kneeland, [1772–74].

An Astronomical Diary: or an Almanack, for the Year . . . [1774, 1775]. [Isaac Warren]. Woburn, Mass.: Isaac Warren, 1774, 1775.

An Astronomical Diary; or an Almanack for the Year . . . 1775 . . . by Nathaniel Ames. Boston: Draper, Edes, and Gill, [1774].

An Astronomical Diary; or, Almanack, for the Year . . . 1775 . . . by Stephen-Row Bradley. Hartford: Ebenezer Watson, [1774].

An Astronomical Diary, or Almanack, for the Year . . . 1776 . . . by Nathanael Low. Worcester, Mass.: Isaiah Thomas, [1775].

An Astronomical Diary; or Almanack, for the Year . . . [1777, 1778] . . . by Nathanael Low. Boston: John Gill, [1776, 1777].

An Astronomical Diary, or Almanack, for the Year . . . 1779 . . . by Nathanael Low. Boston: Powars and Willis, [1778].

An Astronomical Diary, or Almanack, for the Year . . . 1780 . . . by Nathanael Low. Boston: Nathaniel Willis, [1779].

An Astronomical Diary or Almanack, for the Year . . . 1783. Springfield, Mass.: Babcock and Haswell, [1782].

An Astronomical Diary: or Almanack for the Year . . . [1785, 1793, 1797, 1799, 1804] . . . by Nathanael Low. Boston: T. and J. Fleet, [1784, 1792, 1796, 1798, 1803].

An Astronomical Diary: or Almanack, for the Year . . . 1801 . . . by Isaac Bicker-staff. Boston: E. and S. Larkin et al., [1800].

An Astronomical Diary: or Almanack, for the Year . . . 1801 . . . by Seth Chandler. Boston, [1800].

An Astronomical Diary, or Almanack, for the Year . . . 1808 . . . by Daniel Sewall. Portsmouth, N.H.: Stephen Sewall and Co. for Thomas and Tappan, [1807].

An Astronomical Diary, Calendar, or Almanack, for the Year . . . 1804. New Haven: T. Green and Son, [1803].

An Astronomical Ephemeris, Kalendar, or Almanack . . . [1776, 1777]. New Haven: Thomas and Samuel Green, [1775, 1776].

Bailey's Pocket Almanac, for the Year . . . 1796. Philadelphia: Francis and Robert Bailey, [1795].

Bailey's Rittenhouse Almanac, for the Year . . . [1810, 1815, 1819]. Philadelphia: Lydia R. Bailey, [1809, 1814, 1818].

The Baltimore Almanac, or, Time Piece . . . [1819, 1820, 1822]. Baltimore: William Warner, [1818, 1819, 1821].

The Baltimore Almanack, or Time Piece . . . [1810, 1811, 1816]. Baltimore: Warner and Hanna, [1809, 1810, 1815].

Benjamin Banneker's Pennsylvania, Delaware, Maryland and Virginia Almanack and Ephemeris, for the Year . . . 1792. Baltimore: William Goddard and James Angell, [1791].

The Barbados Almanack, for the Year . . . 1752. Philadelphia: B. Franklin and D. Hall, [1751].

Beers's Almanac for the Year . . . [1805, 1807, 1810, 1815, 1816]. Hartford: Hudson and Goodwin, [1804, 1806, 1809, 1814, 1815].

Beers' Almanac, for the Year . . . [1807, 1808]. Poughkeepsie: Bowman, Parsons and Potter, [1806, 1807].

Beers' Almanac, for the Year . . . [1810–12]. Poughkeepsie: Paraclete Potter, [1809–11].

Beers' Almanac, for the Year . . . [1814, 1816]. Poughkeepsie: P. and S. Potter, [1813, 1815].

Beers' Almanack, for the Year . . . 1824. Ithaca: A. P. Searing and Co., and Spencer and Stockton, [1823].

Beers' Calendar; or, Hosford's Almanack, for the Year . . . 1818. Albany: E. & E. Hosford, [1817].

Beers' Calendar; or, Hosford's New-York and Vermont Almanack, for the Year . . . 1821. Albany: E. & E. Hosford, [1820].

Beers' Calendar; or, Southwick's Almanac . . . [1813–16]. Albany: H. C. Southwick, [1812–15].

Bennett & Walton's Almanac, for the Year [1811, 1815, 1826]. Philadelphia: Bennett and Walton, [1810, 1814, 1825].

Bickerstaff's Albany Almanack, for . . . 1776. Albany: Alexander and Jane Robertson, [1775].

Bickerstaff's Almanac, for the Year . . . 1801. Portsmouth, N.H.: Charles Peirce, [1800].

Bickerstaff's Boston Almanack, for . . . [1768, 1769]. Boston: Mein and Fleeming, [1767, 1768].

Bickerstaff's Boston Almanack. For the Year . . . 1770. Boston: Mein and Fleeming, [1769].

Bickerstaff's Boston Almanack. For the Year . . . [1771, 1773]. Boston: John Fleeming, [1770, 1772].

Bickerstaff's Boston Almanack, for the Year . . . [1774, 1775]. Boston: Mills and Hicks, [1773, 1774].

Bickerstaff's Boston Almanack, for the Year . . . 1777. Salem, Mass.: Ezekiel Russell, [1776].

Bickerstaff's Boston Almanack, for the Year . . . [1778, 1779]. Danvers, Mass.: Ezekiel Russell, [1777, 1778].

Bickerstaff's Boston Almanack, for the Year . . . 1780. Danvers, Mass.: Draper and Folsom, [1779].

Bickerstaff's New-England Almanack . . . 1776. Norwich, Conn.: Robertsons and Trumbull, [1775].

Bickerstaff's New-England Almanack . . . [1777–1780]. Norwich, Conn.: John Trumbull, [1776–79].

Bickerstaff's New-York Almanack . . . [1778, 1779]. New York: Mills and Hicks, [1777, 1778].

Bioren's Town and Country Almanack, for the Year . . . [1808, 1810, 1816, 1817]. Philadelphia: John Bioren, [1807, 1809, 1815, 1816].

Birkett, 1738. An Almanack for the Year . . . 1738. New York: William Bradford, 1738.

Bonsal and Niles' Town and Country Almanac . . . 1801. Baltimore: Bonsal and Niles, [1800].

Boston Almanac for the Year . . . 1692. Boston: Benjamin Harris and John Allen, 1692.

Boucher 1744. The Pennsylvania Almanack, for the Year . . . 1744. [Matthew Boucher]. Philadelphia: William Bradford, [1743].

Boucher 1745. The Pennsylvania Almanack, for the Year . . . 1745. [William Boucher]. Philadelphia: Isaiah Warner and Cornelia Bradford, [1744].

Bradford's Tennessee Almanac . . . [1810, 1815, 1816]. Nashville: Thomas Grayson Bradford, [1809, 1814, 1815].

Brother Jonathan's Almanac for 1860. Philadelphia: Sower and Barnes, [1859].

Brown's Almanac Pocket Memorandum and Account Book. 1856. Boston: Brown, Bazin and Co., [1855].

Browne's Cincinnati Almanac... [1810–1812]. Cincinnati: John W. Browne and Co., [1809–11].

Browne & Co's Cincinnati Almanac... 1813. Cincinnati: John. W. Browne and Co., [1812].

Browne's Western Calendar; or, the Cincinnati Almanac... Eighteen Hundred and Six. Cincinnati: John W. Browne, [1805].

Browne's Western Calendar; or the Cincinnati Almanac... [1808, 1809]. Cincinnati: John W. Browne, [1807, 1808].

The Burlington Almanack, for the Year... [1771–1777]. [Timothy Trueman]. Burlington, N.J.: Isaac Collins, [1770–76].

Carey's Franklin Almanac... 1810. Philadelphia: Matthew Carey, [1809].

Carleton's Almanack (Enlarged and Improved) for... 1796. Boston: William P. Blake, [1795].

The Carolina and Georgia Almanack, or Astronomical Ephemeris for the Year... 1784. [Charleston, S.C.]: Printed for the Author, [1783].

The Caroline Almanack, and American Freeman's Chronicle, for 1840. Rochester, N.Y.: Mackenzie's Gazette Office, [1839].

The Christian Almanac, for Connecticut, for the Year... 1831. Hartford: Connecticut Branch of the American Tract Society, [1830].

The Christian Almanac, for Maryland and Virginia, for the Year... 1828. Baltimore: Baltimore Branch of the American Tract Society, [1827].

The Christian Almanac, for New-England. For the Year... [1829, 1830]. Boston: Lincoln and Edmonds, for the American Tract Society, [1828, 1829].

The Christian Almanac, for New-York, Connecticut, and New-Jersey, for the Year... [1827, 1837]. New York: American Tract Society, [1826, 1836].

The Christian Almanac, for New-York, Connecticut, New-Jersey, and Pennsylvania. For the Year... 1828. New York: American Tract Society, [1827].

The Christian Almanac, for the Western District, for the Year... 1828. Utica, N.Y.: Western Sunday School Union, [1827].

The Christian Almanac, for the Western District, for the Year... 1830. Utica, N.Y.: American Tract Society, [1829].

The Christian Almanack... [1822, 1823]. Boston: Published by Lincoln and Edmonds, [1821, 1822].

The Christian Almanack, for the Year... 1825. Philadelphia: American Tract Society and the American Sunday School Union, [1824].

The Christian Almanack, for the Year... 1827. Rochester, N.Y.: Everard Peck, [1826].

The Christian Register and Almanack... [1825, 1827]. Portsmouth, N.H.: Robert Foster, [1824, 1826].

Christie's Family Almanac for the Year 1853. New York: D.C. Morehead, M.D., [1852].

The Church Almanac... [1846, 1860]. New York: The Protestant Episcopal Tract Society, [1845, 1859].

The Churchman's Almanac for . . . 1839. New York: Protestant Episcopal Press, [1838].

The Citizen and Farmer's Almanac, for the Year . . . 1801. Baltimore: Bonsal and Niles, [1800].

The Citizen and Farmer's Almanac, for the Year . . . [1810, 1815]. Morristown, N.J.: Jacob Mann, [1809, 1814].

The Citizen & Farmer's Almanac, for the Year . . . 1816. Morristown, N.J.: Jacob Mann, [1815].

The Citizens' Almanac, for the Year . . . 1846. Baltimore: John T. Hanzsche, [1845].

Citizen's and Farmer's Almanac, for the Year . . . [1801, 1805]. Philadelphia: John M'Culloch, [1800, 1804].

Citizens & Farmers' Almanack for the Year . . . 1826. Philadelphia: Griggs and Dickinson, for Towar and Hogan, [1825].

The Clergyman's Almanack; or, an Astronomical Diary & Serious Monitor, for the Year . . . 1810. Boston: E. G. House, [1809].

The Clergyman's Almanack, or, an Astronomical Diary and Serious Monitor, for the Year . . . [1815, 1816]. Boston: Lincoln and Edmonds, [1814, 1815].

The Clergyman's Almanack, or an Astronomical Diary and Serious Monitor, for the Year . . . 1820. Boston: Parmenter and Balch, [1819].

Clough, [1700–1703]. The New-England Almanack for the Year . . . [MDCC–MDCCIII]. Boston: Bartholomew Green and John Allen, 1700–1703.

Clough, 1704. The New-England Almanack of the Coelestial Motions for the Year . . . 1704. Boston: Bartholomew Green and John Allen, 1704.

Clough, 1705. Kalendarium Nov-Anglicanum, or an Almanack of the Coelestial Motions for the Year . . . 1705. Boston: Bartholomew Green, 1705.

Clough, [1706, 1707]. Kalendarium Nov-Anglicanum, or an Almanack for the Year . . . [1706, 1707]. Boston: Bartholomew Green, 1706, 1707.

Clough's Farewell, 1708. An Almanack for the Year . . . 1708. Boston: Bartholomew Green, 1708.

Cochran's Philadelphia Almanac . . . 1810. Philadelphia: Robert Cochran, [1809].

College Almanack, [1761, 1762]. New Haven: James Parker, [1760, 1761].

College Almanack, for . . . 1773. New Haven: Thomas and Samuel Green, [1772].

The Columbian Almanac for the Year . . . 1798. Philadelphia: Stewart and Cochran, [1797].

The Columbian Almanac for the Year . . . 1816. Philadelphia: David Dickinson, [1815].

The Columbian Almanac, for the Year . . . 1816. New Brunswick, N.J.: Robert Stewart, [1815].

Columbian Almanac, for the Year . . . 1827. Philadelphia: Joseph M'Dowell, [1826].

Columbian Almanac, for the Year [1828, 1831]. Philadelphia: Joseph M'Dowell, [1827, 1830].

Columbian Almanac, for [*1833, 1836, 1847*]. Philadelphia: Joseph M'Dowell, 1833, [1835, 1846].

Columbian Almanac for [*1848, 1850, 1854, 1856, 1858, 1859*]. Philadelphia: Joseph McDowell, [1847, 1849, 1853, 1855, 1857, 1858].

The Columbian Almanac: or, the North-American Calendar . . . [*1797, 1801, 1805, 1810*]. Wilmington, Del.: Peter Brynberg, [1796, 1800, 1804, 1809].

The Columbian Calendar: or Almanac . . . 1801. Dedham, Mass.: Herman Mann, [1800].

The Columbian Calendar, or New-York and Vermont Almanack, for the Year . . . [*1817, 1824, 1826*]. Troy, N.Y.: Francis Adancourt, [1816, 1823, 1825].

The Columbus Almanac, for the Year . . . 1819. Columbus, Ohio: Published by the Author, [1818].

The Columbus Almanac, for the Year . . . 1822. Worthington, Ohio: Published by the Author, [1821].

The Columbus Almanac, for the Year . . . [*1826, 1827*]. Columbus, Ohio: Geo. Nashee and Co., [1825, 1826].

The Columbus Almanac, for the Year . . . 1829. Columbus, Ohio: P. H. Olmsted, [1828].

The Columbus Almanac, for the Year . . . [*1830, 1831*]. Columbus, Ohio: Olmsted and Bailhache, [1829, 1830].

The Columbus Almanac, for the Year . . . 1832. Columbus, Ohio: Jenkins and Glover, [1831].

The Comic Almanac, for the Year 1855. Philadelphia: King and Baird, [1854].

The Common School Almanac . . . 1839. New York: American Common School Society, [1838].

The Common School Almanac, for 1843. New York: Clement and Packard, [1842].

The Complete New-Hampshire & Vermont Almanac, and Farmers Precaution for the Year . . . 1810. Windsor, Vt.: John Cunningham, [1809].

The Connecticut Almanack, for . . . [*1767, 1768, 1770, 1772, 1773*]. New London: Timothy Green, [1766, 1767, 1769, 1771, 1772].

The Connecticut Almanack, for . . . 1778. Hartford: Hannah Watson, [1777].

The Connecticut Almanack, for . . . 1779. Hartford: Watson and Goodwin, [1778].

The Connecticut Almanack, for . . . 1780. Hartford: Hudson and Goodwin, [1779].

The Connecticut Diary; or Almanack for the Year . . . [*1756, 1757*]. New Haven: James Parker, [1755, 1756].

The Connecticut Register, and United States Calendar, for the Year . . . [*1814, 1817, 1822*] . . . *by Nathan Daboll.* New London: Samuel Green, [1813, 1816, 1821].

The Continental Almanac, for the Year . . . [*1780, 1782*]. Philadelphia: Francis Bailey, [1779, 1781].

Continental Almanac, for 1860. Philadelphia: J. Van Court, [1859].

Cottom's New Virginia Almanac, for the Year ... [1815, 1816]. Richmond: Peter Cottom, [1814, 1815].

The Country Almanack ... [1815, 1816]. Greenfield, Mass.: Denis and Phelps, [1814, 1815].

Cramer's Pittsburgh Almanack, for 1815. Pittsburgh: Cramer, Spear, and Eichbaum, [1814].

Cramer's Pittsburgh Almanack, for ... 1816. Pittsburgh: Robert Ferguson and Co., [1815].

Cramer's Pittsburgh Magazine Almanack ... 1810. Pittsburgh: Cramer and Spear, [1809].

The Cultivator Almanac, for the Year 1846. Albany: Luther Tucker, [1845].

The Cultivator Almanac, or Rural Calendar ... 1844. New York: Burgess and Stringer, [1843].

Cumberland Almanac, for the Year ... [1827, 1828, 1830]. Nashville: John S. Simpson, [1826, 1827, 1829].

Cumberland Almanac, for the Year ... [1832–1834]. Nashville: Hunt, Tardiff and Co., [1831–33].

Cumberland Almanac, for the Year ... 1836. Nashville: W. Hasell Hunt and Co., [1835].

Cumberland Almanac, for the Year ... [1838–1841]. Nashville: S. Nye and Co., [1837–40].

Cumberland Almanac, for the Year ... [1842, 1844, 1845]. Nashville: W. F. Bang and Co., [1841, 1843, 1844].

Daboll's New-England Almanack ... 1775. New London: Timothy Green, [1774].

The Dead Man's Almanack, 1744. The American Almanack for the Year 1744. New York: William Bradford, [1743].

The Democrats' Almanac, and Political Register, for [1839, 1840, 1842]. New York: Office of the Evening Post, [1838, 1839, 1841].

The Diary: or Yeoman's Calendar, Manufacturer's Almanack, and Middlesex Fireside, for the Year ... 1837. Lowell, Mass.: Leonard Huntress, [1836].

Dickson's Balloon Almanac ... 1801. Lancaster, Pa.: William and Robert Dickson, [1800].

Dickson's Balloon Almanac ... 1805. Lancaster, Pa.: William Dickson, [1804].

Dr. Wistar's Free Almanac for 1848. Boston: Seth W. Fowle, [1847].

Eddy's Almanack. 1761. Boston: Benjamin Edes and John Gill, [1760].

Edes & Gill's North-American Almanack for ... 1769. Boston: Edes and Gill, [1768].

Ellicott's Maryland and Virginia Almanac, and Ephemeris ... 1791. Baltimore: John Hayes, [1790].

An Ephemeris for the Year, [1721, 1726]. Philadelphia: Andrew Bradford, [1720, 1725].

An Ephemeris ... for the Year ... 1723. Philadelphia: Andrew Bradford, [1722].

An Ephemeris of the Coelestial Motions for the Year ... 1673. Cambridge: Samuel Green, 1673.

An Ephemeris of Coelestial Motions . . . for the Year . . . 1682. Cambridge: Samuel Green, 1682.

An Ephemeris of the Coelestial Motions . . . for . . . MDCCX. Boston: Bartholomew Green, 1710.

Ephemeris Sideralis. A Mathematical Almanack . . . 1706. Philadelphia: Jacob Taylor, [1705].

Ephemeris Sideralis. Or an Almanack . . . 1707. Philadelphia: Tiberius Johnson, [1706].

The Entertaining Almanac for 1836. Philadelphia: M. Fithian, [1835].

The Essex Almanack, for . . . [1769, 1771, 1772]. Salem, Mass.: Samuel Hall, [1768, 1770, 1771].

The Essex Almanack, for . . . 1773. Salem, Mass.: Samuel Hall and Ebenezer Hall, [1772].

Family Almanac, and Franklin Calendar, 1848. Cazenovia, N.Y.: Henry and Sweetlands, [1847].

Family Almanac, and Franklin Calendar, 1849. Troy, N.Y.: Ackley and Brother, [1848].

The Family Christian Almanac for the United States . . . 1847. New York: American Tract Society, [1846].

The Family Doctor, and Medical Almanack for 1846. Boston: Comstock and Ross, [1845].

Farmer's Almanac 1854. Philadelphia: John C. Davis, [1853].

The Farmers Almanac, for the Year . . . 1781. [Andrew Beers]. Danbury, Conn.: Nichols and Rowe, [1780].

The Farmer's Almanac, for the Year . . . 1810. Philadelphia: Robert Cochran, [1809].

The Farmer's Almanac, for the Year . . . [1815, 1816]. Baltimore: William Warner, [1814, 1815].

The Farmer's Almanac, for the Year . . . [1817, 1818]. Poughkeepsie: P. and S. Potter, [1816, 1817].

The Farmer's Almanac for the Year . . . 1820. Hartford: Geo. Goodwin and Sons, [1819].

The Farmer's Almanac, for the Year . . . 1820. Poughkeepsie: P. Potter, [1819].

Farmer's Almanac, for the Year 1824. New York: James A. Burtis, [1823].

The Farmer's Almanac, for the Year . . . 1832. Philadelphia: M'Carty and Davis, 1832.

The Farmer's Almanac, for the Year . . . 1842. Sag-Harbor, N.Y.: O. O. Wickham, [1841].

Farmer's Almanac, for the Year . . . 1845. Newark, N.J.: Benjamin Olds, [1844].

Farmer's Almanac, for the Year . . . [1845, 1846, 1850]. New Brunswick, N.J.: John Terhune, [1844, 1845, 1849].

The Farmer's Almanac, for the Year . . . 1850. Hartford: H. S. Parson's and Co., [1849].

Farmer's Almanac. For the Year . . . [1857, 1858]. New Brunswick, N.J.: John Terhune, [1856, 1857].

The Farmer's Almanac, and Housekeeper's Receipt Book . . . 1851. Philadelphia: King and Baird, [1850].

Farmers Almanac for the Year . . . 1827. Philadelphia: Isaac Pugh, [1826].

The Farmers' Almanac, for the Year . . . 1816. Lexington, Ky.: Thomas T. Skillman, [1815].

The Farmer's Almanack for the Year . . . 1849. Concord, Mass.: John F. Brown, [1848].

The Farmer's Almanack . . . for the Year 1714. Boston: Bartholomew Green, 1714.

The Farmer's Almanack . . . [1801, 1810, 1811] . . . by Father Abraham. Baltimore: Warner and Hanna, [1800, 1809, 1810].

The Farmer's Almanack . . . [1801, 1802] . . . by Robert B. Thomas. Boston: Manning and Loring, [1800, 1801].

The Farmer's Almanack . . . 1803 . . . by Robert B. Thomas. Boston: John West, [1802].

The Farmer's Almanack . . . [1809–1812] . . . by Robert B. Thomas. Boston: John West and Co., [1808–11].

The Farmer's Almanack . . . [1813–1818] . . . by Robert B. Thomas. Boston: West and Richardson, [1812–17].

The Farmer's Almanack . . . for the Year . . . [1815, 1816]. [Andrew Beers]. Kingston, N.Y.: S. S. Freer, [1814, 1815].

The Farmer's Almanack . . . [1822–1824] . . . by Robert B. Thomas. Boston: Richardson and Lord, [1821–23].

The Farmer's Almanack . . . [1826–1828, 1836, 1837, 1840] . . . by Robert B. Thomas. Portland, Me.: William Hyde, [1825–27, 1835, 1836, 1839].

The Farmer's Almanack . . . [1829, 1830] . . . by Robert B. Thomas. Portland, Me.: Shirley and Hyde, [1828, 1829].

The Farmer's Almanack . . . 1831 . . . by Robert B. Thomas. Portland, Me.: Shirley, Hyde and Co., [1830].

The Farmer's Almanack . . . 1838 . . . by Robert B. Thomas. Boston: Charles J. Hendee, [1837].

The Farmer's Almanack . . . 1839 . . . by Robert B. Thomas. Portland, Me.: Colman and Chisholm, [1838].

The Farmer's Almanack . . . [1841–1847] . . . by Robert B. Thomas. Boston: Jenks and Palmer, [1840–46].

The Farmer's Almanack for the Year . . . 1834. New York: David Felt; Boston: William Felt and Co., [1833].

The Farmer's Calendar, for the Year . . . 1848. Baltimore: Cushing and Brother, [1847].

The Farmer's Calendar, for the Year . . . 1849. Baltimore: J. N. Lewis and Son, [1848].

The Farmer's Calendar, or the New-York, Vermont & Connecticut Almanack . . . 1815. Bennington, Vt.: Darius Clark and Co., [1814].

The Farmers' Calendar, or the New-York, Vermont & Connecticut Almanack . . . 1816. Bennington, Vt.: Darius Clark, [1815].

The Farmers' Calendar, or Utica Almanack...[*1810, 1815, 1816*]. Utica, N.Y.: Seward and Williams, [1809, 1814, 1815].

The Farmers' Calendar, or Utica Almanack...[*1819, 1820, 1822, 1823*]. Utica, N.Y.: William Williams, [1818, 1819, 1821, 1822].

Farmers' Calendar or the Utica Almanack...*1825*. Utica, N.Y.: William Williams, [1824].

The Farmer's Calendar, or the Vermont, New York, and Connecticut Almanac...*1810*. Bennington, Vt.: Anthony Haswell, [1809].

Farmers' and Citizens' Almanac...*1816*. Philadelphia: David Dickinson, [1815].

The Farmer's Diary, or Western Almanac...*1813*. Canandaiga, N.Y.: James D. Bemis, [1812].

The Farmer's Diary, or Western Almanac...*1816*. Canandaiga, N.Y.: Bemis and Beach, [1815].

The Farmer's Diary, or Western Almanac...*1836*. Canandaiga, N.Y.: Morse and Harvy, [1835].

The Farmer's Diary or Western Almanac...*1837*. Canandaiga, N.Y.: C. Morse, [1836].

The Farmer's and Family Almanac. For the Year 1856. Philadelphia: Published by Bast and Miller, [1855].

The Farmer's and Family Almanac, for the Year 1858. Philadelphia: Marcus Bast, [1857].

The Farmer's and Farrier's Almanac, for 1849. Philadelphia: John B. Perry, [1848].

The Farmer's & Mechanic's Almanack, for the Year...*1826*. [Massachusetts], [1825].

The Farmer's, Mechanic's, and Gentleman's Almanack...*1829*. Wendell, N.H.: J. Metcalf, [1828].

The Farmer's, Mechanic's, and Gentleman's Almanack...*1840*. Keene, N.H.: J. and J. W. Prentiss, [1839].

The Farmer's, Mechanic's and Gentleman's Almanack, and Farmer's Calendar...*1826*. Chesterfield, N.H.: Published by the Author, [1825].

The Farmer's and Poultry Breeder's Almanac...*1853*. Philadelphia: John H. Seman, [1852].

The Farmers & Mechanics Almanac...*1817*. Philadelphia: Joseph Rakestraw, [1816].

The Farmers and Mechanics Almanack...[*1833, 1834, 1840*]. Philadelphia: George W. Mentz and Son, [1832, 1833, 1839].

The Farmers and Mechanics Almanack...*1835*. Pittsburgh: R. Patterson, [1834].

The Farmers and Mechanics Almanack...[*1844, 1846*]. Philadelphia: Mentz and Rovoudt, [1843, 1845].

The Farmers and Mechanics Almanack...[*1850, 1853, 1856*]. Philadelphia: William G. Mentz, [1849, 1852, 1855].

Father Abraham's Almanac...*for the Year*...[*1760, 1762–1768*]. Philadelphia: William Dunlap, [1759, 1761–67].

Father Abraham's Almanac, for the Year . . . [*1769, 1771–1777, 1779, 1780*]. Philadelphia: John Dunlap, [1768, 1770–76, 1778, 1779].

Father Abraham's Almanac, for the Year . . . *1778*. Lancaster, Pa.: John Dunlap, [1777].

Father Abraham's Almanac, for the Year . . . [*1801, 1810*]. Philadelphia: Peter Stewart, [1800, 1809].

Father Abraham's Almanack . . . *for the Year* . . . *1759*. Philadelphia: William Dunlap, [1758].

Father Abraham's Almanack, for the Year . . . *1782*. Philadelphia: George Kline, [1781].

Father Hutchins' New-York, New-Jersey, and Connecticut Almanack . . . *1776*. New York, 1776.

Father Tammant's Almanac . . . *1801*. Philadelphia: William Young, [1800].

Fisher's Improved House-Keeper's Almanac, and Family Receipt Book. 1858. Philadelphia: Fisher and Brother, [1857].

Fleet's Pocket Almanack for the Year . . . *1801*. Boston: J. and T. Fleet, [1800].

The Franklin Almanac for 1836. Philadelphia: Thomas L. Bonsal, [1835].

The Franklin Almanac, for 1847. Cazenovia, N.Y.: Henry and Sweetlands, [1846].

Franklin Almanac for 1860. Pittsburgh: Wm. G. Johnston and Co., [1859].

The Franklin Almanac, for the Year . . . [*1835, 1838, 1840, 1842, 1844*]. Philadelphia: M'Carty and Davis, 1835, 1838, 1840, [1841, 1843].

The Franklin Almanac, for the Year [*1842, 1845, 1847*]. Pittsburgh: Johnston and Stockton, [1841, 1844, 1846].

The Franklin Almanac, for the Year . . . *1846*. Philadelphia: Thomas Davis, [1845].

Franklin's Legacy: or, the New-York and Vermont Almanac . . . *1801*. Troy, N.Y.: R. Moffitt and Co., [1800].

Franklin's Legacy; or, the New-York & Vermont Almanack . . . *1810*. Troy, N.Y.: Oliver Lyon, [1809].

The Fredericksburg Almanack . . . *1810*. Alexandria, Va.: Cottom and Stewart, [1809].

Freebetter's Connecticut Almanack . . . *1774*. New London: Timothy Green, [1773].

Freebetter's New-England Almanack . . . [*1773, 1776*]. New London: Timothy Green, [1772, 1775].

Freeman's New-York Almanack for . . . [*1767–1772*]. New York: John Holt, [1766–71].

A Friends' Astronomical Diary: or Almanac . . . *1796*. Portsmouth, N.H.: Charles Peirce, [1795].

Gales and Seaton's North-Carolina Almanack . . . *1810*. Raleigh: Gales and Seaton, [1809].

Gales' North-Carolina Almanack . . . *1805*. Raleigh: Joseph Gales, [1804].

Gales's North-Carolina Almanack . . . [*1815, 1816*]. Raleigh: Joseph Gales, [1814, 1815].

Gates' Troy Almanac, for the Year . . . *1841*. Troy, N.Y.: Elias Gates, [1840].

Gen. Zachary Taylor's Old Rough & Ready Almanac. 1848. Philadelphia: R. Magee, [1847].

Gentlemen's and Ladies' Diary, and Almanac . . . 1801. Keene, N.H.: John Prentiss, [1800].

The Genuine Leeds Almanack for the Year . . . 1730. Philadelphia: David Harry, 1730.

The Genuine Leeds Almanack for the Year . . . 1740. Philadelphia: Andrew Bradford, [1739].

The Genuine Leeds Almanack. The American Almanack for the Year . . . [1732, 1735–1738, 1743]. Philadelphia: Andrew Bradford, [1731, 1734–37, 1742].

The Genuine Leeds Almanack. The American Almanack for the Year . . . 1746. Philadelphia: Cornelia Bradford, [1745].

George's Cambridge Almanack or, the Essex Calendar . . . 1776. Salem, Mass.: Ezekiel Russell, [1775].

The Georgia Almanack, for . . . 1771. Charleston, S.C.: Robert Wells, [1770].

The Georgia and South-Carolina Almanac . . . 1801. Augusta, Ga.: John Erdman Smith, [1800].

The Georgia and South-Carolina Almanac . . . [1805, 1816]. Augusta, Ga.: Hobby and Bunce, [1804, 1815].

Georgia and South-Carolina Almanac . . . 1810. Augusta, Ga.: Hobby and Bunce, [1809].

The Georgia and South-Carolina Almanack . . . [1774, 1775]. Charleston, S.C.: Robert Wells, [1773, 1774].

The Georgia and South-Carolina Almanack . . . 1775. Charleston, S.C.: Robert Wells, [1774].

The Girard Almanac for 1837. Philadelphia: Thomas L. Bonsal, [1836].

The Girard Almanac for the Year . . . 1840. Philadelphia: Thomas L. Bonsal, [1839].

The Great Western Almanac for [1844, 1850, 1854, 1856]. Philadelphia: Jos. McDowell, [1843, 1849, 1853, 1855].

Greenleaf's New-York, Connecticut & New Jersey Almanack, or Diary . . . for the Year . . . 1796. New York: Thomas Greenleaf, [1795].

Greenleaf's New York, Connecticut & New Jersey Almanack, or Diary, for the Year . . . 1800. Brooklyn: T. Kirk, [1799].

Green's Almanack and Register, for the State of Connecticut; for the Year . . . [1796, 1797, 1802]. New London: Samuel Green, [1795, 1796, 1801].

Green's New-England Almanack, and Farmer's Friend, for the Year . . . 1826. New London: Samuel Green, [1825].

Griggs' City and Country Almanack . . . 1830. Philadelphia: John Griggs, [1829].

The Hagerstown Town and Country Almanack . . . [1847, 1858, 1860]. Hagerstown, Md.: John Gruber, [1846, 1857, 1859].

Hagers-Town Town and Country Almanack . . . [1854, 1856]. Hagerstown, Md.: John Gruber, [1853, 1855].

Harper's Almanac . . . 1801. Chambersburg, Pa.: Robert and George Kenton Harper, [1800].

The Harrison Almanac 1841. New York: J. P. Giffing, [1840].

Harvards' Ephemeris, or Almanack . . . for the Year . . . 1690. Cambridge: Samuel Green, 1690.

The Health Almanac, for the Year . . . 1842. New York: Health Depository, [1841].

The Health Almanac, for the Year . . . 1843. Boston: Saxton and Pierce, [1842].

The Health Almanac, for the Year . . . 1844. New York: Saxton and Miles, [1843].

The Health and Temperance Almanac, for 1834: Calculated Generally for all Parts of the United States. The Literary Part, on Health and Temperance, by the Editor of the Journal of Health. Philadelphia: Edward C. Mielke, [1833].

Henderson's Almanack, for 1815. Raleigh, N.C.: Thomas Henderson, [1814].

Henderson's Almanack, for . . . 1816. Raleigh, N.C.: Thomas Henderson, [1815].

Der Hoch-Deutsch Americanische Calendar . . . [1739–1758]. Germantown, Pa.: Christopher Sauer, [1738–57].

Hodge & Boylan's North-Carolina Almanack . . . [1801, 1805]. Halifax: Abraham Hodge, [1800, 1804].

Hoff's Agricultural & Commercial Almanac . . . [1815, 1816]. Charleston, S.C.: John Hoff, [1814, 1815].

"Honest John's" Farmer's Almanack . . . for the Year . . . 1847. Worcester, Mass.: J. Grant, Jr., [1846].

Hosfords' Calendar; or the New-York and Vermont Almanack . . . 1827. Albany: E. and E. Hosford, [1826].

Houghton's Genuine Almanac. The Gentleman's and Ladies' Diary, and Almanac . . . [1804, 1810]. Keene, N.H.: John Prentiss, [1803, 1809].

Houghton's Genuine Almanac. The Ladies' and Gentleman's Diary and Almanac . . . 1813. Walpole, N.H.: Isaiah Thomas and Co., [1812].

Howe's Genuine Almanac for the Year . . . [1810, 1815–1817]. Greenwich, Mass.: John Howe, [1809, 1814–16].

Howe's Genuine Almanac, for the Year 1823. Enfield, Mass.: [John Howe], [1822].

Hunt's Almanack, for the Year . . . 1825. Philadelphia: Uriah Hunt, [1824].

Hunt's Family Almanac for 1847. Philadelphia: Uriah Hunt, [1846].

Hunt's Family Almanac for 1851. Philadelphia: Uriah Hunt and Son, [1850].

Hutchings' (Revived) Almanac, for the Year 1825. New York: David D. Smith, [1824].

Hutchins', [1755–1757]. An Almanack . . . for . . . [1755–1757]. [John Nathan Hutchins]. New York: Hugh Gaine, [1754–56].

Hutchins's Almanack . . . for . . . [1758, 1759]. [John Nathan Hutchins]. New York: Hugh Gaine, [1757, 1758].

Hutchins Improved: An Almanac, for the Year . . . 1805. Elizabethtown, N.J.: John Woods, [1804].

Hutchins Improved: Being an Almanack and Ephemeris . . . *[1782, 1789, 1793].*
New York: H. Gaine, [1781, 1788, 1792].

Hutchins Improved: Being an Almanack and Ephemeris . . . *1801.* New York:
Andrew Beers, [1800].

Hutchins Improved: Being an Almanack and Ephemeris . . . *1805.* New York:
Ming and Young, [1804].

Hutchins Improved: Being an Almanack and Ephemeris . . . *[1809, 1810, 1812,*
1815– 1817]. New York: Alexander Ming, [1808, 1809, 1811, 1814–16].

Hutchins' Improved Almanac, for the Year . . . *1836.* New York: Octavius Long-
worth, [1835].

Hutchins' Improved Almanac, and Ephemeris . . . *[1842, 1845].* New York:
H. and S. Raynor, [1841, 1844].

Hutchins' improved: Being an Almanack . . . *for the Year* . . . *[1760–1780].* [John
Nathan Hutchins]. New York: Hugh Gaine, [1759–79].

Hutchins' Revived Almanac, for the Year . . . *[1815, 1816].* New York: Smith
and Forman, [1814, 1815].

Hutchins' Revived Almanac, for the Year 1828. New York: C. Brown, [1827].

The Illustrated Annual Register of Rural Affairs and Cultivator Almanac, for the
Year 1860. Albany: Luther Tucker and Son, [1859].

The Illustrated Family Christian Almanac for the United States . . . *[1849–1852,*
1856, 1859]. New York and Boston: American Tract Society, [1848–51,
1855, 1858].

The Illustrated Family Christian Almanac for the United States . . . *1860.* New
York: American Tract Society, [1859].

The Illustrated Phrenological Almanac for [*1851, 1852, 1854, 1860*]. New York:
Fowlers and Wells, [1850, 1851, 1853, 1859].

Isaiah Thomas, Junr's Massachusetts, Connecticut, Rhodeisland, New-
Hampshire and Vermont Almanack . . . *for the Year* . . . *[1804–1806, 1808,*
1810]. Worcester, Mass.: Isaiah Thomas, Jr., [1803–5, 1807, 1809].

Isaiah Thomas, Junior's Town & Country Almanack, or Complete Farmer's Cal-
endar, for the Year . . . *[1812, 1813, 1815, 1816, 1819].* Worcester, Mass.:
Isaiah Thomas Jr., [1811, 1812, 1814, 1815, 1818].

Isaiah Thomas's Massachusetts, Connecticut, Rhode-Island, Newhampshire
& Vermont Almanack . . . *for* . . . *[1781, 1799].* Worcester, Mass.: Isaiah
Thomas, [1780, 1798].

John Grigg's Almanack, for the Year . . . *1829.* Philadelphia: D. and S. Neall,
[1828].

Johnson and Warner's Almanac, for the Year 1812. Philadelphia: Johnson and
Warner, [1811].

Johnson & Warner's Kentucky Almanac . . . *1810.* Lexington: Johnson and
Warner, [1809].

Johnson's Almanac for . . . *1809.* Philadelphia: Benjamin and Thomas Kite,
[1808].

Johnson's Almanac, for . . . *1810.* Philadelphia: Bennett and Walton, [1809].

Kalendarium Pennsilvaniense, or, American Messenger . . . *for the Year* . . . *1686.*
Philadelphia and New York: William Bradford, [1685].

The Kentucky Almanac for the Year . . . 1801. Lexington: John Bradford, [1800].

The Kentucky Almanack, for the Year . . . 1810. Lexington: Daniel and C. Bradford, [1809].

The Kentucky Farmer's Almanac . . . [1810, 1815]. Lexington: William W. Worsley, [1809, 1814].

Keystone Agricultural Almanac, for 1839. Philadelphia: William W. Walker, [1838].

Kimber's Almanac for 1805. Philadelphia: Emmor Kimber, [1804].

Kite's Town and Country Almanac . . . 1815. Philadelphia: Lydia R. Bailey, [1814].

Kite's Town and Country Almanac . . . 1824. Philadelphia: Benjamin and Thomas Kite, [1823].

Kite's Town and Country Almanac . . . 1831. Philadelphia: Thomas Kite, [1830].

Knickerbocker Almanac, for the Year . . . 1837. New York: Mahlon Day, [1836].

The Lancaster Almanack . . . [1775, 1776, 1778, 1779]. Lancaster, Pa.: Francis Bailey, [1774, 1775, 1777, 1778].

The Lancaster Almanack . . . 1775. Lancaster, Pa.: Stewart Herbert, [1774].

Leavitt's Farmer's Almanack and Miscellaneous Year Book . . . [1850–1852]. Concord, N.H.: John F. Brown, [1849–51].

Leavitt's Genuine Improved New-England Farmer's Almanac, and Agricultural Register . . . [1815, 1816]. Exeter, N.H.: C. Norris and Co., [1814, 1815].

Leavitt's Improved New-England Almanack . . . 1829. Concord, N.H.: Jacob B. Moore, [1828].

Leavitt's Improved New-England Farmer's Almanack and Year Book, for the Year . . . 1848. Concord, N.H.: John F. Brown, [1847].

Leeds, 1704–1710, 1713. The American Almanack for . . . [1704, 1705–1710, 1713]. New York: William Bradford, [1703], 1705–10, 1713.

Leeds, 1711–1712. The American Almanack for . . . [1711, 1712]. New York: William and Andrew Bradford, 1711, 1712.

Leeds, 1714. The American Almanack for . . . 1714. [New York: William Bradford], 1714.

Leeds, 1715–1716, 1725. The American Almanack for . . . [1715, 1716, 1725]. New York: William Bradford, 1715, [1715], 1724 .

Leeds, 1717. The American Almanack for . . . 1717. Philadelphia: William Bradford, [1716].

Leeds, 1718–1722, 1724. The American Almanack for . . . [1718–1722, 1724]. Philadelphia: Andrew Bradford, [1717–21, 1723].

Leeds, 1727. The American Almanack for . . . 1727. Philadelphia: Samuel Keimer, [1726].

Leeds, 1731. The American Almanack for . . . 1731. New York: William Bradford; Philadelphia: Andrew Bradford, [1730].

Leeds, 1733. The American Almanack for . . . 1733. New York and Philadelphia: William Bradford, [1732].

Leeds, 1737. An American Almanack for . . . 1737. New York: William Bradford, 1737.

Leeds. The American Almanack for the Year . . . [1726, 1728]. Philadelphia: Andrew Bradford, [1725, 1727].

Loomis' No. XVI. Pittsburgh Almanac . . . for the Year . . . 1850. Pittsburgh: Luke Loomis, [1849].

Loomis' No. XVII. Pittsburgh Almanac . . . for the year . . . 1851. Pittsburgh: Luke Loomis, [1850].

Low. An Astronomical Diary; or, Almanack . . . [1809, 1810] . . . by Nathanael Low. Boston: Munroe, Francis, and Parker, [1808, 1809].

Low. An Astronomical Diary; or Almanack . . . [1811, 1812] . . . by Nathanael Low. Boston: Munroe and Francis, [1810, 1811].

Low's Almanack, for the Year . . . [1821, 1822] . . . by Nathanael Low. Boston: Munroe and Francis, [1820, 1821].

Low's Almanack, and Agricultural Register, for the Year . . . 1816 . . . by Nathanael Low. Boston: Munroe, Francis and Parker, [1815].

Low's Almanack, and Agricultural Register; for the Year . . . 1817 . . . by Nathanael Low. Boston: Munroe and Francis, [1816].

Low's Almanack and Mechanics and Farmer's Calendar, for the Year 1824 . . . by Nathanael Low. Boston: Munroe and Francis, [1823].

Low's. An Astronomical Diary: or Almanack, for the Year . . . 1801 . . . by Nathanael Low. Boston: John and Thomas Fleet, [1800].

Low's Genuine Almanack for the Year . . . [1813, 1814] . . . by Nathanael Low. Boston: Munroe and Francis, [1812, 1813].

The Maine Farmers' Almanac, for . . . 1832. Portland: Gershom Hyde and Co., [1831].

The Maine Farmers' Almanac, for . . . 1834. Hallowell: Glazier, Masters, and Co., [1833].

The Maine Farmers' Almanac, for . . . [1854, 1858, 1859]. Hallowell: Masters, Smith and Company, [1853, 1857, 1858].

Mary K. Goddard's Pennsylvania, Delaware, Maryland, and Virginia Almanack . . . 1779. Baltimore: Mary K. Goddard, [1778].

The Maryland Almanack for the Year . . . [1761, 1763–1765]. Annapolis: Jonas Green, [1760, 1762–64].

The Maryland Almanack, for the Year . . . 1778. Frederick: Matthias Bartgis, [1777].

The Maryland and Virginia Almanac . . . 1801. Baltimore: Bonsal and Niles, [1800].

The Maryland and Virginia Almanac . . . 1810. Washington City: Daniel Rapine, [1809].

The Massachusetts Calendar, or Almanac, for . . . 1772. Boston: Isaiah Thomas, [1771].

The Massachusetts Calendar, or an Almanack, for . . . 1774. Boston: Isaiah Thomas, [1773].

The Massachusetts Calendar, or Wonderful Almanack . . . 1773. Boston: Ezekiel Russell, [1772].

The Massachusetts and New-Hampshire Almanack, for the Year . . . 1792. Boston: J. White and C. Cambridge, [1791].

The Mathamaticians [sic] *Glory Astronomy and New-England Almanack . . . 1774.* Boston, 1774.

Meanwell's Town and Country Almanack . . . 1774. New York: Hodge and Shober, [1773].

The Mechanics' Almanac, and Astronomical Ephemeris, for 1825. Boston: Stone and Fovell, [1824].

Merchant Gargling Oil Co.'s National Almanac . . . for the Year 1860. Lockport, N.Y.: Published by M. H. Tucker and Co., [1859].

Mercurius Nov-Anglicanus. Or An Almanack . . . [1743, 1747]. Boston: Gamaliel Rogers, John Fowle, and Daniel Fowle, 1743, [1746].

Merry Andrew's Almanack . . . for . . . 1762. Philadelphia: Andrew Steuart, [1761].

Merry Andrew's New Almanack . . . [1774, 1775]. New York: John Anderson, [1773, 1774].

The Methodist Almanac, for the Year . . . [1836, 1837, 1843, 1844, 1846]. New York: Methodist Episcopal Church, [1835, 1836, 1842, 1843, 1845].

Middlebrook's Almanack, for the Year . . . 1816. New Haven: J. Barber, [1815].

Middlebrook's Almanack, for the Year . . . 1822. Norwalk, Conn.: P. Price, [1821].

Middlebrook's Almanack for the Year . . . 1834. Norwalk, Conn.: Weed and Butler, [1833].

Middlebrook's Astronomical Diary, Calendar, or Almanack . . . 1810. New Haven: Sidney's Press, [1809].

Middlebrook's New England Almanac . . . 1847. Bridgeport, Conn.: William B. Oakley, [1846].

Middlebrook's New-England Almanac . . . 1852. Bridgeport, Conn.: J. Barber and Sons, [1851].

Miner's Agricultural and Miscellaneous Almanac, for Pennsylvania & New Jersey, for the Year . . . 1817. Doylestown, Pa.: Asher Miner, [1816].

Miner's Pennsylvania and New-Jersey Almanac . . . 1816. Doylestown, Pa.: Asher Miner, [1815].

Ming's Hutchins' Improved; Being an Almanac and Ephemeris . . . for the Year . . . [1820, 1823]. New York: Alexander Ming, [1819, 1822].

The Mississippi and Louisiana Almanac . . . 1815. Washington, Miss.: Andrew Marschalk, [1814].

The Mississippi and Louisiana Almanac . . . 1816. Natchez: Andrew Marschalk, [1815].

Monthly Observations and Predictions, for . . . 1692. Boston: Benjamin Harris, 1692.

The Moral Almanac, for the Year [1841, 1843]. Philadelphia: Tract Association of Friends, [1840, 1842].

Morehead's Family Almanac for the Year 1858. New York: D. C. Morehead, [1857].

A New Almanack for the Year . . . *1727*. Boston: Thomas Fleet, 1727.

New Brunswick (N.J.) Almanack for the Year . . . *1827*. Philadelphia: Griggs and Dickinson, [1826].

Neu-Eingerichteter Americanischer Geschichts-Calendar . . . *1749*. Philadelphia: Godhart Armbruster, [1748].

Neu-Eingerichteter Americanischer Geschichts-Calendar . . . *1750*. Philadelphia: B. Franklin and Johann Böhm, [1749].

Neu-Eingerichteter Americanischer Geschichts-Calendar . . . *1752*. Philadelphia: B. Franklin, [1751].

Neu-Eingerichteter Americanischer Geschichts-Calendar . . . *[1754–1856]*. Philadelphia: Anthony Armbruster, [1753–1855].

The New-England Almanack for the Year . . . *1686*. Cambridge: Samuel Green, 1686.

The New-England Almanack, for the Year . . . *1745*. [Copernicus]. New York: Henry De Foreest, [1744].

The New-England Almanack, for the Year . . . *1764*. [Benjamin West]. Providence: William Goddard, [1763].

The New-England Almanack, for the Year . . . *1778*. [Nathan Daboll]. Hartford: Nathaniel Patten, [1777].

The New-England Almanack, for the Year . . . *[1809, 1810, 1815, 1816, 1819, 1821, 1822*. [Nathan Daboll]. New London: Samuel Green, [1808, 1809, 1814, 1815, 1818, 1820, 1821].

The New-England Almanack, for the Year . . . *1815*. [Stoddard Capen]. Boston: Charles Callendar, [1814].

The New-England Almanack, for the Year . . . *1816*. [Stoddard Capen]. Boston: Thomas G. Bangs, [1815].

The New-England Almanack, for the Year . . . *1818*. [Stoddard Capen]. Boston: Permenter and Norton, [1817].

The New-England Almanack, and Farmers' Friend . . . *[1823–1825, 1829, 1835–1838]* . . . *by Nathan Daboll*. New London: Samuel Green, [1822–24, 1828, 1834–37].

The New-England Almanack, and Farmers' Friend . . . *1839* . . . *by Nathan Daboll*. New London: E. Williams, [1838].

The New-England Almanac, and Farmers' Friend . . . *[1844,1845,1847–1849]* . . . *by Nathan Daboll*. New London: Bolles and Williams, [1843, 1844, 1846–48].

The New-England Almanac, and Farmers' Friend . . . *[1850–1852]* . . . *by Nathan Daboll*. New London: Bolles and Co., [1849–51].

The New-England Almanac, and Farmers' Friend . . . *[1856–1858, 1860]* . . . *by Nathan Daboll*. New London: Starr and Co., [1855–57, 1859].

The New-England Almanac, and Gentlemen and Ladies' Dairy, for the Year . . . *[1797, 1805]* . . . *by Nathan Daboll*. New London: Samuel Green, [1796, 1804].

The New-England Almanack; and Gentleman's and Lady's Diary . . . *[1777–1780]*. New London: Timothy Green, [1776–79].

The New-England Almanack, and Gentlemen and Ladies' Diary . . . 1801. New London: Samuel Green, [1800].

The New-England Almanack, or Lady's and Gentleman's Diary, for the Year . . . 1765. [Benjamin West]. Providence: William Goddard, [1764].

The New-England Almanack, or Lady's and Gentleman's Diary, for the Year . . . 1766. [Benjamin West]. Providence: Sarah and William Goddard, [1765].

The New-England Almanack, or Lady's and Gentleman's Diary, for the Year . . . 1767. [Benjamin West]. Boston, [1766].

The New-England Almanack, or, Lady's and Gentleman's Diary, for the Year . . . 1768. [Benjamin West]. Providence: Sarah Goddard, [1767].

The New-England Almanack, or Lady's and Gentleman's Diary, for the Year . . . 1769. [Benjamin West]. Boston: Mein and Fleeming, [1768].

The New-England Almanack, or Lady's and Gentleman's Diary, for the Year . . . [1770–1774, 1776, 1778–1780]. [Benjamin West]. Providence: John Carter, [1769–73, 1775, 1777–79].

The New-England Almanack, or Lady's and Gentleman's Diary, for the Year . . . 1799. Providence: Carter and Wilkinson, [1798].

The New-England Almanack, or Lady's and Gentleman's Diary, for the Year . . . [1801, 1804, 1805, 1809, 1810, 1813]. Providence: John Carter, [1800, 1803, 1804, 1808, 1809, 1812].

New England Anti-Masonic Almanac for the Year . . . 1832. Boston: John Marsh and Co., [1831].

New England Anti-Masonic Almanac for the Year . . . 1833. Boston: William Souther, [1832].

The New-England Farmer's Almanack . . . 1816. Kennebunk, Me.: James K. Remich, [1815].

The New England Farmer's Almanack. For the Year . . . 1830. Boston: Carter and Hendee, [1829].

The New-England Farmer's Almanack, and Repository . . . 1815. Boston: Munroe, Francis, and Parker, [1814].

The New-England Farmer's Diary, and Almanac . . . 1815. Weathersfield, Vt.: Eddy and Patrick, [1814].

The New-England Farmer's Diary, and Almanac . . . 1816. Windsor, Vt.: Jessie Cochran, [1815].

The N. England Kalendar, 1703. Boston: Bartholomew Green and John Allen, 1703.

The N. England Kalendar, 1704. Or an Almanack for the Year . . . 1704. Boston: Bartholomew Green and John Allen, 1704.

The N. England Kalendar, [1705, 1706]. Or an Almanack for the Year . . . 1705, 1706. Boston: Bartholomew Green, 1705, 1706.

The New England Odd Fellows' Almanac . . . 1846. Exeter, N.H.: C. C. Dearborn, [1845].

The New-England Town and Country Almanack . . . 1769. Providence: Sarah Goddard, [1768].

The New Farmer's Almanac, for the Year . . . 1848. Boston: Phillips and Sampson, [1847].

New From the Stars. An Almanack . . . for the Year . . . 1691. Boston: Richard Pierce for Benjamin Harris, 1691.

New-Jersey Almanac, for the Year . . . [1828, 1833, 1834] . . . by David Young. Newark: Benjamin Olds, [1827, 1832, 1833].

The New-Jersey Almanack for . . . 1744. [William Ball]. Philadelphia: Isaiah Warner and Cornelia Bradford, [1743].

The New-Jersey Almanack for the Year . . . [1745, 1747, 1752, 1753, 1755]. [William Ball]. Philadelphia: William Bradford, [1744, 1746, 1751, 1752, 1754].

The New-Jersey Almanack . . . for the Year . . . 1768. [William Ball]. New York: James Parker, [1767].

The New-Jersey Almanack . . . for the Year . . . 1769. New York: James Parker, [1768].

The New-Jersey Almanack . . . for the Year . . . 1770. [William Ball]. New York: Richard Draper, [1769].

The New-Jersey Almanack for the Year . . . [1779, 1780]. [Timothy Trueman]. Trenton: Isaac Collins, [1778, 1779].

The New-Jersey and Pennsylvania Almanac . . . 1801. Trenton: Sherman, Mershon, and Thomas, [1800].

The New Jersey and Pennsylvania Almanac . . . 1805. Trenton: Sherman and Mershon, [1804].

The New-Jersey and Pennsylvania Almanac . . . [1810, 1815, 1816]. Trenton: George Sherman, [1809, 1814, 1815].

Newport, 1731. An Almanack for the Year . . . 1731. Newport: James Franklin, 1731.

The Newport Almanac for . . . 1801. Newport: Oliver Farnsworth, [1800].

Newtonian Reflector, or New-England Almanac . . . 1824. Hartford: Roberts and Burr, [1823].

The Newtonian Reflector, or New-England Almanac . . . 1830. Hartford: H. Burr, Jr., [1829].

The Newtonian Reflector, or New-England Almanac . . . 1832. Hartford: H. Burr, [1831].

The New-Year's Gift; or a Pocket Almanack . . . 1741. Philadelphia: Benjamin Franklin, [1740].

The New-York Almanack, for the Year . . . [1747, 1748]. New York: Henry De Foreest, [1746, 1747].

The New-York Almanack, for . . . 1774. [Mark Time]. New York: John Holt, [1773].

The New-York Almanack, for . . . 1780. [Isaac Bickerstaff]. New York: Mills and Hicks, [1779].

The New-York Calendar, or Middle District Almanac; for the Year . . . 1819. Kingston: John Tappen and S. S. and A. Freer, [1818].

The New-York and Country Almanack . . . 1776. New York: Shober and Loudon, [1775].

The New-York and Farmer's Almanac...1836. New York: Charles Small, [1835].

The New-York and Farmer's Almanack...1830. New York: David Felt, [1829].

The New-York Medical Almanac, and Repository of Useful Science and Amusement, for the Year [1824, 1826, 1827]. New York: Samuel Marks, [1823, 1825, 1826].

The New-York Medical Almanac, and Repository of Useful Science and Amusement, for the Year 1825. New York: John C. Totten, [1824].

The New-York Medical Almanac, and Repository of Useful Science and Amusement, for the Year...1828. New York: Caleb Bartlett, [1827].

The New-York Pocket Almanack, for the Year [1758, 1760]. New York: Hugh Gaine, [1757, 1759].

The New-York & Vermont Farmer's Almanack... [1810, 1812]. Lansingburgh, N.Y.: Tracy and Bliss, [1809, 1811].

The North American Almanac, for...1851. Philadelphia: C. G. Sower, [1850].

The North American Almanac, for...1852. Philadelphia: Sower and Barnes, [1851].

The Northamerican Almanack. For the Year...1770. Boston: Samuel Stearns, [1769].

The North-American Almanack...1771. Boston: Richard Draper, John Fleet, et al., [1770].

The North-American Almanack, Being, The Gentlemans and Ladies Diary for...1772. Boston: Richard Draper, [1771].

The North American's Almanack...1777. Worcester, Mass.: William Stearns and Daniel Bigelow, [1776].

The North-American's Almanack, and Gentleman's and Ladies's Diary... [1774, 1775]. Boston: Edes and Gill, [1773, 1774].

The North-American's Almanack, and Gentleman's and Lady's Diary...1776. Worcester, Mass.: Isaiah Thomas, [1775].

The North-American Calendar, or the Columbian Almanac for the Year...1815. Wilmington, Del.: Peter Brynberg, [1814].

The North-American Calendar, or the Columbian Almanac, for the Year... [1816, 1822]. Wilmington, Del.: Robert Porter, [1815, 1821].

The North American Calendar, or the Columbian Almanac, for the Year... [1823, 1824]. Wilmington, Del.: Robert Porter, [1822, 1823].

The North-American's Calendar and Gentleman and Ladies Diary...1773. Boston: Edes and Gill, [1772].

The North-Carolina Almanack...1816. Raleigh: A. Lucas, [1815].

The Ohio Almanac, for the Year...1806. Cincinnati: Joseph Carpenter, [1805].

The Ohio Almanac, for the Year...1807. Cincinnati: David L. Carpenter, [1806].

The Ohio Almanac, for the Year...1810. Cincinnati: Carney and Morgan, [1809].

The Ohio Almanac, for the Year . . . 1814. Cincinnati: Browne and Locker, [1813].

The Ohio Almanac, for the Year . . . [1815, 1816]. Cincinnati: Looker and Wallace, [1814, 1815].

The (old) Farmer's Almanack . . . for the Year . . . [1832, 1833] . . . by Robert B. Thomas. Portland, Me.: G. Hyde and Co., [1831, 1832].

The (old) Farmer's Almanack . . . for the Year . . . 1834 . . . by Robert B. Thomas. Boston: Carter, Hendee and Co., [1833].

The (old) Farmer's Almanack . . . for the Year . . . [1848–1851] . . . by Robert B. Thomas. Boston: Jenks, Palmer and Co., [1847–50].

The (old) Farmer's Almanack . . . for the Year . . . [1852, 1859] . . . by Robert B. Thomas. Portland, Me.: Sanborn and Carter, [1851, 1858].

The (old) Farmer's Almanack . . . for the Year . . . [1853, 1854] . . . by Robert B. Thomas. Boston: Jenks, Hickling and Swan, [1852, 1853].

The (old) Farmer's Almanack . . . for the Year . . . 1855 . . . by Robert B. Thomas. Portland, Me.: Blake and Carter, [1854].

The (old) Farmer's Almanack . . . for the Year . . . [1856, 1857] . . . by Robert B. Thomas. Boston: Hickling, Shaw and Brown, [1855, 1856].

The (old) Farmer's Almanack . . . for the Year . . . 1858 . . . by Robert B. Thomas. Portland, Me.: Francis Blake, [1857].

Oliver & Brother's Pictorial Temperance Almanac for 1850. New York: Oliver and Brother, [1849].

Oneida Almanac, for the Year . . . 1835. Utica, N.Y.: Gardiner Tracy, [1834].

Oram's Almanac, for the Year . . . 1808. New York: James Oram, [1807].

Oram's Almanac for the Year . . . 1810. New York: Charles Harrison, [1809].

Oram's New-Jersey and New-York Almanac . . . 1805. Trenton: James Oram. [1804].

Palladium of Knowledge: or, the Carolina and Georgia Almanac, for the Year . . . [1801, 1804, 1805, 1807, 1813]. Charleston, S.C.: W. P. Young, [1800, 1803, 1804, 1806, 1812].

The Palladium of Knowledge or, the Carolina and Georgia Almanac, for the Year . . . 1816. Charleston, S.C.: W. P. Young, [1815].

Palladium of Knowledge, and Charleston Pilot: or, the Carolina and Georgia Almanac, for the Year . . . 1806. Charleston, S.C.: W. P. Young, [1805].

Palmer's New-England Almanac, for the Year . . . [1832, 1833]. New Haven: Durrie and Peck, [1831, 1832].

Pennsylvania, 1745. An Almanack and Ephemeris . . . 1745. Philadelphia: William Bradford, [1744].

The Pennsylvania Almanac, 1836. Philadelphia: McCarty and Davis, [1835].

The Pennsylvania Almanac, for the Year . . . 1801. Philadelphia: Francis and Robert Bailey, [1800].

The Pennsylvania Almanac, for the Year . . . 1810. Philadelphia: Robert Cochran, [1809].

The Pennsylvania Almanac, for the Year . . . 1815. Philadelphia: Ann Coles, [1814].

Pennsylvania Almanac, for the Year . . . 1830. Philadelphia: McCarty and Davis, 1830.

The Pennsylvania Almanack for the Year . . . [1733, 1736]. [Thomas Godfrey]. Philadelphia: Andrew Bradford, [1732, 1735].

The Pennsylvania Almanack. Or Ephemeris . . . for 1760. Philadelphia: William Dunlap, [1759].

The Pennsylvania, New-Jersey & Delaware Almanac for [1848, 1851]. Philadelphia: John B. Perry, [1847, 1850].

The Pennsylvania, New-Jersey, Delaware, Maryland and Virginia Almanac . . . 1805. Philadelphia: Peter Stewart, [1804].

The Pennsylvania, New-Jersey, Delaware, Maryland & Virginia Almanac . . . 1810. Philadelphia: Peter Stewart, [1809].

The Pennsylvania Town and Country-man's Almanack, for the Year . . . [1754, 1755]. Germantown: Christopher Sauer, [1753, 1754].

The Pennsylvania Town and Country-man's Almanack, for the Year . . . [1756–1766]. [John Tobler]. Germantown: Christopher Sauer, [1755–1765].

The Pennsylvania Town and Country-man's Almanack, for the Year . . . 1767. [John Tobler]. Wilmington, Del.: James Adams, [1766].

The Pennsylvania Town and Country-man's Almanack, for the Year . . . [1768, 1769, 1771–1774, 1777]. Wilmington, Del.: James Adams, [1767, 1768, 1770–73, 1776].

The Pennsylvanian Almanac, for 1849. Philadelphia: John H. Simon, [1848].

Pensilvania, 1737–1738, 1740–1742. An Almanack and Ephemeris . . . 1737– 1738, 1740–1742. Philadelphia: Andrew Bradford, [1736–37, 1739–41].

Pensilvania, 1743. An Almanack, or Ephemeris . . . 1743. Philadelphia: Isaiah Warner, [1742].

Pensilvania, 1744. An Almanack or Ephemeris . . . 1744. Philadelphia: Cornelia Bradford and Isaiah Warner, [1743].

Pensilvania, 1746. An Almanack and Ephemeris . . . 1746. Philadelphia: William Bradford, [1745].

People's Almanac. [1835, 1837]. Boston: Published by Charles Ellms, [1834, 1836].

The People's Almanac of Useful and Entertaining Knowledge. 1836. Boston: Charles Ellms; Baltimore: Custling and Sons, [1835].

The People's Almanac of Useful and Entertaining Knowledge. 1838. Boston: Thomas Groom, [1837].

The People's Illustrated Almanac . . . for 1848. Philadelphia: T. W. Dyott and Sons, and F. W. Brown, [1847].

The People's Illustrated Almanac. [1849, 1850]. New York: Clapp and Townsend, [1848, 1849].

Peter Parley's Almanac for Old and Young. MDCCCXXXVI. New York: Freeman, Hunt and Co.; Philadelphia: Desilver, Thomas and Co.; Boston: Samuel Colman, [1835].

Peter Parley's Almanac, for Old and Young. 1837. Boston: Otis, Broaders and Co., [1836].

The Philadelphia Almanack for the Year . . . 1779. Philadelphia, [1778].

Philadelphia Almanack, for the Year . . . [1829, 1834, 1835]. Philadelphia: Uriah Hunt, [1828, 1833, 1834].

The Philadelphia Newest Almanack . . . [1775, 1776]. Philadelphia: Robert Aitkin, [1774, 1775].

Phillips's United States Diary; or an Almanack . . . 1798. Warren, N.H.: Nathaniel Phillips, [1797].

Philo's Essex Almanack, for . . . 1770. Salem, Mass.: Samuel Hall, [1769].

Phinney's Calendar: or, Western Almanac . . . 1801, 1805. Cooperstown, N.Y.: Elihu Phinney, [1800, 1804].

Phinney's Calendar: or, Western Almanac . . . 1810. Otsego, N.Y.: H. and E. Phinney, [1809].

Phinney's Calendar, or, Western Almanac . . . [1815, 1816, 1826, 1828, 1830, 1831, 1838, 1840–1842, 1846–1849]. Cooperstown, N.Y.: H. and E. Phinney, [1814, 1815, 1825, 1827, 1829, 1830, 1837, 1839–41, 1845–48].

Phinney's Calendar or Western Almanac . . . [1850, 1852]. Buffalo: Phinney and Co., [1849, 1851].

Phinney's Calendar or Western Almanac . . . 1851. Cazenovia, N.Y.: Miles, Crandall and Mosely, [1850].

Phinney's Calendar or Western Almanac . . . 1855. Syracuse: Hall and Hopkins, [1854].

Phinney's Calendar or Western Almanac . . . 1856. Cazenovia, N.Y.: Crandall and Mosely, [1855].

Phinney's Calendar, or, Western Almanac . . . 1859. Utica, N.Y.: Tiffany and Arnott, [1858].

Phinney's Calendar, or Western Almanac . . . 1860. Syracuse: Wynkoop and Bro., [1859].

The Phrenological and Physiological Almanac for 1847. New York: Fowlers and Wells, [1846].

Phrenological and Physiological Almanac for 1848. New York: Fowlers and Wells, [1847].

The Physician's Almanac for 1817. Boston: Tileston and Parmenter, [1816].

The Pictorial Almanac for 1852. Dayton: B. F. Ells, [1851].

The Pittsburgh Almanack, for . . . 1801. Pittsburgh: John Israel, [1800].

The Pittsburgh Almanack, for . . . 1805. Pittsburgh: Zadok Cramer, [1804].

The Pittsburgh Republican Calendar . . . 1805. Pittsburgh: John Israel, [1804].

The Pittsburgh Town & Country Almanac, for Rogues and Honest Folks. 1815. Pittsburgh: Silas Engles, [1814].

The Pittsburgh Town & Country Almanac, for Rogues and Honest Folks. 1816. Pittsburgh: R. Patterson, [1815].

The Planters' and Merchants' Almanac . . . 1817. Charleston, S.C.: A. E. Miller, [1816].

The Planters' & Merchants' Almanac . . . [1818, 1819]. Charleston, S.C.: A. E. Miller, [1817, 1818].

The Planters' & Merchants' City Almanac . . . 1820. Charleston, S.C.: A. E. Miller, [1819].

A Pocket Almanack for the Year [1742–1748]. Philadelphia: Benjamin Franklin, [1741–47].

A Pocket Almanack for the Year [1749–1759]. Philadelphia: B. Franklin and D. Hall, [1748–58].

A Pocket Almanack for the Year 1755. New York: Henry De Foreest, [1754].

The Politician's Register, for [1839–1841]. New York: H. Greeley, 1839–41.

Poor Job, 1750–1755. An Almanack for the Year . . . [1750–1755]. Newport, R.I.: James Franklin, [1749–54].

Poor Job. An Almanack for the Year . . . 1779. Charleston, S.C.: Nicholas Boden and Co., [1778].

Poor Job's Country and Townsman's Almanack for . . . 1758. Newport: James Franklin, [1757].

Poor Joseph, 1759. Being an Almanack . . . for . . . 1759. Boston: Benjamin Mecom, [1758].

Poor Richard, 1733–1747. An Almanack for the Year . . . [1733–1747]. Philadelphia: B. Franklin, [1732–46].

Poor Richard Improved. An Almanack for . . . 1810. Philadelphia: Hall and Pierce, [1809].

Poor Richard improved: Being an Almanack and Ephemeris . . . for the Year, [1748, 1749]. Philadelphia: B. Franklin, [1747, 1748].

Poor Richard improved: Being an Almanack and Ephemeris . . . for the Year . . . [1750–1766]. Philadelphia: B. Franklin and D. Hall, [1749–65].

Poor Richard improved: Being an Almanack and Ephemeris . . . for the Year . . . [1767–1773]. Philadelphia: David Hall and William Sellers, [1766–72].

Poor Richard improved: Being an Almanack and Ephemeris . . . for the Year . . . [1774–1777, 1779–1781, 1787, 1794, 1800]. Philadelphia: Hall and Sellers, [1773–76, 1778–80, 1786, 1793, 1799].

Poor Richard Reviv'd. Being an Astronomical Diary, or Almanack . . . 1801. Newfield, Conn.: Lazerus Beach, [1800].

Poor Richard Revived. or, the Albany Almanack . . . [1801, 1805]. Albany: John Barber, [1800, 1804].

Poor Richard Revived: or, the Albany Almanack . . . 1810. Albany: S. Allen, [1809].

Poor Richard's Almanack for . . . Eighteen Hundred & Five. Boston: Andrew Newell, [1804].

Poor Richard's Almanack, for the Year . . . 1830. Rochester, N.Y.: Marshall, Dean and Co., [1829].

Poor Richard's Almanack, for the Year . . . 1833. Utica, N.Y.: Gardiner Tracy, [1832].

Poor Richard's Genuine New-England Almanack . . . 1806. Boston: A. Newell, [1805].

"Poor Richard's" New Farmer's Almanac . . . 1836. Concord, N.H.: M. G. Atwood, [1835].

Poor Robin's Almanac, for the Year... [*1805, 1815*]. Philadelphia: David Hogan, [1804, 1814].

Poor Robin's Almanac, or the Starry Observer... *1805*. Baltimore: Fryer and Clark, [1804].

Poor Robin's Almanack for the Year [*1742, 1744, 1745*]. Philadelphia: William Bradford, [1741, 1743, 1744].

Poor Robin's Almanack, for the Year... *1833*. Philadelphia: Griggs and Dickinson, [1832].

Poor Robin's Spare Hours... *or Almanack*... [*1751, 1752, 1754, 1755, 1758*]. Philadelphia: William Bradford, [1750, 1751, 1753, 1754, 1757].

Poor Roger, 1756–1758. The American Country Almanack, for the Year... [*1756–1758*]. New York: James Parker and William Weyman, [1755–57].

Poor Roger, 1760. The American Country Almanack, for the Year... *1760*. Woodbridge, N..J.: James Parker, [1759].

Poor Roger, 1761–62, 1767–1769. The American Country Almanack, for the Year... [*1761, 1762, 1767–1769*]. New York: James Parker, [1760, 1761, 1766–68].

Poor Roger, 1763–1765. The American Country Almanack, for the Year... [*1763–1765*]. New York: James Parker and John Holt, [1762–64].

Poor Roger, 1771–1773. The American Country Almanack, for the Year... [*1771–1773*]. New York: Samuel Inslee and Anthony Car, [1770–72].

Poor Thomas improved: Being More's Country Almanack for the Year... [*1760–1768*]. New York: William Weyman, [1759–67].

Poor Thomas improved: Being More's Country Almanack, for the Year... *1770*. New York: Alexander and James Robertson, [1769].

Poor Tom revived: Being More's Almanack, for... [*1771, 1772*]. Charleston, S.C.: Charles Crouch, [1770, 1771].

Poor William's Almanack, for the Year... *1739*. Philadelphia: Andrew Bradford, [1738].

Poor Will's Almanac, for the Year 1818. Philadelphia: Joseph Rakestraw, [1817].

Poor Will's Almanac, for the Year [*1833, 1836–1840, 1842*]. Philadelphia: Joseph M'Dowell, [1832, 1835–39, 1841].

Poor Will's Almanack for... [*1741–1743*]. [William Birkett]. Philadelphia: Andrew Bradford, [1740–42].

Poor Will's Almanack, for... [*1744, 1745*]. [William Birkett]. Philadelphia: Isaiah Warner and Cornelia Bradford, [1743, 1744].

Poor Will's Almanack, for... [*1746, 1750*]. [William Birkett]. Philadelphia: William Bradford, [1745, 1749].

Poor Will's Almanack, for... [*1747, 1748*]. [William Birkett]. Philadelphia: Cornelia Bradford, [1746, 1747].

Poor Will's Almanack, for the Year... [*1771–1780, 1810, 1815*]. Philadelphia: Joseph Crukshank, [1770–79, 1809, 1814].

Poor Will's Almanack, for the Year... *1801*. Philadelphia: Joseph and James Crukshank, [1800].

Poor Will's Almanack, for the Year . . . 1805. Philadelphia: James Crukshank, [1804].

Poor Will's Pocket Almanack, for the Year 1801. Philadelphia: Joseph and James Crukshank, [1800].

Pope's Almanack, for the Year . . . 1795. Boston: John W. Folsom, [1794].

Porter's Health Almanac, for [1832, 1833]. Philadelphia: Henry H. Porter, [1831, 1832].

Poulson's Town and Country Almanac . . . [1794, 1797, 1800]. Philadelphia: Zachariah Poulson, Junior, [1793, 1796, 1799].

Poulson's Town and Country Almanac . . . [1802, 1805]. Philadelphia: John Bioren, [1801, 1804].

Pounder's Wesleyan Almanac . . . [1815, 1816]. Philadelphia: Jonathan Pounder, [1814, 1815].

Prindle's Almanac, for the Year . . . 1837. New Haven: A. H. Maltby, [1836].

Prindle's Almanac, for the Year . . . 1848. New Haven: B. Booth, [1847].

Prindle's Almanac, for the Year . . . 1849. Birmingham, Conn.: S. P. and J. B. Tomlinson, [1848].

Prindle's Almanac, for the Year . . . [1852, 1854, 1855]. New Haven: Durrie and Peck, [1851, 1853, 1854].

Prynne's Almanac for 1841. Albany: Erastus H. Pease, [1840].

The Rhode-Island Almanac, for the Year . . . [1801, 1805]. Newport: Oliver Farnsworth, [1800, 1804].

The Rhode-Island Almanac, for the Year [1836, 1841–1843, 1845, 1846, 1849]. Providence: H. H. Brown, [1835, 1840–1842, 1844, 1845, 1848].

The Rhode-Island Almanack, for the Year . . . [1815, 1816]. Providence: Brown and Wilson, [1814, 1815].

The Rhode-Island Almanack, for the Year . . . 1818. Providence: Hugh H. Brown, [1817].

The Rhode-Island Almanack, for the Year . . . 1821. Providence: Brown and Danforth, [1820].

The Rhode-Island Almanack, or Astronomical Diary, for . . . 1772. Newport: Soloman Southwick, [1771].

Richardson's Virginia and North Carolina Almanac, for 1849. Richmond: J. W. Randolph and Co., [1848].

Richardson's Virginia and North Carolina Almanac, for the Year . . . 1854. Richmond: J. W. Randolph, [1853].

Rivington's New Almanack . . . for . . . [1774, 1775]. New York: James Rivington, [1773, 1774].

Russell's American Almanack, for . . . 1780. Danvers, Mass.: Ezekiel Russell, [1779].

Sanford's Astronomical Diary, or Almanack . . . 1805. Hartford: Elisha Babcock, [1804].

The Scholar's Almanack, and Farmer's Daily Register . . . 1810. Exeter, N.H.: Charles Norris and Co., [1809].

Shelton's New Almanack, for the Year . . . 1815. Bridgeport, Conn.: N.L. Skinner, [1814].

Smith & Forman's New-York and New-Jersey Almanac . . . 1810, 1815. New York: Smith and Forman, [1809, 1814].

Smith & Forman's New-York & New-Jersey Almanac . . . 1816. New York: Smith and Forman, [1815].

The South-Carolina Almanack, for the Year . . . [1755, 1756]. Germantown, Pa.; Charleston: Christopher Sauer, [1754–1755].

The South-Carolina Almanack, for the Year . . . [1757, 1758]. [John Tobler]. Germantown, Pa.: Christopher Sauer, [1756, 1757].

The South-Carolina Almanack, for the Year . . . 1759. [John Tobler]. Charleston: Peter Timothy, [1758].

The South-Carolina Almanack, or Lady's and Gentleman's Diary . . . 1775. Charleston: Charles Crouch, [1774].

The South-Carolina Almanack and Register . . . 1762. Charleston: Robert Wells, [1761].

The South-Carolina & Georgia Almanac . . . [1789, 1794–1796]. Charleston, S.C.: Markland and M'Iver, [1788, 1793–95].

The South Carolina and Georgia Almanac . . . 1797. Charleston, S.C.: J. M'Iver, [1796].

The South Carolina and Georgia Almanac . . . 1798. Charleston, S.C.: S. J. Elliott, [1797].

The South-Carolina & Georgia Almanac . . . [1799, 1800]. Charleston, S.C.: Freneau and Paine, [1798, 1799].

The South-Carolina and Georgia Almanack . . . 1764. Savannah: James Johnston, [1763].

The South-Carolina & Georgia Almanack . . . 1765. Charleston, S.C.: Robert Wells and David Bruce, [1764].

The South-Carolina & Georgia Almanack . . . [1766–1768]. Charleston, S.C.: Robert Wells, [1765–67].

The South-Carolina and Georgia Almanack . . . [1770–1772, 1776]. Charleston, S.C.: Robert Wells, [1769–71, 1775].

The South-Carolina and Georgia Almanack . . . [1777, 1778]. Charleston, S.C.: Robert Wells and Son, [1776, 1777].

The South-Carolina and Georgia Almanack . . . [1779–1781]. Charleston, S.C.: John Wells, [1778–80].

The South-Carolina and Georgia Almanack . . . 1785. Charleston, S.C.: N. Childs and Company, [1784].

The South-Carolina and Georgia Almanack . . . 1786. Charleston, S.C.: Childs, M'Iver and Co., [1785].

Stafford's Almanac, for the Year . . . [1778, 1780]. New Haven: Thomas and Samuel Green, [1777, 1779].

Stafford's Connecticut Almanack . . . 1779. Hartford: Bavil Webster, [1778].

State of New-York Agricultural Almanack for . . . [1823–1825]. Albany: Board of Agriculture, [1822–24].

Steels' Diary; or Columbia Almanac . . . 1810. Hudson, N.Y.: H. and L. Steel, [1809].

Stewart's Columbian Almanac . . . 1815. New Brunswick, N.J.: Robert Stewart, [1814].

Stewart's Washington Almanac . . . 1810. Philadelphia: Robert Stewart, [1809].

Stoddard's Diary: or, the Columbia Almanack . . . 1801. Hudson, N.Y.: Ashbel Stoddard, [1800].

Stoddard's Diary, or, Columbia Almanack . . . [1805, 1810, 1811, 1829]. Hudson, N.Y.: Ashbel Stoddard, [1804, 1809, 1810, 1828].

Stoddard's Diary; or, the Columbia Almanack . . . 1833. Hudson, N.Y.: Ashbel Stoddard, [1832].

Strong's Astronomical Diary, Calendar or, Almanack . . . 1798. West Springfield, Mass.: Edward Gray, [1797].

Taylor, 1726. The Complete Ephemeris for the Year . . . 1726. Philadelphia: Samuel Keimer, [1725].

The Temperance Almanac for . . . 1834. Philadelphia: I. S. Lloyd, [1833].

The Temperance Almanac for . . . 1834. New York: New York State Temperance Society, [1833].

The Temperance Almanac, for . . . 1837. Albany: Packard and Van Benthuysen, [1836].

The Temperance Almanac . . . for 1837. Philadelphia: State Temperance Society, [1836].

The Temperance Almanac, for . . . 1840. Boston: Massachusetts Temperance Union, [1839].

The Temperance Almanac, No. 6, for . . . 1839. New York: Packard, Van Benthuysen and Co., [1838].

The Temperance Almanac, of the Massachusetts Temperance Union, for the Year . . . 1841. Boston: Whipple and Damrell, [1840].

The Temperance Family Almanac for . . . 1835. Boston: Russell, Odiorne and Metcalf, [1834].

Tennery & Stockwell's Calendar, or Newengland & Newyork Almanac . . . 1805. Cambridge, N.Y.: Tennery and Stockwell, [1804].

Der Teutsche Pilgrim . . . MDCCXXXI. Philadelphia: Andrew Bradford, [1730].

Der Teutsche Pilgrim . . . MDCCXXXIII. Philadelphia: Andrew Bradford, [1732].

Thomas, 1762. Being and Almanack and Ephemeris . . . 1762. Philadelphia: William Dunlap, [1761].

Thomas's . . . for . . . [1788, 1789]. Worcester, Mass.: Isaiah Thomas, [1787, 1788].

Thomas's Massachusetts, Connecticut, Rhode-Island, New Hampshire and Vermont Almanack, for . . . [1782–1784]. Worcester, Mass.: Isaiah Thomas, [1781–83].

Thomas's Massachusetts, Connecticut, Rhode Island, New-Hampshire & Vermont Almanack . . . for . . . [1785–1787, 1790]. Worcester, Mass.: Isaiah Thomas, [1784–86, 1789].

Thomas's Massachusetts, Connecticut, Rhode-Island, Newhampshire & Ver-

mont Almanack . . . for . . . [1791–1798]. Worcester, Mass.: Isaiah Thomas, [1790–97].

Thomas's Massachusetts, New-Hampshire, and Connecticut Almanack for . . . [1779–1781]. Worcester, Mass.: Isaiah Thomas, [1778–80].

Thomas's New England Almanack; or, the Massachusetts Calendar, for the Year . . . 1775. Boston: Isaiah Thomas, [1774].

The Thomsonian Almanac for 1838. Philadelphia: Office of the Botanic Sentinel, [1837].

The Thomsonian Almanac for 1839. Philadelphia: A. and J. W. Comfort, [1838].

Thomson's Almanac, for 1841. Boston: Samuel Thomson, [1840].

Thomson's Almanac for the Year 1843. Boston: Samuel Thomson, [1842].

Thomson's Almanac, for the Year 1844. Boston: Nath'l S. Magoon, [1843].

Thomson's Almanac, Calculated on an Improved Plan . . . 1842. Boston: Samuel Thomson, [1841].

Titan's New Almanack for the Year . . . 1729. New York: William Bradford, 1729.

Tobacco and Health Almanac for 1849. New York: Fowlers and Wells, [1848].

The Town and Country Almanac, for . . . 1801. Baltimore: Michael and Joseph Conrad, [1800].

The Town and Country Almanack, for . . . 1801. Boston: Ebenezer Larkin et al., [1800].

The Town and Country Almanack for . . . 1802. Salem, Mass.: Nathaniel Coverly, Jun'r., [1801].

The Town and Country Almanac, for . . . 1805. Alexandria, Va.: Robert and John Gray, [1804].

The Town & Country Almanac, for . . . 1805. Baltimore: John West Butler, [1804].

The Town & Country Almanack, for . . . 1781. [Nathan Daboll]. Norwich, Conn.: John Trumbull, [1780].

Town and Country Almanack, for . . . 1828. Philadelphia: D. and S. Neall, [1827].

The Tribune Almanac for [1859, 1860]. New York: Horace Greeley and Co., [1858, 1859].

The Tribune Almanac and Political Register for [1856–1858]. New York: [Horace Greeley and Co., 1855–57].

The Troy Almanac for 1846. Troy, N.Y.: Young and Hartt, [1845].

Trufant's Family Almanac, and Daily Register . . . 1810. Harvard, Mass.: Sewall Parker, [1809].

Tulley 1687. An Almanack for the Year . . . MDCLXXXVII. Boston: Samuel Green, 1687.

Tulley 1688. An Almanack for the Year . . . MDCLXXXVIII. Boston: Samuel Green, 1688.

Tulley 1689. An Almanack for the Year . . . MDCLXXXIX. Boston: Samuel Green, 1689.

Tulley 1690. An Almanack for the Year . . . MDCXC. Boston: Samuel Green, 1690.

Tulley 1691. An Almanack for the Year . . . MDCXCI. Cambridge: Samuel Green and Bartholomew Green, 1691.

Tulley 1692. An Almanack for the Year . . . MDCXCII. Cambridge: Samuel Green and Bartholomew Green, 1692.

Tulley 1693. An Almanack for the Year . . . MDCXCIII. Boston: Benjamin Harris, 1693.

Tulley, 1694. An Almanack for the Year . . . MDCXCIIII. Boston: Benjamin Harris, 1694.

Tulley, 1695. An Almanack for the Year . . . MDCXCV. Boston: Benjamin Harris, 1695.

Tulley, 1696. An Almanack, for the Year . . . MDCXCVI. Boston: Bartholomew Green and John Allen, 1696.

Tulley, 1697. An Almanack for the Year . . . MDCXCVII. Boston: Bartholomew Green and John Allen, 1697.

Tulley, 1698. An Almanack for the Year . . . MDCXCVIII. Boston: Bartholomew Green and John Allen, 1698.

Tulley, 1699. An Almanack for the Year . . . MDCXCIX. Boston: Bartholomew Green and John Allen, 1699.

Tulley, 1700. An Almanack for the Year . . . 1700. Boston: Bartholomew Green and John Allen, 1700.

Tulley, 1701. An Almanack for the Year . . . 1701. Boston: Bartholomew Green and John Allen, 1701.

Tulley's Farewell 1702. An Almanack for the Year . . . 1702. Boston: Bartholomew Green and John Allen, 1702.

Turner's Comic Almanac 1845. Boston: James Fisher, [1844].

Tuttle's Almanac for 1836. Troy, N.Y.: N. Tuttle, [1835].

Uncle Sam's Almanac, for 1851. Philadelphia: John H. Somon, [1850].

Uncle Sam's Almanac, for 1855. Philadelphia: King and Baird, [1854].

Uncle Sam's Large Almanac, for [1832, 1836]. Philadelphia: Denny and Walker, [1831, 1835].

Uncle Sam's Large Almanac, for [1838, 1839]. Philadelphia: Wm. W. Walker, [1837, 1838].

The United States Almanac, for . . . 1793. Elizabethtown, N.J.: Shepard Kollock, [1792].

The United States Almanac, for the Year . . . [1801, 1810, 1815]. Elizabethtown, N.J.: Shepard Kollock, [1800, 1809, 1814].

The United States Almanac, for the Year . . . 1801. Reading, Pa.: Jungmann and Bruckmann, [1800].

The United States Almanac, for the Year . . . 1815. Wilmington, Del.: Robert Porter, [1814].

United States Almanac, for the Year 1859. Philadelphia: King and Baird, [1858].

The United-States Almanack, for . . . 1783. Hartford: Nathaniel Patten, [1782].

The United States Almanack, for . . . 1784. Hartford: B. Webster, [1783].

The United States Almanack, for the Year . . . 1839 . . . by Charles Frederick Egelmann. Philadelphia: George W. Mentz and Son, [1838].

The United States Almanack, for the Year . . . [1845–1848] . . . by Charles Frederick Egelmann. Philadelphia: Mentz and Rovoudt, [1844–47].

The United States Almanack, for the Year . . . [1854, 1855] . . . by Charles F. Egelmann. Philadelphia: William G. Mentz, [1853, 1854].

The United States Family Almanac, for the Year 1850. New York: Collins and Brothers, [1849].

United States Statistical & Chronological Almanac, for 1846. Rochester, N.Y.: M. Miller, [1845].

The Universal Almanack, for . . . [1773–1777]. Philadelphia: John Humphreys, [1772–76].

The Universal Almanack, for . . . 1801. Boston: Benjamin Edes, [1800].

The Universal American Almanack . . . for . . . [1761, 1762]. Philadelphia: William Bradford, [1760, 1761].

The Universal American Almanack . . . for . . . [1763–1769]. Philadelphia: Andrew Steuart, [1762–68].

The Universal American Almanack . . . for . . . 1770. Philadelphia: Thomas Magee, [1769].

The Universal American Almanack . . . for . . . 1772. Philadelphia: William Evitt, [1771].

The Universal American Almanack: or, Yearly Astronomical Magazine . . . 1760. Philadelphia: William Bradford, [1759].

The Universal Pocket Almanack, for the Year 1758. New York: James Parker and William Weyman, [1757].

The Vermont Almanack, for the Year . . . 1784. Albany: S. Balentine, [1783].

The Vermont and New-York Almanac . . . 1810. Middlebury, Vt.: J.O. Huntington, [1809].

The Vermont & New-York Almanac . . . 1815. Middlebury, Vt.: Slade and Ferguson, [1814].

The Virginia Almanac, for the Year . . . 1815. Alexandria: J.A. Stewart, [1814].

The Virginia Almanack, for . . . [1748–1750]. Williamsburg: William Parks, [1747–49].

The Virginia Almanack, for . . . [1751–1755]. Williamsburg: William Hunter, [1750–54].

The Virginia Almanack, for . . . [1756–1759, 1761]. [Theophilus Wreg]. Williamsburg: William Hunter, [1755–58, 1760].

The Virginia Almanack for . . . [1762, 1764, 1765]. [Theophilus Wreg]. Williamsburg: Joseph Royle, [1761, 1763, 1764].

The Virginia Almanack for . . . 1766. [Theophilus Wreg]. Williamsburg: Alexander Purdie, [1765].

The Virginia Almanack for . . . 1767. [Job Grant]. Williamsburg: William Rind, [1766].

The Virginia Almanack for . . . [1767, 1768]. [Theophilus Wreg]. Williamburg: Purdie and Dixon, [1766, 1767].

The Virginia Almanack for ... 1769–1770. [T.T.]. Williamsburg: Purdie and Dixon, [1768–69].

The Virginia Almanack for ... [1771–1774]. Williamburg: William Rind, [1770–73].

The Virginia Almanack for ... [1771–1774]. Williamsburg: Purdie and Dixon, [1770–73].

The Virginia Almanack for ... 1775. Williamsburg: John Dixon and William Hunter, [1774].

The Virginia Almanack for ... 1775. [David Rittenhouse]. Williamsburg: John Pinkney, [1774].

The Virginia Almanack for ... [1776–1779]. [David Rittenhouse]. Williamsburg: Dixon and Hunter, [1775–78].

The Virginia Almanack for ... 1780. [David Rittenhouse]. Williamsburg: Dixon and Nicholson, [1779].

The Virginia Almanack for ... [1781, 1782]. [Robert Andrews]. Richmond: Dixon and Nicholson, [1780, 1781].

The Virginia Almanack for ... [1783, 1784]. [Robert Andrews]. Richmond: Nicholson and Prentiss, [1782, 1783].

The Virginia Almanack for ... [1785, 1786]. [Robert Andrews]. Richmond: Dixon and Holt, [1784, 1785].

The Virginia Almanack, for ... [1792, 1793]. Petersburg: William Prentiss, [1791, 1792].

The Virginia Almanack, for ... [1797, 1798]. Richmond: T. Nicholson, [1796, 1797].

The Virginia Almanack ... for ... 1799. Petersburg: William Prentiss, [1798].

The Virginia Almanack, for ... 1800. Fredericksburg: T. Green, [1799].

The Virginia Almanack ... for ... 1801. Richmond: Samuel Pleasants, Jr., [1800].

The Virginia Almanack, and Ladies Diary. ... 1769. Williamsburg: William Rind, [1768].

The Virginia and Maryland Almanack ... for ... 1732. Williamsburg: William Parks, [1731].

The Virginia & North Carolina Almanack for the Year 1801. Petersburg: Ross and Douglass, [1800].

The Virginia and North Carolina Almanack for the Year ... 1841. Richmond: John Warrock, [1840].

Wait's York, Cumberland and Lincoln Almanack, for the Year ... 1793. Portland, Me.: Thomas Baker Wait, [1792].

Walton's Vermont Register and Farmers' Almanac, for 1850. Montpelier: E. P. Walton and Sons, [1849].

Warner's Almanack ... for the Year ... 1742. Williamsburg: William Parks, [1741].

Warren's New-England Almanack ... 1775. Norwich, Conn.: Robertson and Trumbell, [1774].

Warrock's Virginia and North Carolina Almanack for the Year ... [1849, 1851, 1856]. Richmond: John Warrock, [1848, 1850, 1855].

The Washington Almanac, for . . . 1801. Baltimore: George Keatinge, [1800].

The Washington Almanac, for the Year . . . 1818. Baltimore: Cushing and Jewett, [1817].

The Washington Almanack, for . . . 1805. New Brunswick, N.J.: Abraham Blauvelt, [1804].

The Washington Almanack, for the Year . . . 1845. Philadelphia: Thomas Cowperthwait and Co., [1844].

Washington's Citizen and Farmer's Almanac . . . 1810. Philadelphia: John M'Colloch, [1809].

Watson's Register, and Connecticut Almanack . . . [1775, 1776]. Hartford: Ebenezer Watson, [1774, 1775].

Weatherwise's Federal Almanack, for the Year . . . 1788. Boston: John Norman, [1787].

Weatherwise's Town and Country Almanack, for the Year . . . 1784. Boston: Norman and White, [1783].

Webster's Calendar, or the Albany Almanac . . . 1847. Catskill, N.Y.: C. Austin, [1846].

Webster's Calendar, or the Albany Almanac . . . 1848. Albany: E. H. Bender, [1847].

Webster's Calendar, or the Albany Almanac . . . 1849. Albany: Joel Munsell, [1848].

Webster's Calendar, or the Albany Almanac . . . 1850. Albany: Aaron Hill, [1849].

Webster's Calendar, or the Albany Almanac . . . 1851. Albany: Gray and Sprague, [1850].

Webster's Calendar, or the Albany Almanac . . . [1852, 1853]. Albany: Gray, Sprague and Co., [1851, 1852].

Webster's Calendar, or the Albany Almanac . . . [1854, 1855]. Albany: Joel Munsell, [1853, 1854].

Webster's Calendar or the Albany Almanac . . . 1860. Albany: P. L. Gilbert's News Office, [1859].

Webster's Calendar: or, the Albany Almanack . . . 1805. Albany: Charles R. and George Webster, [1804].

Webster's Calendar: or, the Albany Almanack . . . [1810, 1811, 1814, 1816]. Albany: Websters and Skinner, [1809, 1810, 1813, 1815].

Webster's Calendar, or the New York, Vermont, and Connecticut Almanac . . . 1810. Bennington, Vt.: Anthony Haswell, [1809].

Western Almanac, for the Year . . . 1829. Rochester, N.Y.: E. Peck and Co., [1828].

The Western Almanac, for 1832. Geneva, N.Y.: Russell Robbins, [1831].

Western Almanac for the Year . . . 1838. Rochester, N.Y.: William Alling and Co., [1837].

Western Almanack, for the Year . . . 1831. Le Roy, N.Y.: Elisha Starr, [1830].

The Western Calendar: or, an Almanack for . . . 1801. Pittsburgh: John Scull, [1800].

The Western "Patriot" and Canton Almanack, for . . . *[1836–1838]* . . . *by Charles F. Egelmann.* Canton, Ohio: Peter Kaufmann, [1835–37].

The Western Patriot and Canton Almanack, for . . . *1840* . . . *by Charles F. Egelmann.* Canton, Ohio: Peter Kaufmann, [1839].

The Western Patriot and Canton Almanack, for . . . *[1842, 1845–1847]* . . . *by Charles F. Egelmann.* Canton, Ohio: Peter Kaufmann and Co., [1841, 1844–46].

The Western Patriot and Canton Almanack, for . . . *[1843, 1844].* Canton, Ohio: Peter Kaufmann and Co., [1842, 1843].

Wheeler's North-American Calendar, or an Almanack . . . *1790.* Providence: Bennett Wheeler, [1789].

The Whig Almanac and Politician's Register for 1838. New York: H. Greeley, 1838.

The Whig Almanac and United States Register for [1843–1855]. New York: Greeley and McElrath, [1842–54].

Whitefield's Almanack for the Year . . . *1760.* Newport, R.I.: James Franklin, [1759].

Whittemore Continued. Being an Almanack for the Year . . . *1740.* Boston: Thomas Fleet, 1740.

Whittemore Revived. An Almanack for the Year . . . *1738.* Boston: Thomas Fleet, 1738.

Williams' Calendar, or the Utica Almanack, for . . . *1830.* Utica, N.Y.: William Williams, [1829].

The Wilmington Almanack . . . *for* . . . *[1762, 1763, 1765–1772, 1774, 1777, 1779, 1781–1789, 1792].* Wilmington, Del.: James Adams, [1761, 1762, 1764–71, 1773, 1776, 1778, 1780–88, 1791].

The Wilmington Almanack . . . *for* . . . *1794.* Wilmington, Del.: Samuel and John Adams, [1793].

Wilson's New-Jersey Almanac . . . *1805.* Trenton: James J. Wilson, [1804].

Wing, improved. An Almanack, for . . . *1764.* New York: Samuel Brown, [1763].

Wing Reviv'd. Being an Almanack . . . *for the Year* . . . *1762.* New York: Samuel Brown, [1761].

Wood's Almanac, for the Year [1814, 1815]. New York: Samuel Wood, [1813–14].

Wood's Almanac for the Year [1817, 1818, 1823, 1825]. New York: Samuel Wood and Sons, [1816, 1817, 1822, 1824].

Wright's Pictorial Family Almanac 1857. Philadelphia: Wm.Wright, [1856].

The Yankee. The Farmer's Almanack for . . . *1832.* Boston: Willard Felt, [1831].

The Yankee. The Farmer's Almanac, for . . . *1835.* Boston: Lemuel Gulliver, [1834].

NOTES

Introduction: Almanacs and the Literature of Popular Health in Early America

1. Stowell, "Influence of Nathaniel Ames," 128; Briggs, *Essays*, 13.

2. Briggs, *Essays*, 13.

3. Clarence S. Brigham, one-time Librarian of the American Antiquarian Society, wrote in 1925 on the value of almanacs to historical study. See his "Report of the Librarian."

4. By the 1860s the almanac had lost its place as a leading secular publication. The emergence of other genres of popular print had reduced the almanac's uniqueness significantly, and the almanac had fallen under the domination of—or, one might argue, been co-opted by—the proprietary medicine industry. For further discussion see the Epilogue.

5. For examples of how almanacs have been used to study American popular culture, see Hall, *Worlds of Wonder*; Nissenbaum, *Battle for Christmas*; Reilly, "Common and Learned Readers"; and McCarter, "Of Physick and Astronomy."

6. Drake, *Almanacs of the United States*, 1:ii. Capp's *English Almanacs* examines the development of the genre in England. For a history of the early years of the Cambridge Press, see Winship, *Cambridge Press, 1638–1692*.

7. Brattle's remarks are in *1694. An Almanack of the Coelestial Motions . . . MDCXCIV*, [16]; Mather, *Christian Philosopher* (London, 1721) is cited in Leventhal, *In the Shadow of the Enlightenment*, 47. Mather's comparison of astrology to Roman Catholicism is from his *Angel of Bethesda*, 301. See also Capp, *English Almanacs*; and Stowell, *Early American Almanacs*. Stowell's work remains, after more than three decades, the best treatment of eighteenth-century American almanacs.

8. Many eighteenth- and nineteenth-century almanac makers hired "philomaths," or local mathematicians and astronomers, to provide the astronomical and astrological calculations (including weather predictions) for their publications.

9. Stowell, *Early American Almanacs*. See also Sagendorph, *America and Her Almanacs*; Kelly, *Practical Astronomy during the Seventeenth Century*; and Drake, *Almanacs of the United States*.

10. The term *aspect* refers to the angular relationship between various points or planets in the horoscope (an astrological chart of the heavens). The five major aspects listed in almanacs were conjunction (0 degrees), sextile (60 degrees),

quartile or square (90 degrees), trine (120 degrees), and opposition (180 degrees). Lewis, *Astrology Encyclopedia*, 40–43.

11. The zodiac is the "belt" constituted by the twelve astrological signs. The foundation of medical astrology is a system of correspondences between the signs of the zodiac and the various organs and parts of the human body. The Anatomy was a pictorial representation of that relationship. Ibid., 354–57, 535–37.

12. Other astrological information sometimes included "Vulgar Notes," which indicated numbers, letters of the alphabet, and days thought to have magical significance for the coming year. Butler, "Magic, Astrology, and the Early American Religious Heritage," 330.

13. In 1786, the almanac maker Nathanael Low referred to almanacs' importance in telling time when he boasted that they "serve as clocks and watches for nine-tenths of mankind." Low's *Astronomical Diary, or Almanack for the Year . . . 1786* (Boston, [1785]) is cited in Drake, *Almanacs of the United States*, 1:viii.

14. Bidwell, "Printers' Supplies and Capitalization," 163–64; Green, "English Books and Printing in the Age of Franklin," 266; Amory, "Reinventing the Colonial Book," 45, 51. As Amory points out, a run of five hundred copies was considered a large edition for a full-length book in colonial America, whereas editions of five thousand to fifty thousand were common for such steady sellers as primers, spelling books, and almanacs. For information on Marshall's *Life of George Washington*, see Casper, *Constructing American Lives*, 22–23. See also Wroth, *Colonial Printer*; Lehmann-Haupt, *Book in America*; Silver, *American Printer, 1787–1825*; and Tebbel, *History of Book Publishing*.

15. Wroth, *Colonial Printer*, 228; Hall, *Worlds of Wonder*, 58. Almanacs were sold in bookshops and general stores, and by printers, merchants, and peddlers. They also circulated in taverns, coffee houses, and post offices. Stowell, *Early American Almanacs*, 30–31.

16. *An Almanack for the Year 1705. An Ephemeris of the Motions and Aspects of the Planets*, [4]. The remarks of "B. A. Philo-Astro" (probably Andrew Bradford) come from *An Astronomical Diary, or an Almanack for the Year . . . 1723* and are cited in Ruffin, "Urania's Dusky Vails," 308; Franklin, *Writings* (New York: Library of America, 1987), is cited in Anderson, *Radical Enlightenments of Benjamin Franklin*, 106; Low's remarks are from his *Astronomical Diary, or, an Almanack for the Year . . . 1762*, [2]; Ames's remarks are from his *Astronomical Diary: or, an Almanack, for the Year . . . 1754*, [2].

17. I use the term *semi-literate* to refer to a person who possesses basic reading skills but lacks the ability to write.

18. For the classical influence see Gummere, "Classical Element in Early New England Almanacs." For regional differences between early American almanacs, see Appendix, table 1.

19. Elliott's *Connecticut Almanack, for . . . 1767*, [3]. West's *Bickerstaff's Boston Almanac for 1768* (Boston, [1767]) is cited in Reilly, "Common and Learned Readers," 245; Goddard's *Pennsylvania, Delaware, Maryland, and Virginia Almanack and Ephemeris for 1787* (Baltimore, [1786]) is cited in Wenrick, "For Education and Entertainment," 24; Thomas's quotation is from

Thomas's Massachusetts, Connecticut, Rhode-Island, New Hampshire and Vermont Almanack, for . . . 1782, [2]; George's remarks are in his *Almanack for the Year . . . 1786*, [2]. *The Farmer's Almanack, for the Year . . . 1811* (Baltimore, [1810]) contains "Directions to Servants," indicating that its compiler envisioned a readership that included individuals and families affluent enough to afford domestic and/or enslaved help. Almanacs were often interleaved with blank sheets of paper and used as diaries and account books. Reilly studied several almanac–diaries and found that they were "used by urban as well as rural people and by wealthy and common readers." Quoted in Reilly, "Common and Learned Readers," 407.

20. Wenrick, "For Education and Entertainment," 83–88; Hayes, *Colonial Woman's Bookshelf*, 80–101. See also Tannenbaum, *Healer's Calling*; Norton, *Founding Mothers and Fathers*; Ulrich, *Midwife's Tale*; and Leavitt, *Brought to Bed*, for the various roles played by women in health care in America during the eighteenth and nineteenth centuries. For a survey of the contents of American almanacs from 1776 to 1800, see Dodge, *Topical Index*.

21. For a discussion of almanac makers particularly and printers generally as cultural mediators, see Reilly, "Common and Learned Readers," 330, 409–11. The social background of almanac makers and printers is discussed in Gronim, "At the Sign of Newton's Head," 58; and Amory, "New England Book Trade," 334. Amory cites the Federal Census of 1790, which placed Boston printer-booksellers at the top of the artisan class, just below sea captains.

22. Miller, "Franklin's *Poor Richard Almanacs*," 98; Green and Stallybrass, *Benjamin Franklin*, 104; Stowell, *Early American Almanacs*, x. See also Horrocks, "Poor Richard's Offspring."

23. *Greenleaf's New York Journal*, November 4, 1797; Reilly and Hall, "Customers and the Market for Books," 392. McCarter, in "Of Physick and Astronomy," 59, notes that Thomas's *Farmer's Almanack*, which was printed in Boston, had an annual circulation that was close to eight thousand customers larger than all the newspapers combined, at a time when seven to fifteen almanacs were published in Massachusetts during any one year.

24. A survey of Drake's *Almanacs of the United States* demonstrates the rate at which almanac production expanded during the eighteenth century. According to Drake, in 1700 there were only 4 almanac titles printed in America. By 1750 there were 25 titles, and by 1800, the number of titles had reached 135. This expansion continued unabated during the first half of the nineteenth century.

25. The expansion of popular print in late eighteenth-century and early nineteenth-century America has received increased scholarly attention in the past three decades. Several of these studies have examined long-neglected genres. See, for example, Neuburg, "Chapbooks in America"; Nord, "A Republican Literature"; Davidson, *Revolution and the Word*; Cohen, *Pillars of Salt*; Reynolds, *Beneath the American Renaissance*; Tompkins, *Sensational Designs*; Baym, *Novels, Readers, and Reviewers*; Reilly, "Common and Learned Readers"; and Lehuu, *Carnival on the Page*. For the rise of the newspaper in the America, see Clark, *Public Prints*; Schudson, *Discovering the News*; and Mott, *American Journalism*. In 1790, there were 92 weeklies and bi-weeklies published in the United

States. By 1810 this figure had increased to 371. That year saw Americans buy 24 million copies of newspapers. Appleby, *Inheriting the Revolution*, 99–100. See O'Malley, *Keeping Watch*; and Bartky, *Selling the True Time*, for two concise studies of the advent of the clock and wristwatch in America.

26. Drake, *Almanacs of the United States*, xii; Michael A. Lofaro, Introduction to [Davy Crockett], *Tall Tales of Davy Crockett*, xvi–xix; Tebbell, *History of Book Publishing*, 1:545–46.

27. Bailyn and Hench, *The Press and the American Revolution*.

28. Remer, in *Printers and Men of Capital*, presents a thorough treatment of the development of early American publishing by looking at the emergence of the book trade in Philadelphia. See also Green, "Transformation of the 1790s"; and idem, "From Printer to Publisher." On the political roles of printers in the early republic, see Pasley, *Tyranny of Printers*. On the creation of the American postal system and its impact on printing and publishing, see John, *Spreading the News*. See also idem, "Early American Origins of the Information Age."

29. On the reading revolution in America, see Davidson, *Revolution and the Word*; Gilmore, *Reading Becomes a Necessity of Life*; and Hall, "Uses of Literacy in New England." Hall surveys scholarship on this subject up to 1993 in "Readers and Reading in America." The idea, implied by the phrase "reading revolution," that nineteenth-century America was a unified nation of readers is challenged by Zboray in *Fictive People*. Davidson qualifies her earlier support for an American reading revolution in "Towards a History of Books and Readers," 14–18. Studies of literacy rates and reading skills in early America have concentrated on early New England. See, for example, Monaghan, "Literacy Instruction and Gender in Colonial New England"; idem, "Family Literacy in Early Eighteenth-Century Boston"; idem, *Learning to Read and Write in Colonial America*; Beales and Monaghan, "Literacy and Schoolbooks"; and Lepore, "Literacy and Reading in Puritan New England." The role of technological innovations in explaining the growth of reading in America has been challenged by Zboray in "Antebellum Reading and the Ironies of Technological Innovation" and in *Fictive People*. According to Lehuu, historians of technology have begun to recognize that the popularization of reading stimulated as much as resulted from technological change. Lehuu, *Carnival on the Page*, 24. See also, Remer, *Printers and Men of Capital*; and Green, "From Printer to Publisher." The figures concerning the numbers of publishing firms, booksellers, and printing houses in mid-nineteenth-century America come from Brown, *Word in the World*, 47.

30. Remer, *Printers and Men of Capital*, 100–124; Zboray, *Fictive People*.

31. Remer, *Printers and Men of Capital*, 100–124.

32. Porter's publishing career is covered in Horrocks, "Poor Man's Riches"; and idem, "Promoting Good Health."

33. Horrocks, "Promoting Good Health." On the emergence of the middle class in America, see Blumin, *Emergence of the Middle Class*; Bledstein, *Culture of Professionalism*; Johnson, *Shopkeeper's Millennium*; Boyer, *Urban Masses and Moral Order*; and Ryan, *Cradle of the Middle Class*.

34. These publications tended to emphasize the idea of learning and virtue

that was part of an older eighteenth-century republican ideology. Reilly, "Common and Learned Readers"; Halttunen, *Confidence Men and Painted Women*; Kasson, *Rudeness and Civility*; Hemphill, *Bowing to Necessities*. See also Howe, *Making the American Self*; and Augst, *Clerk's Tale*.

35. For comprehensive listings of medical publications, including those intended for lay audiences, printed in seventeenth- and eighteenth-century America, see Austin, *Early American Medical Imprints*; and Guerra, *American Medical Bibliography*. See also Hoolihan, *Catalog of the Edward C. Atwater Collection*. Slack, "Mirrors of Health and Treasures of Poor Men"; Wear, *Knowledge and Practice in English Medicine*, 112–15; and Smith, "Prescribing the Rules of Health," provide useful introductions to the British scene. On *Aristotle's Masterpiece*, see Fissell, "Making a Masterpiece"; Porter and Hall, "Medical Folklore in High and Low Culture"; Blackman, "Popular Theories of Generation"; Beall, "*Aristotle's Master Piece* in America"; and Bullough, "Early American Sex Manual." *Erra Pater* is discussed in Fissell, "Readers, Texts, and Contexts." It should be mentioned that other genres of print, such as newspapers and broadsides, also disseminated health information to laypersons.

36. There are few adequate surveys of pre–Civil War lay health publications. Two useful studies are Murphy, *Enter the Physician*; and Blake, "From Buchan to Fishbein." For a concise introduction to pre-1860 American popular health literature, see Rosenberg, "Health in the Home." For a survey of domestic health publications in the Antebellum South, see Keeney, "Unless Powerful Sick." For discussions of the works of William Buchan and John Gunn, two of the most popular authors of lay health books in America, see Rosenberg, "Medical Text and Social Context"; and idem, introduction to [Gunn], *Domestic Medicine*.

37. Sellers, *Market Revolution*, examines how the rapid development of the marketplace radically transformed American life in the three decades that followed the War of 1812. See also Watts, *Republic Reborn*; and Stokes and Conway, *Market Revolution in America*. For overviews of the period, see Feller, *Jacksonian Promise*; and Watson, *Liberty and Power*.

38. Walters, *American Reformers*; Mintz, *Moralists and Modernizers*; and Dorsey, *Reforming Men and Women*, offer concise reviews of the various antebellum reform movements. See also Halttunen, *Confidence Men and Painted Women*; Smith, *Revivalism and Social Reform*; Hatch, *Democratization of American Christianity*; Abzug, *Cosmos Crumbling*; Brown, *Word in the World*; and Augst, *Clerk's Tale*.

39. Walters, *American Reformers*, 145–46; Blake, "Health Reform," 4. William Alcott, John H. Griscom, Robert Hartley, and Sylvester Graham are just four examples of health reformers who linked piety with hygienic improvement. See Whorton, "Christian Physiology"; Rosenberg and Smith-Rosenberg, "Pietism and the Origins of the American Public Health Movement"; and Nissenbaum, *Sex, Diet, and Debility*. See also Whorton, *Crusaders for Fitness*; and Fellman and Fellman, *Making Sense of Self*. In *Cosmos Crumbling*, Abzug argues that, while social and economic factors influenced health reform (as well as other reform movements), religious forces were central to the movement. Alcott, Graham, and Orson S. Fowler, according to Abzug, saw themselves as religious

prophets. During the second third of the nineteenth century, the American Tract Society and the American Sunday-School Union established their own publishing networks, issuing affordably priced bibles, biographies, memoirs of ministers and other religious leaders, and other publications that promoted the pious and moral life. See Casper, *Constructing American Lives*, 80; Harris, "Spiritual Cakes upon the Waters"; Nord, "Religious Reading and Readers"; Wosh, *Spreading the Word*; Brown, *Word in the World*; and Gutjahr, *American Bible*.

40. Murphy, *Enter the Physician*; Horrocks, "Promoting Good Health"; Rosenberg, "Catechisms of Health"; Halttunen, *Confidence Men and Painted Women*; Kasson, *Rudeness and Civility*; Hemphill, *Bowing to Necessities*; Augst, *Clerk's Tale*.

41. Rosenberg, preface to Rosenberg, ed., *Right Living: An Anglo-American Tradition of Self-Help Medicine and Hygiene* (Baltimore: Johns Hopkins University Press, 2003), viii. Guerra, "Medical Almanacs of the American Colonial Period"; idem, *American Medical Bibliography*; and McCarter, "Of Physick and Astronomy," are the only studies of early American almanacs and the health information they contained. Guerra's work, while useful, lacks analysis. McCarter's study focuses solely on New England from 1700 to 1764.

42. Rosenberg, "Health in the Home"; idem, "Medical Text and Social Context"; idem, introduction to [Gunn], *Domestic Medicine*; idem, "Catechisms of Health"; Murphy, *Enter the Physician*; Blake, "Complete Housewife"; idem, "From Buchan to Fishbein."

43. Casper, "Antebellum Reading Proscribed and Described." For a review of issues of concern to historians of the book, see Darnton, "What Is the History of Books?"

44. See, for example, Rosenberg, "Health in the Home"; idem, "Medical Text and Social Context"; idem, introduction to [Gunn], *Domestic Medicine*; idem, "Catechisms of Health"; Fissell, "Making a Masterpiece"; idem, "Readers, Texts, and Contexts"; Blake, "From Buchan to Fishbein"; idem, "Complete Housewife"; Murphy, *Enter the Physician*; and Horrocks, "Poor Man's Riches."

1. Heavenly Guidance

1. *The Methodist Almanac for the Year . . . 1846*, [3].

2. Rawcliffe, *Medicine and Society*, 83–85. See also Willis and Curry, *Astrology, Science, and Culture*; Berlinski, *Secrets of the Vaulted Sky*; Whitfield, *Astrology*; Holden, *History of Horoscopic Astrology*; Tester, *History of Western Astrology*; Newman and Grafton, *Secrets of Nature*; Curry, *Prophecy and Power*; Eade, *Forgotten Sky*; and McCaffery, *Astrology*. Throughout the Middle Ages and well into the modern period, most educated men and women believed that the planets and stars exerted a profound influence on the earth and the weather. Eisenstadt, "Weather and Weather Forecasting," 60.

3. Rawcliffe, *Medicine and Society*, 86–87; Palmer, *Admirable Secrets*, 3. A scholarly study of the history of medical astrology has yet to be done. Mercier's *Astrology in Medicine*, though dated, is useful. Ebertin's *Astrological Healing* concentrates on the late nineteenth century and most of the twentieth.

4. Capp, *English Almanacs*, 15–16, 20–21, 64, 180, 190–91; Thomas, *Religion and the Decline of Magic*, 283–85, 296. See also McDonald, "Career of Astrological Medicine in England"; idem, *Mystical Bedlam*; Traister, "Medicine and Astrology in Elizabethan England"; idem, *Notorious Astrological Physician of London*; Chapman, "Astrological Medicine"; and Roos, "Luminaries in Medicine."

5. Thomas, *Religion and the Decline of Magic*, 288–89. See also Curth, "Medical Content of English Almanacs." Eisenstein, *Printing Press as an Agent of Change*, provides a useful overview of print culture and the popularization of print in the late fifteenth century and the early modern period. Spufford, *Small Books and Pleasant Histories*, provides a good introduction to the rise of the English market in popular literature.

6. *Erra Pater*, [5, 8]. Popular health publications, such as the *Erra Pater*, were serious competitors of the almanac at the low end of the English print market. For an excellent introduction to *Erra Pater*, see Fissell, "Readers, Texts, and Contexts." Verse often used as mnemonic device was encountered often in cheap print, such as *Aristotle's Masterpiece* and almanacs.

7. Capp, *English Almanacs*, 23. Capp cites distribution figures presented in Blagden, "Distribution of Almanacs."

8. Capp, *English Almanacs*, 24, 191; Thomas, *Religion and the Decline of Magic*, 287, 324; Furdell, *Publishing and Medicine*, 30, 158; and Winkler, "Technical Aspects of Eighteenth-Century Common Almanacs," 11–12. The importance of the moon's place for bloodletting is discussed in Palmer, *Admirable Secrets*, 3; and Chapman, "Astrological Medicine," 293–94.

9. Eisenstadt, "Weather and Weather Forecasting," 93–94. Although Foster established the second printing press in America, he can be considered this country's first commercial printer, producing the first printed map and portrait in New England. Amory, "Printing and Bookselling in New England," 90–92. I wish to thank James N. Green for bringing this fact and reference to my attention.

10. Eisenstadt, "Weather and Weather Forecasting," 93–95, 99; *1695. The New England Almanack for . . . MDCXCV*, [15–16].

11. Capp, *English Almanacs*, 206; Stowell, *Early American Almanacs*, 53–62. Guerra states that at least 90 percent of colonial American almanacs contained the "Anatomy." See his "Medical Almanacs of the Colonial Period," 237. My own findings counter Guerra's inflated claim. Less than half of the almanacs printed in colonial New England contained an image of the Anatomy (see Appendix, table 1). Astrology was a basic component of the Pennsylvania German almanacs. See Winkler, "Pennsylvania German Astronomy and Astrology XIII"; and idem, "Pennsylvania German Astronomy and Astrology XIV." On popular astrology-related health publications that circulated among early American German communities, see Cowen and Wilson, "Traffic in Medical Ideas." See also Wells, "Small Herbal of Little Cost"; and Sauer, *Herbal Cures*.

12. *An Almanack for the Year . . . 1694* (William Bradford), [20]; *An Almanack for the Year . . . 1695* (William Bradford), [19].

13. *The American Almanack for the Year . . . 1715*, [20]; *MDCCXV. An*

Almanack for the Year . . . *1715*, [2]; *MDCCXXIII. An Almanack of Coelestial Motions* . . . *1723*, [16].

14. *Boston Almanack for the Year* . . . *1692*, 17–18.

15. *Tulley 1689*, [16]; *Tulley, 1694*, [22–23].

16. Travis's remarks are in *MDCCIX. An Almanack of Coelestial Motions and Aspects* . . . *1709* (New York, 1709) and are cited in McCarter, "Of Physick and Astronomy," 157.

17. *An Astronomical Diary: or, an Almanack for the Year* . . . *1752* . . . *by George Wheten*, [16].

18. McCarter, "Of Physick and Astronomy," 33–42. In the calendar columns designating the moon's place in the zodiac, the part of the body influenced by the moon's place on a particular day was represented in three basic formats: use of the zodiacal symbol representing the part of the body (e.g., the lion denoting the heart), the word denoting the part or organ (e.g., "heart"), and the zodiacal symbol or word with a number indicating the place or degree in the sign (1–30 degrees) in which the moon was located. This format was followed by most American almanacs from the late seventeenth century through the mid-nineteenth century.

19. Cupping is a process, intended to improve circulation, by which blood is drawn to a part of the body by suction from a cup placed over the part. Bleeding involves drawing blood from the body through an incision made by a sharp instrument, such as a lancet.

20. *Columbian Almanac, for 1833*, 6.

21. Lewis, *Astrology Encyclopedia*, 24.

22. See, for example, *The South-Carolina Almanack, for the Year* . . . *1755*.

23. The Maryland almanacs that used Eagelmann's astrological and astronomical calculations were the *Farmer's Calendar, for the Year* . . . *1848*; the *Farmer's Calendar, for the Year* . . . *1849*; and the *Hagers-Town Town and Country Almanack* . . . *1854*. The Ohio almanac with which Eagelmann was involved was the *Western "Patriot" and Canton Almanack, for* . . . *1836*. Eagelmann prepared the calculations for this almanac throughout the 1830s and 1840s.

24. For German American interest in astrology, see n. 11. For a complete list of German-language almanacs with which Eagelmann was involved, see Drake, *Almanacs of the United States*, vol. 2.

25. See Appendix, table 1.

26. *Poor Richard 1733*, [3]. Franklin did not include the Anatomy in the 1748 *Poor Richard* and offered no explanation for the omission. Louis Winkler suggests that the woodcut of the figure Franklin had been using had worn out. Winkler's evidence for this claim is that Franklin used a larger, improved cut in his 1749 almanac. See Winkler, "Pennsylvania German Astronomy and Astrology XIV," 38–39. Reilly, *Dictionary of Colonial American Printers' Ornaments*, 443–56, presents the various artistic renderings of the Anatomy used by colonial almanac makers.

27. *1678. An Almanack of Coelestial Motions*, [2].

28. *The Virginia Almanack for* . . . *1768* [Theophilus Wreg], [3].

29. *Tulley, 1696*, [16].

30. Clough's remarks appeared in his *1706. Kalendarium Nov-Anglicanum* (Boston, 1706) and are cited in McCarter, "Of Physick and Astronomy," 168.

31. *An Almanack for the Year . . . 1753* [John Nathan Hutchins], [2].

32. "Student in Mathematics and Astrology": Samuel Atkins, philomath for *Kalendarium Pennsilvaniense, or, America's Messenger . . . for the Year . . . 1686*; "A Student in Astronomy and Astrology": Joseph Stafford, philomath for *An Almanack for the Year . . . 1744*; "dealer in astrology": Elisha Stimson, philomath for *The Mathamaticians* [sic] *Glory Astronomy and New-England Almanack . . . 1744*.

33. *An Astronomical Diary: or, Almanack for the Year . . . 1764 . . . by Nathaniel Ames*, [2]. For biographical information on Ames, see Briggs, *Essays.*

34. Ames's remarks are in his *Astronomical Diary, or, an Almanack for the Year . . . 1727* (Boston, [1726]) and are cited in Eisenstadt, "Weather and Weather Forecasting," 120.

35. Ames's remarks are in his *Astronomical Diary, or, an Almanack for the Year . . . 1745* (Boston, 1745) and are cited in McCarter, "Of Physick and Astronomy," 185.

36. *An Astronomical Diary, or an Almanack for the Year . . . 1729 . . . by Nathaniel Ames*, [2]. See also Eisenstadt, "Weather and Weather Forecasting," 122–23.

37. *Clough, 1703. The New-England Almanack*, [3].

38. James Franklin's remarks are in *MDCCXXIX. The Rhode-Island Almanack . . . 1729* (Newport, 1729) and are cited in McCarter, "Of Physick and Astronomy," 273. Franklin's prediction of the death of Titan Leeds is in his *Poor Richard, 1733.*

39. Robie's remarks are in his *Letter to a Certain Gentleman* (Boston, 1719) and are cited in Eisenstadt, "Weather and Weather Forecasting," 125.

40. Taylor's remarks are in his *Pensilvania, 1746. An Almanack, and Ephemeris*, [24].

41. *Poor Joseph, 1759*, [1].

42. The remarks of "Frank Freeman" are in *Freeman's New-York Almanack for . . . 1767*, [2–3].

43. *Johnson and Warner's Almanac, for the Year 1812*, [19].

44. *The Mechanics' Almanac, and Astronomical Ephemeris, for 1825*, [2].

45. Leeds's poem is in *The American Almanack for 1725* (New York, [1724]) and is cited in Stowell, *Early American Almanacs*, 22.

46. *Clough, 1702*, [2]; *Clough, 1704*, [3].

47. Freeman's remarks are in his *Freeman's New-York Almanack, for . . . 1768* (New York, [1767]) and are cited in Gronim, "At the Sign of Newton's Head," 62.

48. Thomas's remarks are in *Isaiah Thomas's Massachusetts, Connecticut, Rhode-Island, Newhampshire & Vermont Almanack . . . for . . . 1799* (Worcester, [1798]) and are cited in Eisenstadt, "Weather and Weather Forecasting," 127.

49. *The Virginia & North Carolina Almanack for the Year 1801*, [22]; *Stoddard's Diary; or, the Columbia Almanack . . . 1833*, [2].

50. *Webster's Calendar or the Albany Almanac . . . 1855*, [27–28].

51. Astrological, magic, and occult practices in early New England are discussed in Butler, "Magic, Astrology, and the Early American Religious Heritage"; and idem, *Awash in a Sea of Faith*, 67–98. A detailed study of astrology in early America has yet to be written. Butler's works, Hall's *Worlds of Wonder*, and Stahlman's "Astrology in Colonial America," are useful for their coverage of seventeenth- and eighteenth-century America. See also Kelly, *Practical Astronomy during the Seventeenth Century*.

52. *1695. The New England Almanack*.

53. Winship, "Cotton Mather, Astrologer"; Watson, *Angelical Conjunction*; and Godbeer, *Devil's Dominion*.

54. John Tulley's printers obtained licenses for his almanacs every year they applied. McCarter, "Of Physick and Astronomy," 80. New England almanacs issued between 1646 and 1700 also include a list of signs (8 percent) and general astrological information (6 percent) (see Appendix, table 1).

55. Astrology in the Pennsylvania German community is discussed in Cowan and Wilson, "Traffic in Medical Ideas"; Wells, "Small Herbal of Little Cost"; Winkler, "Pennsylvania German Astronomy and Astrology XIII"; and idem, "Pennsylvania German Astronomy and Astrology XIV." See also Butler, "Magic, Astrology, and the Early American Religious Heritage."

56. McCarter, "Of Physick and Astronomy," 131, 135, 138–39.

57. Butler, "Magic, Astrology, and the Early American Religious Heritage," 326; idem, "Thomas Teackle's 333 Books." Butler, *Awash in a Sea of Faith*, 77, states that books by Culpeper and Salmon led the list of occult titles in late seventeenth- and early eighteenth-century libraries of Virginians. The works of both Culpeper and Salmon were collected by the noted Virginia bibliophile William Byrd II of Westover. Hayes, *Library of William Byrd of Westover*. Ebenezer Sibly is a classic example of a trained physician who mixed science and astrology in his writings, many of which were quite popular with learned readers. See, for example, *New and Complete Illustration of the Occult Sciences*. Debus, "Scientific Truth and Occult Tradition."

58. Mead, *Treatise Concerning the Influence of the Sun and Moon*, 82–83. See also Roos, "Luminaries in Medicine."

59. Eliot's remarks are in his *Essays Upon Field Husbandry in New England* (Boston, 1760) and are cited in Reilly, "Common and Learned Readers," 416.

60. African Americans possessed a fairly sophisticated knowledge of herbs and plants—when they should be picked and when they were most potent as remedies—suggesting a familiarity with astrology. Fett, *Working Cures*, 6–76.

61. Stiles's remarks are in *Literary Diary of Ezra Stiles* (New York, 1910), and are cited in Brooke, "True Spiritual Seed," 107.

62. Eisenstadt, "Weather and Weather Forecasting"; and idem, "Almanacs and the Disenchantment of Early America." See also Stahlman, "Astrology in Colonial America"; and Goldberg, "Eighteenth-Century Philadelphia Almanac."

63. Butler, in "Magic, Astrology, and the Early American Religious Heritage," 345–46, states that astrology survived especially in the nineteenth-century south and among German-speaking residents in parts of Pennsylvania. See also

Brooke, "True Spiritual Seed"; and Leventhal, *In the Shadow of the Enlighten-ment*, 64.

64. See *Complete Fortune Teller*, and Russel, *Complete Fortune Teller, and Dream Book*, as examples of the few astrology books published in America dur-ing the eighteenth century and early decades of the nineteenth.

65. One of the most successful of these periodicals was *Broughton's Monthly Planet Reader and Astrological Journal*, which was published first in Philadelphia and then in New York by L. D. Broughton from 1860 to 1869. Lewis, *Astrology Encyclopedia*, 258–59; Broughton, *Elements of Astrology*, x–xiii. See also Lewis, *Beginnings of Astrology in America*; and Gardner, *Bibliotheca Astrologica*.

66. Lamon, *Life of Abraham Lincoln*, 44–45. Lamon's observations were based on interviews conducted by Lincoln's one-time law partner, William Herndon, for the latter's own biography of Lincoln, which was published in 1888. Herndon's interviews have been criticized by many Lincoln scholars as being highly unreliable. Yet, in this instance, the belief in and practice of as-trology referred to in Lamon's passage is in keeping with other contemporary sources. Moreover, similar beliefs and practices were, according to former Presi-dent Jimmy Carter, still adhered to in rural Georgia in the 1930s. For a discus-sion of William Herndon as a biographer, see Wilson, *Honor's Voice*, 3–18; and idem, "Keeping Lincoln's Secrets." For astrological beliefs and practices in rural Georgia in the 1930s, see Carter, *Hour before Daylight*, 170.

67. Baldwin, *Diary of Christopher Columbus Baldwin*, 176–78. Thomas Hague, a Philadelphia "Astrologer and Meteorologist," advertised his services to "Tradesman, Insurance Brokers, Merchants," and others, including those in debt, and ship captains desiring astrological predictions. Hague offered advice about such things as "favorable periods for marriage, journeys, setting up in business, lawsuits, speculations in funds . . . hiring and purchasing houses . . . taking a sea voyage." [Hague], *Astrology*.

68. Benes, "Fortunetellers, Wise-Men, and Magical Healers," 128–29.

69. *Webster's Calendar, or the Albany Almanac . . . 1849*, [4].

2. Advice for the Afflicted

1. See Appendix, table 1, for national and regional percentages.

2. *The American Farmers' Almanac 1854*, 5, 7, 9, 11 includes a list of vari-ous roots and herbs, noting the medicinal uses of each one. Of the almanacs consulted for this study, only this one offers extensive information on the me-dicinal uses of a variety of herbs. Almanacs that include this kind of information tend to concentrate on only one or two herbs or plants. By the beginning of the nineteenth century, according to J. Worth Estes, every American practitioner of medicine, whether a trained physician or a layperson, depended on botani-cal remedies that were readily available in home gardens, in forests, and from apothecaries and physicians. Although several botanical remedies had been bor-rowed from Native American practice or introduced by local practitioners and botanists, most were transplants from England and Europe. Estes, "Therapeutic Practice in Colonial New England." According to William Rothstein, "botanicals

were usually dried, ground into powder or stored in leaf form. When needed, the leaves were brewed into a tea or a teaspoonful of the powder was added to some sweetened hot water and drunk by the patient. Occasionally the powder was sniffed like snuff. Sometimes a number of drugs were combined according to a recipe, dissolved in water, vinegar, brandy, or wine, and kept in a bottle to be used as needed. The resulting medicine was often made more concentrated by boiling off most of the liquid. . . . Occasionally they were cooked with oils, fats, or beeswax for long periods of time as used as ointments. Some botanicals were ground and mixed with a liquid and corn meal or some other substance for use as poultices on wounds, bites, or sores." Rothstein, "Botanical Movements and Orthodox Medicine," 33. African Americans, especially those enslaved on southern plantations, were known for their detailed knowledge of wild-growing herbs and plants. Fett, *Working Cures*, 72.

3. See Rosenberg, "Therapeutic Revolution," for a concise examination of traditional therapeutic assumptions. See also Warner, *Therapeutic Perspective*; Estes, "Therapeutic Practice in Colonial New England"; idem, *Naval Surgeon*, 65–73; idem, "Patterns of Drug Use in Colonial America"; Gifford, "Botanic Remedies in Colonial Massachusetts"; Gevitz and Sullivan-Fowler, "Making Sense of Therapeutics in Seventeenth-Century New England"; and Moss, *Southern Folk Medicine*. Belief in the relationship of the body to its environment is the subject of Valencius's *Health of the Country*, which studies the attitudes of settlers in the American West, concerning the relationship between the health of the land and the health of their bodies. Estes, *Dictionary of Protopharmacology*; Sauer, *Herbal Cures*; and Crellin and Philpott, *Herbal Medicine Past and Present*, are useful introductions to the therapeutic practices of laypersons and trained physicians during the period covered. See Nutten, "Medicine in the Greek World," 23–25; and idem, "Humoralism," for an introduction to humoralism. Porter, "Lay Medical Knowledge in the Eighteenth Century," offers a case study that shows what little difference there was between lay and professional medical knowledge in the eighteenth century.

4. The therapeutic theories of Paracelsus are discussed in Wear, "Medicine in Early Modern Europe"; Webster, "Alchemical and Paracelsian Medicine"; Debus, *Chemical Philosophy*; idem, "Paracelsus and the Chemical Revolution"; and Gevitz and Sullivan-Fowler, "Making Sense of Therapeutics in Seventeenth-Century New England," 90. See also Furdell, *Publishing and Medicine*, 42–43.

5. Estes, "Yellow Fever Syndrome," 8–9; idem, "Patterns of Drug Use in Colonial America," 38. See also King, *Medical World of the Eighteenth Century*, 59–93; Shryock, *Medicine and Society in America*, 51, 66–67; and Lindeboom, "Boerhaave's Concept of the Basic Structure of the Body."

6. The medical beliefs and practices of African American slave communities are discussed in Fett, *Working Cures*; Gorn, "Black Magic"; and Savitt, *Medicine and Slavery*. Seventeenth-century Puritan views of health and disease are discussed in Watson, *Angelical Conjunction*; Wear, "Puritan Perceptions of Illness"; and Mutschler, "Province of Affliction."

7. See, as examples, [Tennent], *Every Man His Own Doctor*; Buchan, *Domestic Medicine*; Ewell, *Planter's and Mariner's Medical Companion*; Rishel,

Indian Physician; [Gunn], *Domestic Medicine*; Thomson, *New Guide to Health* (1822); Smith, *American Physician*; and Simons, *Planter's Guide.*

8. According to Estes, this general definition of dropsy had become obsolete by the mid- to late nineteenth century, at least within the medical profession. By the middle of the nineteenth century, physicians had begun to link dropsy with heart, liver, and kidney disease, or with malnutrition. Estes, "Dropsy." See also Peitzman, "From Bright's Disease to End-Stage Renal Disease."

9. *The Wilmington Almanack . . . for . . . 1787*, [3]. See also Estes, "Dropsy." Saltpeter or *Sal niter* (potassium nitrate) was used primarily as a diuretic. It was also used as a refrigerant (to reduce the heat of the body), resolvent (to dissolve and disperse humors through exhalation or circulation), mild cathartic, and diaphoretic (to produce perspiration). Estes, *Dictionary of Protopharmacology*, 137; Thacher, *American New Dispensatory*, 166–67; Simons, *Planter's Guide*, 43.

10. *Poor Richard improved . . . 1764*, [32]; *The South-Carolina & Georgia Almanack . . . 1767*, [17]; *Poor Will's Almanack, for the Year . . . 1771*, [26]. The juice and leaves of the artichoke (*Cynara scolamus*) were known for their diuretic properties. Estes, *Dictionary of Protopharmacology*, 47.

11. *The South Carolina & Georgia Almanack . . . 1766*, [20]. The root, leaves, and berries of the dwarf elder (*Sambucus ebulus*) were used primarily for their cathartic properties. Estes, *Dictionary of Protopharmacology*, 72. Dwarf elder's roots and berries were also used for diuretic purposes. Sauer, *Herbal Cures*, recommends dwarf elder for dropsy, 129.

12. *The Burlington Almanack, for the Year . . . 1772*, [38]. *Raphanus rusticanus* (root of horseradish) has diuretic properties. The bark of the elderberry (*Sambucus nigra*) was used as a cathartic, deobstruent (used to facilitate urination, sweating, defecation, etc.), diaphoretic, and diuretic. Besides their diaphoretic, aperient (a weak cathartic), tonic, and antisyphilitic properties, the wood, root, and bark of *Laurus sassafras* were used to promote urination. *Petroselinum* (root and seed of parsley) has diuretic properties. The seeds of fennel (*Foeniculum vulgare*) were used as a carminative (to expel gas from intestines), resolvent, expectorant (to promote secretion of fluids from lungs and trachea), and diuretic. Scurvy grass (*Cochlearia officinalis*), while used primarily to treat scurvy, was also used as a diuretic in cases of dropsy. Burdock, the seeds of *Arctium lappa*, was used as a strong diuretic. The root of elecampane (*Enula campana*) is known for its expectorant, diaphoretic, cathartic, and diuretic properties. Garlic (*Allium sativum*), which could be taken orally or applied externally, was used for its various properties, including diuretic. Iron (*Ferrum*) was often used as a tonic, diaphoretic, cathartic, and diuretic. Iron rust (*Ferri rubigo*), however, was often used for its properties as a tonic for stomach pain or to promote menstruation. Its use in this remedy is unclear. It is possible that iron rust was used to ease the pain associated with dropsy. Likewise, molasses or *Saccharum officinarum* would have been used to "sugarcoat" the concoction by disguising the taste. Estes, *Dictionary of Protopharmacology*, 24, 51, 78, 82, 84, 88, 150, 163, 170–71, 173; Sauer, *Herbal Cures*, 74–75, 129–32, 136–38, 171–72, 236–38, 274, 280–82; Thacher, *American New Dispensatory*, 83, 109, 144, 201, 210–11. Horserad-

ish and parsley were popular ingredients in early American dropsy remedies. Crellin and Philpott, *Herbal Medicine Past and Present*, 199–200, 253–54, 282–84, 320–32.

13. *Hutchins Improved . . . 1793*, [7]. *Sinapi [alba* or *nigra]* (white and black mustard seed) has diuretic properties. Estes, *Dictionary of Protopharmacology*, 178; Thacher, *American New Dispensatory*, 109; Sauer, *Herbal Cures*, 220–22. Horseradish and parsley are described in n. 12.

14. *The South Carolina & Georgia Almanac . . . 1800*, [34]. Cream of tartar (or cremor tartar), powdered sodium potassium tartrate, was considered a mild cathartic. It was also used as a diuretic. Estes, *Dictionary of Protopharmacology*, 55; Thacher, *American New Dispensatory*, 220.

15. *Bioren's Town and Country Almanack . . . 1810*, [49]; *The Citizen & Farmer's Almanac . . . 1816*, [30]. *Scillae* or *Scilliticae* refers to a "Squill Pill," which was, according to Estes, "usually made with *scilla, Gum ammoniac, Glyc-errihiza, Cardamomum minus*, and simple syrup." It was used primarily "as a strong diuretic, but occasionally as a diaphoretic." Oxymel referred to a drink or syrup consisting of vinegar and honey. Estes, *Dictionary of Protopharmacology*, 154, 174. Parsley and horseradish are described in n. 12, mustard seed in n. 13.

16. *Farmer's Almanac, for the Year 1824*, [18]. *Juniperus communis* (berries and tops of juniper) "was most commonly used in the form of an infusion . . . as a diuretic drink in dropsy." Thacher, *American New Dispensatory*, 139. See also Sauer, *Herbal Cures*, 181–83; Estes, *Dictionary of Protopharmacology*, 108.

17. *Agricultural Almanac, for the Year . . . 1838*, [33].

18. *Agricultural Almanac, for the Year . . . 1840*, [34]. The broom seed referred to in this remedy could be either *Genista* or *Scoparius*, though probably the latter. The former includes the tops and seeds of various genera of broom that would have been used as a cathartic and emetic. *Scoparius* includes fresh tops of broom that would have been used as a diuretic, cathartic, and emetic. Estes, *Dictionary of Protopharmacology*, 31, 88, 174.

19. Moses Appleton, Receipt book. See n. 15 for descriptions of ingredients contained in Appleton's remedy.

20. Moss, *Southern Folk Medicine*, 11–12, 88.

21. Buchan, *Domestic Medicine*, 288. Ipecacuanha (root of *Cephaelis ipeca-cuanha*) was used primarily as a mild emetic and, in small doses, as a diaphoretic and expectorant. Thacher calls jalap "an efficacious and safe purgative." Sauer espouses its use as a diuretic, claiming it is "an excellent medicine for operat-ing against superfluous watery humors." Estes identifies calomel (mercurous chloride) as the most widely used mercurial drug in early America. It was used as a cathartic diuretic, emetic, expectorant, and antivenereal. Mustard seed is described in n. 13, cream of tartar in n. 14, juniper berries in n. 16, broom in n. 18. Bolus was a stiffened soft paste that could be shaped into a pill that usu-ally contained many ingredients (in this case camphor, opium, and syrup of or-ange peel). Camphor, an extract of *Cinnamomum camphora*, was administered both internally and externally, usually in compound preparations, and was used, among other things, as a narcotic, anti-inflammatory, diaphoretic, diuretic, and tonic. Today opium is an illegal drug, but in the period covered by this study it

was widely available and used as a sedative and a narcotic. When taken internally, as it would have been in this case, opium, according to Estes, "induces serenity and drowsiness, slows the pulse, dilates the veins, causes sweating, and reduces bowel discharge by inhibiting intestinal muscular activity." It is difficult to determine exactly what Buchan meant when he prescribed orange peel. He might have meant orange peel water or simply orange peel, which was used as a stomachic (a medicine that warms and strengthens the stomach). Orange peel used in this remedy, however, might have been the bark or rind used as another term for cinchona. Cinchona referred to different species of pale or colored barks that contained various quantities of quinine. It was widely used as a tonic (a drug that strengthens the body, via the stomach, by increasing circulation, heat, secretions, digestion, or muscular action), astringent (a drug that strengthens the body when it is relaxed, or that diminishes excessive evacuations), and antiseptic (used to prevent putrefaction), especially for patients with intermittent fevers (malaria). Estes, *Dictionary of Protopharmacology*, 29, 34–35, 47–49, 104, 142–43; Thacher, *American New Dispensatory*, 100–106, 113, 135–37, 174–79, 290–92, 313; Sauer, *Herbal Cures*, 81–84, 177–78, 181, 187–89, 233–34; Simons, *The Planter's Guide*, 36.

22. [Gunn], *Domestic Medicine*, 208–9. For a longer version of the dropsy cure, see *Agricultural Almanac, for the Year . . . 1829*, [29–30]. Bark and leaves of common elder are described in n. 12, calomel and jalap in n. 21.

23. In his 1830 textbook, William Potts Dewees, a faculty member of the medical school at the University of Pennsylvania, lists dropsy remedies that call for bleeding, purging (including cream of tartar and jalap), and the use of diuretics and emetics. His treatments comprise an even mix of plant, vegetable, chemical, and mineral components. Dewees, *A Practice of Physic*, 2:645–63. In a book published two decades later, George Bacon Wood, also on the University of Pennsylvania medical faculty, recommends a therapeutic approach that, like Dewees's, calls for a mix of bleeding, diuretics, and cathartics for various forms of dropsy. Unlike Dewees and scores of other writers of domestic health guides, however, Wood advocated treatments containing much higher percentages of chemical and mineral components. Wood, *Treatise on the Practice of Medicine*, 1:335–46.

24. For the publication history of Samuel Thomson's works, especially his *New Guide to Health*, see Estes, "Samuel Thomson Rewrites Hippocrates." Thomsonianism and Thomsonian publications were especially popular in the South. Keeney, "Unless Powerful Sick." For the publication history of Wooster Beach's *American Practice of Medicine*, see Haller, *Medical Protestants*, 74.

25. Thomson, *New Guide to Health* (1832), 43. For an overview of Thomson and Thomsonian Practice, see Estes, "Samuel Thomson Rewrites Hippocrates"; Haller, *People's Doctors*; Berman and Flannery, *America's Botanico-Medical Movements*; and Whorton, *Nature Cures*, 25–49. For a review of botanical movements in general, see Rothstein, "Botanical Movements and Orthodox Medicine."

26. Beach, *American Practice of Medicine*, 1:17, 130, 134. See also Berman and Flannery, *America's Botanico-Medical Movements*, 10–11; Haller, *Medical*

Protestants, 69–75; Rothstein, "Botanical Movements and Orthodox Medicine"; and Berman, "Wooster Beach and the Early Eclectics."

27. The popularity of mercury in early nineteenth-century therapeutics is discussed in Rosenberg, "Therapeutic Revolution," 9.

28. Infection from both amebic and bacillary dysentery is by the fecal-oral route. Fecal contamination of food and water is the most common mode of transmission, and crowding and poor sanitary conditions encourage its spread. Patterson, "Dysentery"; idem, "Amebic Dysentery"; idem, "Bacillary Dysentery"; idem, "Disease Environments in the Antebellum South"; Grob, *Deadly Truth*, 53, 85; Duffy, *Epidemics in Colonial America*, 215.

29. Grob, *Deadly Truth*, 84.

30. *The Pennsylvania Town and Country-man's Almanack . . . 1754*, 23. Ginger (*Zingiber officinale*) was "used in tonics, to stimulate weak organs." Estes, *Dictionary of Protopharmacology*, 214. Ginger, according to Sauer, "strengthens a cold stomach, promotes digestion [and] dispels crudities in the stomach." Rhubarb, or *Rheum officinale*, should not be confused with the culinary rhubarb used today. Only the root of this highly toxic plant was used (as a cathartic). Nutmeg (*Myristica fragrans*) was used for its tonic, narcotic, stomachic, and astringent properties. Sauer proclaims its value in strengthening the stomach. Sauer, *Herbal Cures*, 155, 227–28, 260–61.

31. *The American Calendar; or an Almanack . . . 1767*, [15]; *Poor Richard improved . . . 1770*, [30]. Ipecacuanha is described in n. 21. Thacher describes chamomile, or *Anthemis nobilis*, a plant indigenous to the south of England, as possessing two components: "bitter extractive and essential oil." *American New Dispensatory*, 79. The latter was known for its "antiseptic, carminative, cordial, and diaphoretic effects," the former for "promoting digestion." Moreover, "chamomile is also capable of exciting vomiting." Crellin and Philpott, *Herbal Medicine Past and Present*, 147–50.

32. *Poor Will's Almanack . . . 1771*, [29]; *Poor Will's Almanack . . . 1779*, [6, 8, 10]. Rhubarb is described in n. 30. Sanders, or *Santalum*, was known for its astringent tonic properties. Cinnamon, or *Lauris cinnamomum*, the bark of the cinnamon tree, was used as an aromatic (a spicy drug), stomachic, carminative, and tonic. *Crocus martis* was used as a deobstruent and emmenagogue (used to promote menstruation). "Lucatellus's" balsam, or Balsam of Lucatelli, was used as an emollient (produces warmth and moisture) and astringent. Estes, *Dictionary of Protopharmacology*, 49, 56, 118, 172. Ipecac is described in n. 21, chamomile tea in n. 31.

33. *Poulson's Town and Country Almanac . . . 1797*, [40]. Castor oil (*Ricinus communis*), an oil expressed from seeds of castor bean, was used as a cathartic. Whereas Thacher calls castor oil "a gentle and useful" cathartic, Sauer describes it as an "overly violent emetic" that "should never be used internally, except by those who are definitely known to possess extraordinary strong constitutions." Glauber's salt, or sodium sulfate, was named for Johann Rudolph Glauber, a German physician and chemist, who introduced the remedy in the middle of the seventeenth century. The salts were used for their cathartic and diuretic properties. Ladanum, an aromatic gum resin, was used as a stomachic. Whey or lac, a

term referring to milk, was used, according to Estes, to promote all natural secretions. Thacher, *American New Dispensatory*, 195–96, 261–62; Sauer, *Herbal Cures*, 87–88; Estes, *Dictionary of Protopharmacology*, 90, 111–12, 166, 205; Crellin and Philpott, *Herbal Medicine Past and Present*, 138–39.

34. *The United States Almanac, for the Year . . . 1801* (Reading, Pa.), [23]. Jalap and calomel are described in n. 21, rhubarb in n. 30.

35. *Smith & Forman's New-York & New-Jersey Almanac . . . 1816*, [26]. Saffron, or *Crocus sativus*, was used as an aromatic, cordial (a mild stimulant), and narcotic. Sauer claims, however, that saffron is a "very effective powder for bloody flux." Sauer, *Herbal Cures*, 85–86, 269–71. Cardamom, or *Eletteria cardamomum*, was used as an aromatic, carminative, diuretic, and diaphoretic. Estes, *Dictionary of Protopharmacology*, 39, 56; Thacher, *American New Dispensatory*, 115–16.

36. The almanac remedy is cited in Moss, *Southern Folk Medicine*, 69. The combination of jalap and tartar produced a strong purgative (a strong cathartic). Cream of tartar is described in n. 14, ipecacuanha in n. 21.

37. Buchan, *Domestic Medicine*, 263.

38. Dewees, *Practice of Physic*, 2:565–66.

39. Ibid, 1:64.

40. Wilson, "Fever." For the discussion on fever in this chapter, I relied primarily on ibid. and "Of Fevers," chapter 5 in King, *Medical World of the Eighteenth Century*. For early nineteenth-century observations on fever, see Wilson, "Fevers and Science"; and Smith, "Quinine and Fever."

41. Wilson, "Fevers and Science," 394–97. See also Wear, *Knowledge and Practice in English Medicine*, 455–60.

42. King, *Medical World of the Eighteenth Century*, 127. See also Wilson, "Fevers and Science," 397–99.

43. Wilson, "Fevers and Science," 399–400; Bynum, "Cullen and the Study of Fevers in Britain," 137–40; King, *Transformations in American Medicine*, 43–55. See also Sullivan, "Sanguine Practices"; and Kopperman, "Venerate the Lancet."

44. Buchan, *Domestic Medicine*, 266–68. Ipecacuahna and opium are described in n.. 21, rhubarb in n. 30, and chamomile in n. 31.

45. [Gunn], *Domestic Medicine*, 191–92. Calomel is described in n. 21. Red or slippery elm, or *Ulmus rubra*, was used as an emollient, diet drink, expectorant, and antidiarrheal. Its inner bark was used in dysentery treatments. Estes, *Dictionary of Protopharmacology*, 199; Thacher, *American New Dispensatory*, 223–24; Sauer, *Herbal Cures*, 133–34; Crellin and Philpott, *Herbal Medicine Past and Present*, 202–4.

46. William Dewees, for example, says bleeding "is almost constantly necessary" in combating dysentery in order to reduce inflammation and fever. He also recommends purges to restore normal defecation and, once the pulse is sufficiently reduced, laudanum or opium to relieve the pain associated with the complaint. Dewees, *Practice of Physic*, 2:575–78. George B. Wood recommends a similar treatment, though he advises caution with bleeding, calling for it only "when there is much pain and tenderness in the abdomen," when fever is

present, and when there is "a vigorous pulse." He prescribes emetics of ipecac, mild purges of calomel and castor oil, and diaphoretics to cleanse the stomach of "acrid accumulations," free the bowels "from irritating secretions," restore normal evacuations, revive normal circulation, and promote perspiration. Wood also advocates the use of opium to ease the pain, facilitate the "action of the cathartics," and help the patient sleep. Wood, *Treatise on the Practice of Medicine*, 1:567–74. Ipecac and calomel are described in n. 21, castor oil in n. 33.

47. Thomson, *New Guide to Health* (1822), 190–91. See also Smith, *American Physician*, 159–60, for similar views of heat.

48. Thomson, *New Guide to Health* (1822), 232–33.

49. Beach, *American Practice of Medicine*, 1:610–11. Rhubarb is described in n. 30, slippery elm in n. 45. Potash, or potassium carbonate, was used for its diaphoretic, diuretic, deobstruent, and aperient properties. Peppermint, or *Mentha piperita*, was used as a warm tonic, carminative, antispasmotic, and stomachic. Cinnamon is described in n. 32. Olive oil, when taken internally, was used as a laxative. It may also have been used in this case to mitigate the purge's strong effect on the stomach. Hops, or *Humulus lupulus*, was used in early America primarily for brewing and cooking. The flowers of the plant were also used in medicine as an astringent, diuretic, tonic, and narcotic. Tansy, or *Tanacetum vulgare*, the flowers, leaves, or seeds of the tansy plant, was used as a deobstruent, tonic, and emmenagogue. Horehound, or *Marrubium vulgare*, was used as an aperient, cathartic, diuretic, diaphoretic, and expectorant. Catnip, or *Nepeta cataria*, was used as a tonic, antispasmodic, and emmenagogue. Estes, *Dictionary of Protopharmacology*, 117–19, 123, 128, 136, 190; Thacher, *American New Dispensatory*, 131, 141–42, 152–53, 156–57, 167–68, 254–55; Sauer, *Herbal Cures*, 88, 101–2, 169–71, 319–20; Crellin and Philpott, *Herbal Cures Past and Present*, 139–41, 247–49, 250–51, 301–3, 423–25.

50. Buchan, *Domestic Medicine*, 295.

51. Wood, *Treatise on the Practice of Medicine*, 1:422.

52. Buchan, *Domestic Medicine*, 295–96.

53. Dewees, *Practice of Physic*, 2:76.

54. This remedy appeared in the following almanacs: *Freeman's New-York Almanack . . . 1768*, [47]; *The American Calendar; or an Almanack . . . 1768*, [24]; *Freeman's New-York Almanack . . . 1772*, [33]; and *Poor Richard improved . . . 1774*, [10]. Seneca snakeroot, or rattlesnake root, was used as a tonic, expectorant, anti-inflammatory, diuretic, diaphoretic, and cathartic. Besides being used as a diuretic (see n. 12), garlic was also used as a diaphoretic, expectorant, and carminative. It was administered both internally and externally. The "Gum Ammoniac" referred to in this remedy probably was *Ammoniacum*, a gum resin originally imported from Egypt and the West Indies. It was used generally as a stimulant and contained cathartic, diaphoretic, diuretic, antispasmodic, deobstruent, and expectorant properties. Estes, *Dictionary of Protopharmacology*, 8, 88, 176; Thacher, *American New Dispensatory*, 76–77.

55. *Poor Will's Almanack . . . 1771*, [26]. The leaves of senna (*Cassia acutifolia*) were used for their cathartic and diuretic properties. Hermodactylus, known as "Finger of Hercules," was used as a cathartic, as were turpethum,

the bark of root of turbith, and scammony, in an electuary or as a powder. The root of zedoary (*Curcuma zedoaria*) was used as an aromatic tonic. According to Sauer, zedoary would have been useful to those suffering from rheumatism because it "warms all internal organs afflicted by cold." Cubebs, fruit of the vine *Piper cubeba*, was used as a stimulant. Ginger, or *Zingiber officinale*, was popular among early Americans as a cooking and medicinal herb. Sauer asserts that ginger "strengthens a cold stomach, promotes digestion, dispels crudities in the stomach and gut . . . and all manner of stomach aches brought on by taking chill or sleeping uncovered." Estes, *Dictionary of Protopharmacology* 56, 95, 174, 176, 197, 213; Sauer, *Herbal Cures*, 155, 285–86, 362.

56. *The Burlington Almanack . . . 1773*, [33]. Cochineal is a red dye that was used primarily as a diaphoretic. According to Estes, it was used in the late eighteenth century chiefly to color various drugs. Estes, *Dictionary of Protopharmacology*, 50. Burdock and garlic are described in n. 12, snakeroot in n. 54.

57. *The New-England Almanack, or Lady's and Gentleman's Diary . . . 1804*, [23]. Gum guaiacum, or *Guaiacum officinale*, the resin and wood of lignum vitae, was used primarily as a diaphoretic. J. Hugh Simons claims that guaiacum is good for "rheumatism and gout of long standing." It was also used as a diuretic, cathartic, and stimulant. Simons, *Planter's Guide*, 36; Estes, *Dictionary of Protopharmacology*, 92; Thacher, *American New Dispensatory*, 129. Sir John Pringle (1707–1782) studied medicine at Leyden under Boerhaave and later served as physician to the king and president of the Royal Society of London. He is noted for his influential book *Observations on the Diseases of the Army*, published in 1745. King, *Medical World of the Eighteenth Century*, 133–38. This cure also appeared earlier in *The South-Carolina and Georgia Almanack . . . 1772*, [25]; and *Poor Richard improved . . . 1772*.

58. *The Baltimore Almanac, or, Time Piece . . . 1822*, [27]. The wood, root, and bark of the *Laurus sassafras* are described in n. 12.

59. *Phinney's Calendar, or, Western Almanac . . . 1826*, [23]. According to Sauer, the leaves of cabbage "are highly praised for their ability to keep blisters flowing and clean." Moreover, fresh leaves should be applied "every two hours, and indeed heated as hot as the patient can bear them. Therein lies the secret and advantage of this cure." *Herbal Cures*, 79. See also Estes, *Dictionary of Protopharmacology*, 30.

60. *The American Farmer's Almanac 1853*, [17]. Honey, according to Thacher, is a "very useful aperient and expectorant." The term *flour of sulfur* probably refers to "flowers of sulfur," or sublimed sulfur, which was used as a cooling cathartic, diaphoretic, and resolvent. Nutmeg, or *Myristica fragrans*, was used as an aromatic tonic, narcotic, stomachic, and astringent. This, according to Estes, was probably added to the remedy to strengthen the stomach after the other components had depleted the system. Estes, *Dictionary of Protopharmacology*, 97, 138, 186; Thacher, *American New Dispensatory*, 143, 162, 219; Sauer, *Herbal Cures*, 225–26; Crellin and Philpott, *Herbal Medicine Past and Present*, 224–26.

61. *Hagers-Town Town and Country Almanack . . . 1854*, [11]. Saltpeter is described in n. 9.

62. Moss, *Southern Folk Medicine*, 82, 84. *Ammoniacum* is described in n. 54.

63. Buchan, *Domestic Medicine*, 296–97.

64. [Gunn], *Domestic Medicine*, 149–52.

65. Thomson, *New Guide to Health* (1822), 233.

66. Smith, *American Physician*, 184–85.

67. Beach, *American Practice of Medicine*, 1:441–45. Sarsaparilla, the root of the *Smilax sarsaparilla*, was used both as a tonic and as a diaphoretic. Burdock is described in n. 12. Estes, *Dictionary of Protopharmacology*, 172–73; Thacher, *American New Dispansatory*, 211.

68. Rosenberg, "Therapeutic Revolution"; Warner, "Selective Transport of Medical Knowledge."

3. Prescribing Prevention

1. See Appendix, table 1.

2. *Trattato de la vita sobria . . .* (Padua, 1558) was the first edition of Luigi Cornaro's much-reprinted and often translated work *Discourses on the Sober and Temperate Life*. Very popular in early America, the first American edition of Cornaro's work, issued in 1788, was titled *The Probable Way of Attaining a Long and Healthful Life*. Five years later Mason Locke Weems issued a version of this work entitled *Sure and Certain Methods of Attaining a Long and Healthy Life*. See Walker, "Luigi Cornaro"; and Gruman, "Rise and Fall of Prolongevity Hygiene." Cheyne's *Essay on Health and Long Life*, in which he advocates temperance, exercise, proper diet, and adequate sleep as some of the key elements of a long and healthy life, was first issued in the United States in 1813. See also his *Essays on Regimen*. See Guerrini, *Obesity and Depression in the Enlightenment*; and King, "George Cheyne." On the "non-naturals," see Wear, *Knowledge and Practice in English Medicine*, 156–59; Emch-Deriaz, "Non-Naturals Made Easy"; Berryman, "Tradition of the 'six things non-natural'"; Niebyl, "Non-Naturals"; and Rather, "Six things non-natural." For a discussion of the tenets of the non-naturals as they were expounded in Diderot and d'Alembert's *Encyclopedie*, see Coleman, "Health and Hygiene in the *Encyclopedie*."

3. See Coleman's comments on the elitist message of hygiene advice in "Health and Hygiene in the *Encyclopedie*."

4. On regimen advice in seventeenth-century almanacs, see Curth, "Medical Content of English Almanacs." Both Culpeper's and Wesley's works were quite popular in early America. Culpeper's career is discussed in Thulesius, *Nicholas Culpeper*. The first American edition of Culpeper's *English Physician* was published in Boston in 1720. See Cowen, "Boston Editions of Nicholas Culpeper." On Wesley, see Rouseau, "John Wesley's *Primitive Physic*"; and Rogal, "Pills for the Poor." The first American edition of Wesley's *Primitive Physick* was printed in 1764 in Philadelphia.

5. Rosenberg, "Medical Text and Social Context"; *Thomas's Massachusetts, New-Hampshire and Connecticut Almanack . . . 1781*, [21].

6. *The Pennsylvania Town and Country-man's Almanack . . . 1754*, [22];

An Astronomical Diary, or an Almanack for the Year . . . 1761 . . . by Nathaniel Ames (Boston, [1760]) is cited in Briggs, *Essays*, 319. *The New-England Almanack, and Gentleman's and Lady's Diary . . . 1784* (New London, [1783]) is cited in Meyer, "Colonial Values," 172. Low. *An Astronomical Diary; or Almanack . . . 1812*, [14].

7. *An Astronomical Diary; or, Almanack for the Year . . . 1767 . . . by Nathaniel Ames* (Boston, [1766]) is cited in Briggs, *Essays*, 385. Nathaniel Ames, founder of *An Astronomical Diary*, compiled the annual from 1726 until his death in the summer of 1764. His son, Nathaniel Jr., carried on the almanac from 1765 to 1775.

8. *The Columbian Calendar, or New-York and Vermont Almanack . . . 1817*, [8].

9. *Poor Richard, 1742*, [22–23].

10. *Poor Richard improved . . . 1749*, [9]; *Poor Richard improved . . . 1756*, [17].

11. *Beers' Calendar; or, Southwick's Almanack . . . 1816*, [5]; *Bennett & Walton's Almanac . . . 1826*, [31]; *Tuttle's Almanac for 1836*, [14].

12. Augst, *Clerk's Tale*, 1–11.

13. *The (old) Farmer's Almanack . . . for the Year . . . 1854 . . . by Robert B. Thomas*, [11]; *The Rhode-Island Almanac, for the Year 1843*, [19]. The article was originally issued in the *Journal of Health* 1 (1829–30): 351.

14. *Cumberland Almanac . . . 1839*, [24].

15. *The Burlington Almanack . . . 1772*, [20].

16. *The New-England Almanack, or Lady's and Gentleman's Diary . . . 1799*, [4–18]. The poem was continued from month to month in the calendar section of the almanac.

17. *The Baltimore Almanack, or, Time Piece . . . 1811*, [4].

18. *Poor Will's Almanac . . . 1836*, [26–27]. Only representative stanzas are reproduced.

19. *Isaiah Thomas's Massachusetts, Connecticut, Rhode-Island, Newhampshire & Vermont Almanack . . . 1799*, 34, 38–39; *The Town & Country Almanac . . . 1805*, [9, 11]; *Hunt's Almanack, for the Year . . . 1825*, [30]; "*Poor Richards*" *New Farmer's Almanac . . . 1836*, [8].

20. Arner, "Politics and Temperance in Boston and Philadelphia."

21. Rush, *Enquiry into the Effects of Spirituous Liquors*. Although this work is undated, evidence suggests that it was published in 1784; idem, "Moral and Physical Thermometer." For a bibliographic history of Rush's writings on the harmful effects of spirituous liquors, including "Moral and Physical Thermometer," see Fox, Miller, and Miller, *Benjamin Rush*. Of the almanacs I consulted, the following offer extracts of Rush's *Enquiry: Poor Richard improved . . . 1787*, [2]; and *Ellicott's Maryland and Virginia Almanac, and Ephemeris . . . 1791*, [21–22]. Almanacs that reprint Rush's "Moral and Physical Thermometer" along with extracts of the *Enquiry* are *Thomas's Massachusetts, Connecticut, Rhode Island, New-Hampshire & Vermont Almanack . . . 1787*, [33–39]; and *Wait's York, Cumberland and Lincoln Almanack . . . 1793*, [30–32]. *Bioren's Town and Country Almanack . . . 1817*, [30], contains a chart titled "Of the Physical,

moral, and immoral effects of certain liquors upon the body and mind of Man, and upon his conditions in society" that is similar to Rush's scale, except that it does not include the thermometer motif.

22. Buchan, *Domestic Medicine*, 68–69.

23. [Gunn], *Domestic Medicine*, 74–75.

24. *Journal of Health* 1 (1829–30): 13–14, and 4 (1832–33): 285–87, cited in Horrocks, "Poor Man's Riches," 124–26. The earliest American medical journal published for the layperson was the *Medical and Agricultural Register*. Published in Boston and edited by Daniel Adams, the periodical was issued in twenty-four parts from December 1806 through December 1807.

25. *Journal of Health* 1 (1829–30): 13–14, 212, 238, and 2 (1830–31): 273, cited in Horrocks, "Poor Man's Riches," 125–26. The temperance movement's activities during the antebellum period are discussed in Dorsey, *Reforming Men and Women*, 90–135; Appleby, "Personal Roots"; Rorabaugh, *Alcoholic Republic*, 187; Nissenbaum, *Sex, Diet, and Debility*, 69–85; and Gusfield, *Symbolic Crusade*.

26. The notion that water is of value to health and a useful alternative to alcohol did not originate in the nineteenth century; it had been espoused by several writers of eighteenth-century guides to regimen. George Cheyne, for example, claimed that water is "the only beverage designed and fitted by nature for *long* life, health, and serenity." Cheyne, *Essay on Regimen*, xxiv.

27. *Poor Will's Almanac . . . 1842*, [28]. Only two of the poem's several stanzas are reproduced.

28. *The North American Almanac . . . 1852*, [33].

29. *The United States Almanac . . . 1793*, [23].

30. *The Columbian Almanac: or, the North-American Calendar . . . 1797*, [21].

31. *The Columbian Almanac for the Year . . . 1798*, [5, 7–8].

32. *Isaiah Thomas's Massachusetts, Connecticut, Rhode-Island, Newhampshire & Vermont Almanack . . . 1799*, [34].

33. *Low's Almanack, for the Year . . . 1822*, [25].

34. *The (old) Farmer's Almanack . . . for the Year . . . 1833 . . . by Robert B. Thomas*, [9].

35. *Poor Robin's Almanack, for the Year . . . 1833*, [25–26]; *Cumberland Almanac, for the Year . . . 1834*, [28–29].

36. William A. Alcott and Sylvester Graham were two of the most prominent leaders of the antebellum health reform movement. For discussions of their works, see Murphy, *Enter the Physician*, 115–34; Whorton, *Crusaders for Fitness*; and Nissenbaum, *Sex, Diet, and Debility*.

37. *Journal of Health* 4 (1832–33): 97–100, cited in Horrocks, "Poor Man's Riches," 126–27.

38. Horrocks, "Poor Man's Riches, " 125. John Bell, co-editor of the *Journal of Health*, clearly admired Broussais's doctrines. He translated the latter's *Treatise of Physiology Applied to Pathology* (Philadelphia: Carey, Lea and Carey) in 1826 and edited the 1828 edition. See also Nissenbaum, *Sex, Diet, and Debility*,

and Whorton, *Crusaders for Fitness*, for discussions of Broussais's influence on the early nineteenth-century dietary and temperance movements.

39. *An Astronomical Diary: or an Almanack for the Year . . . 1755 . . . by Nathaniel Ames*, [15].

40. *New-Jersey Almanac, for the Year . . . 1828*, [31]; *Phinney's Calendar, or Western Almanac . . . 1840*, [26].

41. *Thomas's Massachusetts, Connecticut, Rhode-Island, New Hampshire and Vermont Almanack . . . 1783*, [33].

42. *Hutchins' Improved Almanac, and Ephemeris . . . 1845*, 27. Years before this, Benjamin Rush advocated walking as beneficial to health. See his *Sermons to Gentlemen*, 30–31. See also *Journal of Health* 1 (1829–30): 74, for similar recommendations.

43. *The Farmer's Almanack . . . 1816 . . . by Robert B. Thomas*, [17].

44. *John Grigg's Almanack . . . 1829*, [19]. See Buchan, *Domestic Medicine*, 62 for the original version of the passage. One will note that Buchan's phrase "lolling a-bed" reads as "lying a-bed" in the almanac version. This change can be attributed either to an error that occurred during the transcription or to a conscious decision by the almanac compiler.

45. Buchan, *Domestic Medicine*, 62.

46. *Journal of Health* 1 (1829–30): 249, and 2 (1830–31): 262, cited in Horrocks, "Poor Man's Riches, " 120–21. Echoing the romantic view of country life advanced by many writers of the period, the journal's editors, both of whom were city dwellers, once wrote that middle-class Americans are those "in the medium conditions of life" who enjoy "the greatest amount of health and the fairest prospect of surviving . . . to an advanced age," because they are country people or the "rural classes—the decent people—people possessed of education and employment . . . the farmer and the moderate proprietor—the man of action and enterprise." *Journal of Health* 1 (1829–30): 357–58. Nineteenth-century reformers' and writers' negative views of city life are discussed in Boyer, *Urban Masses and Moral Order*; Halttunen, *Confidence Men and Painted Women*; and Kasson, *Rudeness and Civility*.

47. *The (old) Farmer's Almanack . . . 1833 . . . by Robert B. Thomas*, [19]; *The Farmer's Almanack . . . 1839 . . . by Robert B. Thomas*, [11]; *Phinney's Calendar, or Western Almanac . . . 1846*, [26].

48. Cornaro and Cheyne are cited in Horrocks, "Poor Man's Riches," 121–22. See also Rosenberg, "Body and Mind in Nineteenth-Century Medicine." Although Rosenberg concentrates on the nineteenth century, he does discuss briefly how ideas about the relationship between body and mind evolved in an earlier period.

49. *Father Abraham's Almanac . . . 1766*, [33].

50. *The New-York Almanack, for . . . 1780*, [23].

51. *The South Carolina and Georgia Almanac . . . 1795*, [31]. Cheyne's rules concerning the passions can be found on his *Essay on Health and Long Life*, 144–45.

52. *Poor Richard improved . . . 1800*, [16–17].

53. *Philadelphia Almanack, for the Year ... 1834*, [23]; *Phinney's Calendar or Western Almanac ... 1855*, [4]; *The Hagerstown Town and Country Almanack ... 1860*, [15].

54. *The Clergyman's Almanack, or, an Astronomical Diary and Serious Monitor ... 1815*, [19].

55. *The Rhode-Island Almanac, for the Year 1849*, 18.

56. *Middlebrook's New-England Almanac ... 1852*, [26].

4. Health Advice with an Agenda

1. *Prynne's Almanac for 1841*, [1].

2. One genre of specialty almanac, the agricultural almanac, tended not to espouse prevention as part of a moral agenda. These almanacs were similar to general almanacs in that both kinds offered astrological, therapeutic, and regimen advice and general almanacs often contained advice and information directed to a rural, farming audience.

3. Horrocks, "Promoting Good Health"; and idem, "Poor Man's Riches."

4. Bell and Condie criticized not only alternative medical systems, such as Thomsonianism, but also domestic practice. They believed that therapeutic advice offered in domestic health guides—and, by implication, similar advice that appeared in many almanacs—was "little short of quackery." Quoted in Horrocks, "Poor Man's Riches," 132.

5. Ibid., 123.

6. Haller, *People's Doctors*; Berman and Flannery, *America's Botanico-Medical Movements*; Estes, "Samuel Thomson Rewrites Hippocrates."

7. *Thomson's Almanac, for the Year 1844*, [3]; *Thomson's Almanac for the Year 1843*, [3, 27].

8. *Thomson's Almanac, Calculated on an Improved Plan ... 1842*, [17]; *Thomson's Almanac for the Year 1843*, [3].

9. See Rosenberg, "Catechisms of Health," for a concise and insightful analysis of early nineteenth-century anatomy and physiology textbooks. Kaestle's *Pillars of the Republic* provides a useful overview of the rise of the common school movement in America.

10. *The Health Almanac, for the Year ... 1842*, [18]; *The Health Almanac, for the Year ... 1844*, [46].

11. See Appendix, table 2, for information on health advice found in specialty almanacs.

12. Except for agricultural and medical almanacs, therapeutic advice was rarely offered by specialty almanacs. See Appendix, table 2.

13. On the religious publishing empire in antebellum America, see Harris, "Spiritual Cakes upon the Waters"; Nord, "Free Grace"; idem, "Evangelical Origins of Mass Media"; idem, "Religious Reading and Readers"; idem, *Faith in Reading*; Schantz, "Religious Tracts"; Wosh, *Spreading the Word*; Gutjahr, *American Bible*; and Brown, *Word in the World*. For the link between spiritual and physical health, see Walters, *American Reformers*; Mintz, *Moralists and Modernizers*; Dorsey, *Reforming Men and Women*; Abzug, *Cosmos Crumbling*;

Blake, "Health Reform"; Nissenbaum, *Sex, Diet, and Debility*; and Whorton, *Crusaders for Fitness.*

14. *The Christian Almanack, for the Year . . . 1827*, [21, 23]; *The Christian Almanac, for Connecticut . . . 1831*, [5, 14].

15. *The Illustrated Family Christian Almanac for the United States . . . 1850*, 46; *The Illustrated Family Christian Almanac for the United States . . . 1851*, 24.

16. *The Christian Almanac, for New-York, Connecticut, and New-Jersey . . . 1837*, [8–18].

17. *The Illustrated Family Christian Almanac for the United States . . . 1849*, [13]. On the history of cleanliness in early America, see Bushman and Bushman, "Early History of Cleanliness"; Hoy, *Chasing Dirt*; and Brown, "Maternal Physician."

18. *The Methodist Almanac, for the Year . . . 1844*, [32–33].

19. *The Methodist Almanac for the Year . . . 1846*, [3]. The other religious almanac that openly criticized astrology was *The Christian Almanac, for New-York, Connecticut, New-Jersey, and Pennsylvania . . . 1828*, [2].

20. Of the seventeen religious almanac titles consulted, eight list a purchase price. Five of those eight were published by the American Tract Society. Of the almanacs that do not list prices, several were issued by the American Tract Society, which probably means that they, too, were both sold on the market and given away. On the economics of early nineteenth-century religious publishing in America, see Nord, "Free Grace."

21. For an introduction to the tradition of printed medical advertisements in general and in almanacs in particular, see Furdell, *Publishing and Medicine*, 135–46; and Curth, "Medical Content of English Almanacs," 276. For proprietary medicine advertisements in early American newspapers, see Helfand, "Advertising Health to the People," 23, 28. See also Helfand, *Quack, Quack, Quack*, 45.

22. *Kalendarium Pennsilvaniense, or America's Messenger . . . for the Year . . . 1685* (Philadelphia, 1685) is cited in Guerra, *American Medical Bibliography*, 278.

23. *An Almanack for the Year . . . 1698* (New York, 1698) is cited in Guerra, *American Medical Bibliography*, 283.

24. Helfand, "Advertising Health to the People," 26–28; Young, *Toadstool Millionaires*, 32.

25. Helfand, "Advertising Health to the People," 39; idem, *Quack, Quack, Quack*, 35–36.

26. *Beers' Almanac, for the Year . . . 1816*, 45.

27. Helfand, *Quack, Quack, Quack*, 37–38; idem, "Advertising Health to the People," 28.

28. *Phinney's Calendar, or, Western Almanac . . . 1826*, [35].

29. Young, *Toadstool Millionaires*, 76–77.

30. *Phinney's Calendar, or Western Almanac . . . 1838*, 32.

31. *Phinney's Calendar, or Western Almanac . . . 1848*, 28–35.

32. For the development of lithography and color printing and the impact

these processes exerted on advertising, see Helfand, "Advertising Health to the People," 27, 40–43.

33. *The Family Almanac, and Franklin Calendar, 1848*, [36].

34. Townsend also claimed that his Compound "cured 35,000 cases of severe disease, of which at least 5,000 had been deemed incurable." Townsend is cited in Young, *Toadstool Millionaires*, 187.

35. *The People's Illustrated Almanac . . . for 1848*, [11]; *The People's Illustrated Almanac. 1849*, [9].

36. Dr. William B. Moffat, whose New York City firm produced Moffat's Vegetable Life Pills and Phoenix Bitters among other nostrums, issued an almanac that included the phrase "For Gratuitous Distribution" on the front cover. See his *Agricultural and Family Almanac . . . 1847* and *Agricultural and Family Almanac . . . 1848*. The firm that produced and sold Wistar's Balsam of Wild Cherry and other "Wistar" medicines published an almanac whose title included the word *Free*. See *Dr. Wistar's Free Almanac for 1848*.

37. Briggs, *Essays*, 13.

38. *The People's Illustrated Almanac. 1850*, [6].

39. Whorton, *Inner Hygiene*.

40. *Agricultural and Family Almanac . . . 1847*, [6].

41. *Wright's Pictorial Family Almanac 1857*, [5].

42. *Christie's Family Almanac for the Year 1853*, 3. Galvanism was an eighteenth-century practice of applying electricity to the body to stimulate the muscles or nerves. The practice was named for Luigi Galvani (1737–1798), an Italian physiologist who discovered that electricity can result from chemical action.

Epilogue

1. See Rosenberg, "Health in the Home"; and Fellman and Fellman, *Making Sense of Self* for views of the popular health publication tradition as it evolved since 1860.

2. Tyler, *History of American Literature*, 1:120.

3. *An Astronomical Diary, or, an Almanack for the Year . . . 1752 . . . by Nathaniel Ames*, [15].

4. *Thomas's Massachusetts, Connecticut, Rhode-Island, New Hampshire and Vermont Almanack, . . . 1783*, [33].

5. *The Christian Almanac, for New-England. For the Year . . . 1830*, [16]; *The Christian Almanac, for the Western District, for the Year . . . 1830*, [10].

6. *Peter Parley's Almanac for Old and Young. MDCCCXXXVI*, 30.

7. Rosenberg, "Catechisms of Health," 189.

8. Ibid.

9. Lindman and Tarter, *Centre of Wonders*; Chaplin, *Subject Matter*; Sappol, *Traffic in Dead Bodies*.

10. Fett, *Working Cures*; Gorn, "Black Magic"; Savitt, *Medicine and Slavery*; Watson, *Angelical Conjunction*; Wear, "Puritan Perceptions of Illness"; Mutschler, "Province of Affliction."

11. Fett, *Working Cures*; Gorn, "Black Magic."

BIBLIOGRAPHY

Primary Works

Appleton, Moses. Receipt book, Waterville, Maine, 1791–1796 [B MS b149.1, p. 53]. Boston Medical Library in the Francis A. Countway Library of Medicine, Boston, Mass.

Baldwin, Christopher Columbus. *The Diary of Christopher Columbus Baldwin, Librarian of the American Antiquarian Society, 1829–1835.* Worcester, Mass.: American Antiquarian Society, 1901.

Beach, Wooster. *The American Practice of Medicine.* 3 vols. New York: Betts and Anstice, 1833.

Bowron, John S. *Observations on Planetary and Celestial Influences in the Production of Epidemics, and on the Nature and Treatment of Diseases.* New York: Published by John S. Taylor, 1850.

Briggs, Samuel, ed. *The Essays, Humor, and Poems of Nathaniel Ames, Father and Son, of Dedham, Massachusetts, From Their Almanacks 1726–1775, with Notes and Comments by Sam. Briggs.* Cleveland: The Subscribers, 1891.

Broughton, L. D. *The Elements of Astrology.* New York: L. D. Broughton, 1906.

Buchan, William. *Domestic Medicine; or, the Family Physician.* Philadelphia: Joseph Crukshank, for R. Aitken, 1774.

Cheyne, George. *An Essay on Health and Long Life.* London: George Strahan and J. Leake, 1724. Reprint, New York: Edward Gillesby, 1813.

———. *Essay on Regimen. Together With Five Discourses, Medical, and Philosophical: Serving to Illustrate the Principles and Theory of Philosphical Medicin* [sic], *and Point Out Some of Its Moral Consequences.* London: C. Rivington, 1740.

The Complete Fortune Teller; or, An Infallible Guide to the Hidden Decrees of Fate; Being a New and Regular System for Foretelling Future Events, by Astrology, Phisiognomy [sic], *Palmistry, Moles, Cards, Dreams.* Boston: Printed for the Booksellers, 1797.

Cornaro, Luigi. *The Probable Way of Attaining a Long and Healthful Life.* Portsmouth, N.H.: George Jerry Osborne, 1788.

[Crockett, Davy]. *The Tall Tales of Davy Crockett: The Second Nashville Series of Crockett Almanacs 1839–1841.* Knoxville: University of Tennessee Press, 1987.

Culpeper, Nicholas. *Culpeper's Family Physician. The English Physician Enlarged . . . Revised, Corrected, and Enlarged by James Seammon.* Exeter: Published by James Seammon, 1824.

————. *Pharmacopoeia Londinensis; or, the London Dispensatory*. Boston: Printed by John Allen, 1720.

Dewees, William P. *A Practice of Physic.* . . . 2 vols. Philadelphia: Carey and Lea, 1830.

Erra Pater. *The Book of Knowledge, Treating of the Wisdome of the Ancients.* Suffield: Edward Gray, 1799.

Ewell, James. *The Planter's and Mariner's Medical Companion*. Philadelphia: Printed by James Bioren, 1807.

Franklin, Benjamin. *The Complete Poor Richard Almanacks*. 2 vols. Barre, Mass.: Imprint Society, 1970.

[Gunn, John]. *Gunn's Domestic Medicine, or Poor Man's Friend*. Knoxville: [John Gunn], 1830. Reprint, with an introduction by Charles E. Rosenberg. Knoxville: University of Tennessee Press, 1986.

[Hague, Thomas]. *Astrology*. Philadelphia: n.p., ca. 1830s. [Broadside]

Lamon, Ward H. *The Life of Abraham Lincoln from His Birth to His Inauguration as President*. Boston: James R. Osgood and Company, 1872.

Mackay, Charles. *Life and Liberty in America; or, Sketches of a Tour in the United States and Canada, in 1857–8*. New York: Harper and Brothers, 1859.

Mather, Cotton. *The Angel of Bethesda: An Essay Upon the Common Maladies of Mankind*. Edited with an introduction and notes by Gordon W. Jones. Barre, Mass.: American Antiquarian Society and Barre Publishers, 1972.

Mayhew, Ira. *Popular Education: For the Use of Parents and Teachers, and for Young Persons of Both Sexes*. New York: Harper and Brothers, 1850.

Mead, Richard. *A Treatise Concerning the Influence of the Son and Moon upon Human Bodies, and Diseases Thereby Produced*. London: Printed by J. Brindley, 1748.

Nordhoff, C. "Fortune-Telling," *Ladies' Repository* 17 (1857): 547–49.

"Observations of the Influence of the Moon on Climate and the Animal Economy, with a Proper Method of Treating Diseases when under the Power of that Luminary. Philadelphia. Folwell, 8 vo. Pp. 24 1798." [Book review] *Medical Repository* 4 (1801): 285–90.

Palmer, Thomas. *The Admirable Secrets of Physick and Chryrurgery*. Edited by Thomas Rogers Forbes. New Haven: Yale University Press, 1984.

Rishel, Jonas. *The Indian Physician . . . for the Use of Families and Practitioners of Medicine*. New Berlin, Pa.: Joseph Miller, 1828.

Rush, Benjamin. *An Enquiry into the Effects of Spirituous Liquors upon the Human Body, and Their Influence upon the Happiness of Society*. Philadelphia: Thomas Bradford, [1784?].

————. "A Moral and Physical Thermometer, or a Scale of the Progress of Temperance." *Columbian Magazine* 3 (1789): 31.

————. *Sermons to Gentlemen Upon Temperance and Exercise*. Philadelphia: Printed for John Dunlap, 1772.

Russell, Chloe. *The Complete Fortune Teller, and Dream Book, by Which Every Person May Acqui'nt Themselves With the Most Important Events that Shall Attend Them Through Life . . . by Astrology—Physiognomy, and Palmistry,*

Anatomy—Geometry—Moles, Cards and Dreams. Exeter, N.H.: Abel Brown, 1824.

Salmon, William. *Synopsis Medicinae. Compendium of Physick, Chirurgery, and Anatomy.* London: Printed for Th[omas] Dawks, 1681.

Sauer, Christopher. *Sauer's Herbal Cures: America's First Book of Botanic Healing, 1762–1778.* Edited and translated by William Woys Weaver. New York: Routledge, 2001.

Sibly, Ebenezer. *A New and Complete Illustration of the Celestial Science of Astrology.* London: Printed for . . . the Proprietor, 1817.

———. *A New and Complete Illustration of the Occult Sciences: or, the Art of Foretelling Future Events and Contingencies, by the Aspects, Positions, and Influences, of the Heavenly Bodies.* London: Printed for the Proprietor, 1790.

Simons, J. Hume. *The Planter's Guide and Family Book of Medicine.* Charleston, S.C.: James J. McCarter, 1848.

Smith, Elias. *The American Physician, and Family Assistant.* Boston: E. Bellamy, 1826.

Smith, Robert. *The Astrologer, of the Nineteenth Century, or the Master Key of Futurity, Being a Complete System of Astrology, Geomancy & Occult Science.* London: William Charlton Wright, [1825].

[Tennent, John]. *Every Man His Own Doctor: or, The Poor Planter's Physician.* Williamsburg and Annapolis: Wil[liam] Parks, 1763.

Thacher, James. *The American New Dispensatory.* Boston: T. B. Wait and Co., 1810.

Thomson, Samuel. *New Guide to Health; or Botanic Family Physician.* Boston: E. G. House, 1822.

———. *New Guide to Health; or, Botanic Physician.* Boston: J. Howe, 1832.

Tyler, Moses Coit. *A History of American Literature.* 2 vols. New York: G. P. Putnam's Sons, 1878.

Weems, Mason Locke. *Sure and Certain Methods of Attaining a Long and Healthy Life, With Means of Correcting a Bad Constitution.* Philadelphia: Reprinted for the Rev. M. L. Weems, 1793.

Willey, Aaron C. "Observations on Magical Practice, by Dr. Aaron C. Willey, of Block Island, addressed to the Editors." *Medical Repository*, Third Hexade, 3 (1812): 377–82.

Wood, George B. *A Treatise on the Practice of Medicine.* 2 vols. Philadelphia: Grigg, Elliot, and Co., 1849.

Periodicals

Greenleaf's New York Journal. November 4, 1797.

Journal of Health (Philadelphia). 1829–33.

Medical and Agricultural Register (Boston). 1806–7.

Medical News-Paper; or, The Doctor and the Physician (Boston). Vol. 1, 1822–24.

Medical Tract, and Singular Miscellany (Boston). Vol. 1, 1830.

Secondary Works

Abzug, Robert H. *Cosmos Crumbling: American Reform and the Religious Imagination.* New York: Oxford University Press, 1994.

Amory, Hugh. "The New England Book Trade, 1713–1790." In Amory and Hall, *Colonial Book in the Atlantic World,* 314–46.

———. "Printing and Bookselling in New England, 1638–1713." In Amory and Hall, *Colonial Book in the Atlantic World,* 83–116.

———. "Reinventing the Colonial Book." In Amory and Hall, *Colonial Book in the Atlantic World,* 26–54.

Amory, Hugh, and David D. Hall. *The Colonial Book in the Atlantic World.* Vol. 1 of *A History of the Book in America.* Cambridge: Cambridge University Press; Worcester, Mass.: American Antiquarian Society, 2000.

Anders, Richard. "A Cataloguer and His Almanacs." *The Book* 20 (March 1990): 4–5.

Anderson, Douglas. *The Radical Enlightenments of Benjamin Franklin.* Baltimore: Johns Hopkins University Press, 1997.

Appleby, Joyce. *Inheriting the Revolution: The First Generation of Americans.* Cambridge, Mass.: Harvard University Press, 2000.

———. "The Personal Roots of the First American Temperance Movement." *Proceedings of the American Philosophical Society* 141 (1997): 141–59.

Armbruster, Carol, ed. *Publishing and Readership in Revolutionary France and America: A Symposium at the Library of Congress.* Westport, Conn.: Greenwood Press, 1993.

Arner, Robert. "Politics and Temperance in Boston and Philadelphia: Benjamin Franklin's Journalistic Writings on Drinking and Drunkenness." In *Reappraising Benjamin Franklin: A Bicentennial Perspective,* edited by J. A. Leo Lemay, 52–77. Newark: University of Delaware Press, 1993.

Augst, Thomas. *The Clerk's Tale: Young Men and Moral Life in Nineteenth-Century America.* Chicago: University of Chicago Press, 2003.

Austin, Robert B. *Early American Medical Imprints, 1668–1820.* Bethesda, Md.: National Library of Medicine, 1961.

Bailyn, Bernard, and John B. Hench, eds. *The Press and the American Revolution.* Boston: Northeastern University Press, 1981.

Bartky, Ian R. *Selling the True Time: Nineteenth-Century Timekeeping in America.* Stanford: Stanford University Press, 2000.

Baym, Nina. *Novels, Readers, and Reviewers: Responses to Fiction in Antebellum America.* Ithaca: Cornell University Press, 1984.

Beales, Ross W., and E. Jennifer Monaghan. "Literacy and Schoolbooks." In Amory and Hall, *Colonial Book in the Atlantic World,* 380–86.

Beall, Otho T. "*Aristotle's Master Piece* in America: A Landmark in the Folklore of Medicine." *William and Mary Quarterly* 20 (1963): 207–22.

Beier, Lucinda McCray. *Sufferers and Healers: The Experience of Illness in Seventeenth-Century England.* London: Routledge and Kegan Paul, 1987.

Benes, Peter. "Fortunetellers, Wise-Men, and Magical Healers in New England,

1644–1850." In *Wonders of the Invisible World: 1600–1900*, edited by Peter Benes, 127–48. Boston: Boston University Press, 1992.

Berlinski, David. *The Secrets of the Vaulted Sky: Astrology and the Art of Prediction*. New York: Harcourt, 2003.

Berman, Alex. "Neo-Thomsonianism in the United States." *Journal of the History of Medicine and Allied Sciences* 11 (1956): 133–55.

———. "The Thomsonian Movement and Its Relations to American Pharmacy and Medicine." *Bulletin of the History of Medicine* 25 (1951): 405.

———. "Wooster Beach and the Early Eclectics." *University of Michigan Medical Bulletin* 24 (1958): 277–86.

Berman, Alex, and Michael Flannery. *America's Botanico-Medical Movements: Vox Populi*. New York: Pharmaceutical Products Press, 2001.

Berryman, Jack W. "The Tradition of the 'six things non-natural': Exercise and Sport Medicine from Hippocrates through Antebellum America." *Exercise and Sport Review* 17 (1989): 515–59.

Berryman, Jack W., and Roberta J. Park, eds. *Sport and Exercise Science: Essays in the History of Sport Medicine*. Urbana: University of Illinois Press, 1992.

Betts, John Rickards. "American Medical Thought on Exercise as the Road to Health, 1820–1860." *Bulletin of the History of Medicine* 45 (1971): 138–52.

Bidwell, John. "Printers' Supplies and Capitalization." In Amory and Hall, *Colonial Book in the Atlantic World*, 163–82.

Blackman, Janet. "Popular Theories of Generation: The Evolution of Aristotle's Works: The Study of an Anachronism." In *Health Care and Popular Medicine in Nineteenth-Century England*, edited by John Woodward and David Richards, 56–88. New York: Holmes and Meier, 1977.

Blagden, Cyprian. "The Distribution of Almanacks in the Second Half of the Seventeenth Century." *Studies in Bibliography* 11 (1958): 108–17.

Blake, John B. "The Complete Housewife." *Bulletin of the History of Medicine* 49 (1975): 30–42.

———. "Early American Medical Literature." *Clio Medica* 11 (1976): 147–60.

———. "From Buchan to Fishbein: The Literature of Domestic Medicine." In *Medicine Without Doctors: Home Health Care in American History*, edited by Guenter B. Risse, Ronald L. Numbers, and Judith Walzer Leavitt, 11–30. New York: Science History Publications, 1977.

———. "Health Reform." In *The Rise of Adventism: Religion and Society in Mid-Nineteenth-Century America*, edited by Edwin S. Gausted, 30–49. New York: Harper and Row, 1974.

Bledstein, Burton. *The Culture of Professionalism: The Middle Class and the Development of Higher Education in America*. New York: W. W. Norton, 1976.

Blumin, Stuart M. *The Emergence of the Middle Class: Social Experience in the American City, 1760–1900*. New York: Cambridge University Press, 1989.

Boyer, Paul. *Urban Masses and Moral Order in America, 1820–1920*. Cambridge, Mass.: Harvard University Press, 1978.

Briggs, Samuel. *The Origin and Development of the Almanack*. Cleveland: Leader Printing Company, 1887.

Brigham, Clarence S. "Report of the Librarian," *Proceedings of the American Antiquarian Society* 35 (1925): 190–218.

Brodhead, Richard H. *Cultures of Letters: Scenes of Reading and Writing in Nineteenth-Century America*. Chicago: University of Chicago Press, 1993.

Bromell, Nicholas K. *By the Sweat of the Brow: Literature and Labor in Antebellum America*. Chicago: University of Chicago Press, 1993.

Brooke, John. " 'The True Spiritual Seed': Sectarian Religion and the Persistence of the Occult in Eighteenth-Century New England." In *Wonders of the Invisible World: 1600–1900*, edited by Peter Benes, 107–26. Boston: Boston University Press, 1992.

Brown, Candy Gunther. *The Word in the World: Evangelical Writing, Publishing, and Reading in America, 1789–1880*. Chapel Hill: University of North Carolina Press, 2004.

Brown, Kathleen. "The Maternal Physician: Teaching Mothers to Put the Baby in the Bathwater." In *Right Living: An Anglo-American Tradition of Self-Help Medicine and Hygiene*, edited by Charles E. Rosenberg, 88–111. Baltimore: Johns Hopkins University Press, 2003.

Brown, Richard D. *Knowledge is Power: The Diffusion of Information in Early America, 1700–1865*. New York: Oxford University Press, 1989.

Bullough, Vern L. "An Early American Sex Manual, or, Aristotle Who?" *Early American Literature* 7 (1972): 236–46.

Burbick, Joan. *Healing the Republic: The Language of Health and the Culture of Nationalism in Nineteenth-Century America*. Cambridge: Cambridge University Press, 1994.

Bushman, Richard L., and Claudia L. Bushman. "The Early History of Cleanliness in America." *Journal of American History* 74 (1988): 1213–38.

Butler, Jon. *Awash in a Sea of Faith: Christianizing the American People*. Cambridge, Mass.: Harvard University Press, 1990.

———. "Magic, Astrology, and the Early American Religious Heritage, 1600–1760." *American Historical Review* 84 (1979): 317–46.

———. "Thomas Teackle's 333 Books: A Great Library on Virginia's Eastern Shore, 1697." *William and Mary Quarterly* 49 (1992): 449–91.

Bynum, W. F. "Cullen and the Study of Fevers in Britain, 1760–1820." In *Theories of Fever from Antiquity to the Enlightenment*, edited by W. F. Bynum and V. Nutten, 135–47. London: Wellcome Institute for the History of Medicine, 1981.

Callaway, C. Wayne. "John Wesley's *Primitive Physick*: An Essay in Appreciation." *Mayo Clinic Proceedings* 49 (1974): 318–24.

Capp, Bernard. *English Almanacs 1500–1800: Astrology and the Popular Press*. Ithaca: Cornell University Press, 1979.

Carlson, Douglas W. " 'Drinks He to His Own Undoing': Temperance Ideology in the Deep South." *Journal of the Early Republic* 18 (1998): 659–91.

Carter, Jimmy. *An Hour before Daylight: Memories of a Rural Boyhood*. New York: Simon and Schuster, 2001.

Casper, Scott E. "Antebellum Reading Prescribed and Described." In *Perspectives on American Book History: Artifacts and Commentary*, edited by Scott

E. Casper, Joanne D. Chaison, and Jeffrey D. Groves, 135–64. Amherst and Boston: University of Massachusetts Press, 2002.

———. *Constructing American Lives: Biography and Culture in Nineteenth-Century America.* Chapel Hill: University of North Carolina Press, 1999.

Cassidy, James H. "The Flourishing and Character of Early American Medical Journalism, 1797–1860." *Journal of the History of Medicine and Allied Sciences* 38 (1983): 135–50.

Cavender, Anthony. *Folk Medicine in Southern Appalachia.* Chapel Hill: University of North Carolina Press, 2003.

Cayleff, Susan E. "Gender, Ideology, and the Water-Cure Movement." In *Other Healers: Unorthodox Medicine in America*, edited by Norman Gevitz, 82–98. Baltimore: Johns Hopkins University Press, 1988.

———. "Self-Help and the Patent Medicine Business." In *Women, Health, and Medicine in America: A Historical Handbook*, edited by Rima D. Apple, 311–36. New York: Garland, 1990.

———. *Wash and Be Healed: The Water-Cure Movement and Women's Health.* Philadelphia: Temple University Press, 1987.

Chaplin, Joyce E. *Subject Matter: Technology, the Body, and Science on the Anglo-American Frontier, 1500–1676.* Cambridge, Mass.: Harvard University Press, 2001.

Chapman, Allan. "Astrological Medicine." In *Health, Medicine and Mortality in the Sixteenth Century*, edited by Charles Webster, 275–300. Cambridge: Cambridge University Press, 1979.

Charvat, William. *Literary Publishing in America, 1790–1850.* Philadelphia: University of Pennsylvania Press, 1959.

———. *The Profession of Authorship in America, 1800–1870: The Papers of William Charvat.* Edited by Matthew J. Bruccoli. Columbus: Ohio State University Press, 1968.

Christianson, Eric. "Medicine in New England." In *Medicine in the New World: New Spain, New France, and New England*, edited by Ronald L. Numbers, 101–53. Knoxville: University of Tennessee Press, 1987.

Clark, Charles E. *The Public Prints: The Newspaper in Anglo-American Culture, 1665–1740.* New York: Oxford University Press, 1994.

Cohen, Daniel A. *Pillars of Salt, Monuments of Grace: New England Crime Literature and the Origins of American Popular Culture.* New York: Oxford University Press, 1993.

Coleman, William. "Health and Hygiene in the *Encyclopedie*: A Medical Doctrine for the Bourgeoisie." *Journal of the History of Medicine and Allied Sciences* 29 (1974): 399–421.

Cordasco, Francesco. *Homoeopathy in the United States: A Bibliography of Homoeopathic Medical Imprints, 1825–1925.* Fairview, N.J.: Junius-Vaughn Press, 1991.

———. *Medical Publishing in 19th-Century America.* Totowa, N.J.: Rowman and Littlefield, 1990.

Cowan, David L. "The Boston Editions of Nicholas Culpeper." *Journal of the History of Medicine and Allied Sciences* 11 (1956): 156–65.

Cowan, David L., and Renate Wilson. "The Traffic in Medical Ideas: Popular Medical Texts as German Imports and American Imprints." *Caduceus* 13 (Spring 1997): 67–80.

Crellin, John K., and Jane Philpott. *A Reference Guide to Medicinal Plants.* Vol. 2 of *Herbal Medicine Past and Present.* Durham: Duke University Press, 1990.

Cunz, Dieter. "John Gruber and His Almanac." *Maryland Historical Magazine* 47 (1952): 89–102.

Curry, Patrick. *Prophecy and Power: Astrology in Early Modern England.* Oxford: Polity Press, 1989.

———, ed. *Astrology, Science, and Society: Historical Essays.* Wolfboro, N.H.: Boydell Press, 1987.

Curth, Louise Hill. "The Medical Content of English Almanacs, 1640–1700." *Journal of the History of Medicine and Allied Sciences* 60 (2005): 255–82.

Daniels, Bruce C. *Puritans at Play: Leisure and Recreation in Colonial New England.* New York: St. Martin's Press, 1995.

Darnton, Robert. "What Is the History of Books?" In *Reading in America: Literature and Social History*, edited by Cathy N. Davidson, 27–52. Baltimore: Johns Hopkins University Press, 1989.

Davidson, Cathy N. *Revolution and the Word: The Rise of the Novel in America.* New York: Oxford University Press, 1986.

———. "Towards a History of Books and Readers." In *Reading in America: Literature and Social History*, edited by Cathy N. Davidson, 1–26. Baltimore: Johns Hopkins University Press, 1989.

Davies, John D. *Phrenology Fad and Science: A Nineteenth-Century Crusade.* New Haven: Yale University Press, 1955.

Davis, Richard Beale. *A Colonial Bookshelf: Reading in the Eighteenth Century.* Athens: University of Georgia Press, 1979.

Debus, Allen G. *The Chemical Philosophy: Paracelsian Science and Medicine in the Sixteenth and Seventeenth Centuries.* New York: Science History Publications, 1977.

———. "Paracelsus and the Chemical Revolution in Sixteenth-Century Medicine." *Gazette of the Grolier Club* n.s. 53 (2002): 49–70.

———. "Scientific Truth and Occult Tradition: The Medical World of Ebenezer Sibly (1751–1799)." *Medical History* 26 (1982): 259–78.

de Vore, Nicholas. *Encyclopedia of Astrology.* Totowa, N. J.: Roman and Littlefield, 1976.

Dodge, Robert K. "Access to Popular Culture: Early American Almanacs." *Kentucky Folklore Record* 25 (1979): 11–15.

———. "Didactic Humor in Almanacs of Early America." *Journal of Popular Culture* 5 (1971–72): 592–605.

———. *A Topical Index of Early American Almanacs, 1776–1800.* Westport, Conn.: Greenwood Press, 1997.

Donegan, Jane B. *"Hydropathic Highway to Health": Women and Water-Cure in Antebellum America.* Westport, Conn.: Greenwood Press, 1986.

Dorn, Michael L. "(In)temperate Zones: Daniel Drake's Medico-Moral Geographies of Urban Life in the Trans-Appalachian American West." *Journal of the History of Medicine and Allied Sciences* 55 (2000): 256–91.

Dorsey, Bruce. *Reforming Men and Women: Gender in the Antebellum City.* Ithaca: Cornell University Press, 2002.

Drake, Milton, comp. *Almanacs of the United States.* 2 vols. New York: Scarecrow Press, 1962.

Duffy, John. *Epidemics in Colonial America.* Baton Rouge: Louisiana State University Press, 1953.

Eade, J. C. *The Forgotten Sky: A Guide to Astrology in English Literature.* Oxford: Clarendon Press, 1984.

Ebert, Myrl. "The Rise and Development of the American Medical Periodical 1797–1850." *Bulletin of the Medical Library Association* 40 (1952): 243–76.

Ebertin, Reinhold. *Astrological Healing: The History and Practice of Astromedicine.* York Beach, Me.: Samuel Weiser, 1989.

Eisenstadt, Peter. "Almanacs and the Disenchantment of Early America." *Pennsylvania History* 65 (1998): 143–69.

———— "The Weather and Weather Forecasting in Colonial America." Ph.D. diss., New York University, 1990.

Eisenstein, Elizabeth L. *The Printing Press as an Agent of Change.* Cambridge: Cambridge University Press, 1979.

Emch-Deriaz, Antoinette. "The Non-Naturals Made Easy." In *The Popularization of Medicine 1650–1850*, edited by Roy Porter, 134–59. London: Routledge, 1992.

Estes, J. Worth. *Dictionary of Protopharmacology: Therapeutic Practices, 1700–1850.* Canton, Mass.: Science History Publications, 1990.

————. "Dropsy." In *The Cambridge World History of Human Disease*, edited by Kenneth F. Kiple, 689–96. Cambridge: Cambridge University Press, 1993.

————. *Naval Surgeon: Life and Death at Sea in the Age of Sail.* Canton, Mass.: Science History Publications, 1998.

————. "Patterns of Drug Use in Colonial America." *New York State Journal of Medicine* 87 (1987): 37–45.

————. "Samuel Thomson Rewrites Hippocrates." In *Medicine and Healing*, edited by Peter Benes, 113–32. Boston: Boston University Press, 1992.

————. "Therapeutic Practice in Colonial New England." In *Medicine in Colonial Massachusetts 1620–1820*, edited by Philip Cash, Eric H. Christianson, and J. Worth Estes, 289–383. Boston: Colonial Society of Massachusetts, 1980.

————. "The Yellow Fever Syndrome and Its Treatment in Philadelphia, 1793." In *A Melancholy Scene of Devastation: The Public Response to the 1793 Philadelphia Yellow Fever Epidemic*, edited by J. Worth Estes and Billy G. Smith, 1–18. Canton, Mass.: Published for the College of Physicians of Philadelphia and the Library Company of Philadelphia by Science History Publications, 1997.

Feller, Daniel. *The Jacksonian Promise: America, 1815–1840.* Baltimore: Johns Hopkins University Press, 1995.

Fellman, Anita Clair, and Michael Fellman. *Making Sense of Self: Medical Advice Literature in Late Nineteenth-Century America*. Philadelphia: University of Pennsylvania Press, 1981.

Fett, Sharla M. *Working Cures: Healing, Health, and Power on Southern Slave Plantations*. Chapel Hill: University of North Carolina Press, 2002.

Fissell, Mary E. "Making a Masterpiece: The Aristotle Texts in Vernacular Medical Culture." In *Right Living: An Anglo-American Tradition of Self-Help Medicine and Hygiene*, edited by Charles E. Rosenberg, 59–87. Baltimore: Johns Hopkins University Press, 2003.

————. "Readers, Texts, and Contexts: Vernacular Medical Works in Early Modern England." In *The Popularization of Medicine 1650–1850*, edited by Roy Porter, 72–96. London: Routledge, 1992.

Fox, Claire G., Gordon L. Miller, and Jacquelyn C. Miller, comps. *Benjamin Rush, M.D.: A Bibliographic Guide*. Westport, Conn.: Greenwood Press, 1996.

Fuller, Robert C. *Alternative Medicine and American Religious Life*. New York: Oxford University Press, 1989.

Furdell, Elizabeth Lane. *Publishing and Medicine in Early Modern England*. Rochester: University of Rochester Press, 2002.

Gardner, F. Leigh. *Bibliotheca Astrologica: A Catalog of Astrological Publications of the 15th through the 19th Centuries*. Hollywood, Calif.: Symbols & Signs, 1977.

Gartrell, Ellen. "Women Healers and Domestic Remedies in 18th Century America: The Recipe Book of Elizabeth Coates Paschall." *New York State Journal of Medicine* 87 (1987): 23–39.

Gevitz, Norman, and Micaela Sullivan-Fowler. "Making Sense of Therapeutics in Seventeenth-Century New England." *Caduceus* 11 (1995): 87–102.

Gifford, George E. Jr. "Botanic Remedies in Colonial Massachusetts, 1620–1820." In *Medicine in Colonial Massachusetts 1620–1820*, edited by Philip Cash, Eric H. Christianson, and J. Worth Estes, 263–88. Boston: Colonial Society of Massachusetts, 1980.

Gilmore, William J. "Literacy, the Rise of and Age of Reading, and the Cultural Grammar of Print Communications in America, 1735–1850." *Communications* 11 (1988): 23–45.

————. *Reading Becomes a Necessity of Life: Material and Cultural Life in Rural New England, 1780–1835*. Knoxville: University of Tennessee Press, 1989.

Gilreath, James. "American Book Distribution." *Proceedings of the American Antiquarian Society* 95 (1985): 501–83.

Godbeer, Richard. *The Devil's Dominion: Magic and Religion in Early New England*. Cambridge: Cambridge University Press, 1992.

Goldberg, Joseph Philip. "The Eighteenth-Century Philadelphia Almanac and Its English Counterpart." Ph.D. diss., University of Maryland, 1962.

Gorn, Elliott J. "Black Magic: Folk Beliefs of the Slave Community." In *Science and Medicine in the Old South*, edited by Ronald L. Numbers and Todd L. Savitt, 295–326. Baton Rouge: Louisiana State University Press, 1989.

Green, Harvey. *Fit for America: Health, Fitness, Sport and American Society.* New York: Pantheon Books, 1986.

Green, James N. "Benjamin Franklin as Publisher and Bookseller." In *Reappraising Benjamin Franklin: A Bicentennial Perspective,* edited by J. A. Leo Lemay, 98–114. Newark: University of Delaware Press, 1993.

———. "English Books and Printing in the Age of Franklin." In Amory and Hall, *Colonial Book in the Atlantic World,* 248–97.

———. "From Printer to Publisher: Mathew Carey and the Origins of Nineteenth-Century Book Publishing." In *Getting the Books Out: Papers of the Chicago Conference on the Book in 19th-Century America,* edited by Michael Hackenberg, 26–44. Washington, D.C.: Library of Congress, 1987.

——— "The Transformation of the 1790s: Mathew Carey and Mason Locke Weems." Book Publishing in Early America, A.S.W. Rosenbach Lectures for 1993, University of Pennsylvania.

Green, James N., and Peter Stallybrass. *Benjamin Franklin: Writer and Printer.* New Castle, Del., Philadelphia, and London: Oak Knoll Press, Library Company of Philadelphia, and the British Library, 2006.

Greenough, Chester Noyes. "New England Almanacs, 1766–1775, and the American Revolution." *Proceedings of the American Antiquarian Society* 45 (1935): 288–316.

Grob, Gerald N. *The Deadly Truth: A History of Disease in America.* Cambridge, Mass.: Harvard University Press, 2002.

Gronim, Sara S. "At the Sign of Newton's Head: Astronomy and Cosmology in British Colonial New York." *Pennsylvania History* 66 (suppl.) (1999): 55–85.

Gross, Robert A. "Much Instruction from Little Reading: Books and Libraries in Thoreau's Concord." *Proceedings of the American Antiquarian Society* 97 (1988): 129–88.

———. "Printing, Politics, and the People." *Proceedings of the American Antiquarian Society* 99 (1990): 375–97.

Grover, Kathryn, ed. *Fitness in American Culture: Images of Health, Sport, and the Body, 1830–1940.* Amherst: University of Massachusetts Press, 1989.

Gruman, Gerald J. "The Rise and Fall of Prolongevity Hygiene, 1558–1873." *Bulletin of the History of Medicine* 35 (1961): 221–29.

Guerra, Francisco. *American Medical Bibliography 1639–1783.* New York: Lathrop C. Harper, 1962.

———. "Medical Almanacs of the American Colonial Period." *Journal of the History of Medicine and Allied Sciences* 16 (1961): 234–55.

Guerrini, Anita. *Obesity and Depression in the Enlightenment: The Life and Times of George Cheyne.* Norman: University of Oklahoma Press, 2000.

Gummere, Richard M. "The Classical Element in Early New England Almanacs." *Harvard Library Bulletin* 9 (1955): 181–96.

Gura, Philip F. "The Study of Colonial American Literature, 1966–1987: A Vade Mecum." *William and Mary Quarterly* 45 (1988): 305–41.

Gusfield, Joseph R. *Symbolic Crusade: Status Politics and the American Temperance Movement.* Urbana: University of Illinois Press, 1963.

Gutjahr, Paul C. *An American Bible: A History of the Good Book in the United States, 1777–1880.* Stanford: Stanford University Press, 1999.

Hall, David D. "On Native Ground: From the History of Printing to the History of the Book." *Proceedings of the American Antiquarian Society* 93 (1983): 313–36.

———. "Readers and Reading in America: Historical and Critical Perspectives." *Proceedings of the American Antiquarian Society* 103 (1993): 337–58.

———. "The Uses of Literacy in New England, 1600–1850." In *Printing and Society in Early America*, edited by William L. Joyce, David D. Hall, Richard D. Brown, and John B. Hench, 1–47. Worcester, Mass.: American Antiquarian Society, 1983.

———. *Worlds of Wonder, Days of Judgment: Popular Religious Belief in Early New England.* Cambridge, Mass.: Harvard University Press, 1989.

Hall, David D., and John B. Hench, eds. *Needs and Opportunities in the History of the Book: America, 1639–1876.* Worcester, Mass.: American Antiquarian Society, 1987.

Haller, John S. *Medical Protestants: The Eclectics in American Medicine, 1825–1939.* Carbondale: Southern Illinois University Press, 1994.

———. *Medicine in Transition, 1840–1910.* Urbana: University of Illinois Press, 1981.

———. *The People's Doctors: Samuel Thomson and the American Botanical Movement, 1790–1860.* Carbondale: Southern Illinois University Press, 2000.

Halttunen, Karen. *Confidence Men and Painted Women: A Study of Middle-Class Culture in America, 1830–1870.* New Haven: Yale University Press, 1982.

Harris, Michael H. "'Spiritual Cakes upon the Waters': The Church as Disseminator of the Printed Word on the Ohio Valley Frontier to 1850." In *Getting the Books Out: Papers of the Chicago Conference on the Book in Nineteenth-Century America*, edited by Michael Hackenberg, 98–120. Washington, D.C.: Library of Congress, 1987.

Hatch, Nathan O. *The Democratization of American Christianity.* New Haven: Yale University Press, 1989.

Hayes, Kevin J. *A Colonial Woman's Bookshelf.* Knoxville: University of Tennessee Press, 1996.

———, comp. *The Library of William Byrd of Westover.* Madison, Wis.: Madison House, 1997.

Helfand, William H. "Advertising Health to the People." In *Right Living: An Anglo-American Tradition of Self-Help Medicine and Hygiene*, edited by Charles E. Rosenberg, 170–85. Baltimore: Johns Hopkins University Press, 2003.

———. *Quack, Quack, Quack: The Sellers of Nostrums in Prints, Posters, Ephemera, and Books.* New York: Grolier Club, 2002.

———. "Advertising Health to the People." In *"Every Man His Own Doctor": Popular Medicine in Early America*, edited by Charles E. Rosenberg, William H. Helfand, and James N. Green, 23–50. Philadelphia: Library Company of Philadelphia, 1998.

Hemphill, C. Dallett. *Bowing to Necessities: A History of Manners in America, 1620–1860.* New York: Oxford University Press, 1999.

Hill, A. Wesley. *John Wesley among the Physicians: A Study of Eighteenth-Century English Medicine.* London: Epworth Press, 1958.

Holden, James Herschel. *A History of Horoscopic Astrology: From the Babylonian Period to the Modern Age.* Tempe, Ariz.: American Federation of Astrologers, 1996.

Hoolihan, Christopher, comp. *A Catalog of the Edward C. Atwater Collection of American Popular Medicine.* Vol. 1. Rochester: University of Rochester Press, 2002.

Horrocks, Thomas A. "'The Poor Man's Riches, The Rich Man's Bliss': Regimen, Reform, and the *Journal of Health*, 1829–1833." *Proceedings of the American Philosophical Society* 139 (1995): 115–34.

———. "Poor Richard's Offspring: Benjamin Franklin's Influence on the American Almanac Trade." *Harvard Library Bulletin* 17 (2006): 41–46.

———. 'Promoting Good Health in the Age of Reform: The Medical Publications of Henry H. Porter of Philadelphia, 1829–1832." *Canadian Bulletin of Medical History* 12 (1995): 259–87.

———. "Rules, Remedies, and Regimens: Health Advice in Early American Almanacs." In *Right Living: An Anglo-American Tradition of Self-Help Medicine and Hygiene*, edited by Charles E. Rosenberg, 112–46. Baltimore: Johns Hopkins University Press, 2003.

———. "Rules, Remedies, and Regimens: Health Information in Early American Almanacs." Ph.D. diss., University of Pennsylvania, 2003.

Howe, Daniel Walker. *Making the American Self: Jonathan Edwards to Abraham Lincoln.* Cambridge, Mass.: Harvard University Press, 1997.

Hoy, Suellen. *Chasing Dirt: The American Pursuit of Cleanliness.* New York: Oxford University Press, 1995.

Hudak, Leona M. *Early American Women Printers and Publishers, 1639–1820.* Metuchen, N. J.: Scarecrow Press, 1978.

Hurry, Robert J. "An Archeological and Historical Perspective on Benjamin Banneker." *Maryland Historical Magazine* 84 (1989): 361–69.

John, Richard. "Early American Origins of the Information Age." In *A Nation Transformed by Information: How Information Has Shaped the United States from Colonial Times to the Present*, edited by Alfred D. Chandler Jr. and James W. Cortada, 56–105. New York: Oxford University Press, 2001.

———. *Spreading the News: The American Postal System from Franklin to Morse.* Cambridge, Mass.: Harvard University Press, 1996.

Johnson, Paul E. *A Shopkeeper's Millennium: Society and Revivals in Rochester, New York, 1815–1837.* New York: Hill and Wang, 1978.

Jorgenson, Chester F. "The New Science in the Almanacs of Ames and Franklin." *New England Quarterly* 8 (1935): 555–61.

Kaestle, Carl F. *Pillars of the Republic: Common Schools and American Society, 1780–1860.* New York: Hill and Wang, 1983.

Kassan, John F. *Rudeness and Civility: Manners in Nineteenth-Century Urban America.* New York: Hill and Wang, 1990.

Kaufman, Martin. *Homeopathy in America: The Rise and Fall of a Medical Heresy.* Baltimore: Johns Hopkins University Press, 1971.

Keeney, Elizabeth Barnaby. "Unless Powerful Sick: Domestic Medicine in the Old South." In *Science and Medicine in the Old South*, edited by Ronald L. Numbers and Todd L. Savitt, 276–94. Baton Rouge: Louisiana State University Press, 1989.

Kelly, John T. *Practical Astronomy during the Seventeenth Century: Almanac-Makers in America and England.* New York: Garland, 1991.

Kett, Joseph F. *The Formation of the American Medical Profession: The Rule of Institutions, 1780–1860.* New Haven: Yale University Press, 1968.

King, Lester S. "George Cheyne, Mirror of Eighteenth-Century Medicine." *Bulletin of the History of Medicine* 48 (1974): 517–39.

———. *Medical Thinking: A Historical Preface.* Princeton: Princeton University Press, 1982.

———. *Transformations in American Medicine from Benjamin Rush to William Osler.* Baltimore: Johns Hopkins University Press, 1991.

———. *The Medical World of the Eighteenth Century.* Huntington, N.Y.: Robert E. Krieger, 1971.

Kitson, Annabella, ed. *History and Astrology: Clio and Urania Confer.* Boston: Unwin, 1989.

Kittredge, George Lyman. *The Old Farmer and His Almanack.* New York: Benjamin Blom, 1967.

Kopperman, Paul E. " 'Venerate the Lancet': Benjamin Rush's Yellow Fever Therapy in Context." *Bulletin of the History of Medicine* 78 (2004): 539–74.

Larkin, Jack. *The Reshaping of Everyday Life, 1790–1840.* New York: Harper and Row, 1988.

Lawrence, Christopher. "William Buchan: Medicine Laid Open." *Medical History* 19 (1975): 20–35.

Leavitt, Judith Walzer. *Brought to Bed: Childbearing in America, 1750–1950.* New York: Oxford University Press, 1986.

Lehmann-Haupt, Hellmut. *The Book in America: A History of the Making and Selling of Books in the United States.* New York: R. R. Bowker, 1952.

Leighton, Ann. *American Gardens in the Eighteenth Century: "For Use or for Delight."* Amherst: University of Massachusetts Press, 1976.

———. *Early American Gardens: "For Meate or Medicine."* Amherst: University of Massachusetts Press, 1970.

Lehuu, Isabelle. *Carnival on the Page: Popular Print Media in Antebellum America.* Chapel Hill: University of North Carolina Press, 2000.

Leonard, Thomas C. "News at the Hearth: A Drama of Reading in Nineteenth-Century America." *Proceedings of the American Antiquarian Society* 102 (1992): 379–402.

———. "News for a Revolution: The Exposé in America, 1768–1773." *Journal of American History* 67 (1980): 26–40.

———. *The Power of the Press: The Birth of American Political Reporting.* New York: Oxford University Press, 1986.

Lepore, Jill. "Literacy and Reading in Puritan New England." In *Perspectives on American Book History: Artifacts and Commentary*, edited by Scott E. Casper, Joanne D. Chaison, and Jeffrey D. Groves, 17–46. Amherst and Boston: University of Massachusetts Press, 2002.

Leventhal, Herbert. *In the Shadow of the Enlightenment: Occultism and Renaissance Science in Eighteenth-Century America*. New York: New York University Press, 1976.

Lewis, James R. *The Astrology Encyclopedia*. Detroit: Visible Ink Press, 1994.

———, ed. *The Beginnings of Astrology in America: Astrology and the Re-Emergence of Cosmic Religion*. New York: Garland, 1990.

Lindeboom, G. A. "Boerhaave's Concept of the Basic Structure of the Body." *Clio Medica* 5 (1970): 203–8.

Lindman, Janet Moore, and Michele Lise Tarter, eds. *A Centre of Wonders: The Body in Early America*. Ithaca: Cornell University Press, 2001.

Littlefield, George Emery. "Notes on the Calendar and Almanac." *Proceedings of the American Antiquarian Society* 24 (1914): 11–64.

Lockridge, Kenneth A. *Literacy in Colonial New England: An Enquiry into the Social Context of Literacy in the Early Modern West*. New York: W. W. Norton, 1974.

Lockwood, Rose. "The Scientific Revolution in Seventeenth-Century New England." *New England Quarterly* 53 (1980): 76–95.

Lovely, N. W. "Notes on New England Almanacs." *New England Quarterly* 8 (1935): 264–77.

Marsh, Margaret. "Popular Medical Guides and the Study of Women's History." *Fugitive Leaves from the Library of the College of Physicians of Philadelphia*, 3rd. ser., 6 (Spring 1991): [1]–3.

McCaffery, Ellen. *Astrology: Its History and Influence in the Western World*. New York: Charles Scribner's Sons, 1942.

McCarter, David. "Dr. Ames Defines His Profession." *Transactions and Studies of the College of Physicians of Philadelphia*, ser. 5, 17 (1995): 115–31.

———. "'Of Physick and Astronomy': Almanacs and Popular Medicine in Massachusetts, 1700–1764." Ph.D. diss., University of Iowa, 2000.

McClary, Ben H. "Introducing a Medical Classic: *Gunn's Domestic Medicine*." *Tennessee Historical Quarterly* 45 (1986): 210–16.

McDonald, Michael. "The Career of Astrological Medicine in England." In *Religio Medici: Medicine and Religion in Seventeenth-Century England*, edited by Ole Peter Grell and Andrew Cunningham, 62–90. Brookfield, Vt.: Scolar Press, 1996.

———. *Mystical Bedlam: Madness, Anxiety, and Healing in Sixteenth-Century England*. Cambridge: Cambridge University Press, 1981.

McKenzie, D. F. *Bibliography and the Sociology of Texts*. London: British Library, 1986.

Merchant, Carolyn. *Ecological Revolutions: Nature, Gender, and Science in New England*. Chapel Hill: University of North Carolina Press, 1989.

Mercier, Charles Arthur. *Astrology in Medicine*. London: Macmillan; St. Martin's Press, 1914.

Meyer, Richard E. "Colonial Values and the Development of the American Nation as Expressed in Almanacs, 1700–1790." Ph.D. diss., University of Kansas, 1970.

Miller, C. William. "Franklin's *Poor Richard Almanacs*: Their Printing and Publication." *Studies in Bibliography* 14 (1961): 97–115.

Mintz, Steven. *Moralists and Modernizers: America's Pre-Civil War Reformers.* Baltimore: Johns Hopkins University Press, 1995.

Monaghan, E. Jennifer. "Family Literacy in Early Eighteenth-Century Boston: Cotton Mather and His Children." *Reading Research Quarterly* 26 (1991): 342–70.

———. *Learning to Read and Write in Colonial America.* Amherst and Boston: University of Massachusetts Press, 2005.

———. "Literary Instruction and Gender in Colonial New England," *American Quarterly* 40 (1988): 18–41.

Morantz, Regina Markell. "Making Women Modern: Middle-Class Women and Health Reform in 19th-Century America." In *Women and Health in America: Historical Readings*, edited by Judith Walzer Leavitt, 346–58. Madison: University of Wisconsin Press, 1984.

———. "Nineteenth-Century Health Reform and Women: A Program of Self-Help." In *Medicine without Doctors: Home Health Care in American History*, edited by Guenter B. Risse, Ronald L. Numbers, and Judith Walzer Leavitt, 73–93. New York: Science History Publications, 1977.

Moss, Kay K. *Southern Folk Medicine 1750–1820.* Columbia: University of South Carolina Press, 1999.

Mott, Frank Luther. *American Journalism: A History of Newspapers in the United States Through 250 Years, 1690–1940.* New York: Macmillan, 1941.

Mullins, Jeffrey Allan. "Making of the Moral Mind: Contestations Over Self-Government, Personal Responsibility, and the Body in American Culture, 1780–1860." Ph.D. diss., Johns Hopkins University, 1997.

Murphy, Lamar Riley. *Enter the Physician: The Transformation of Domestic Medicine, 1760–1860.* Tuscaloosa: University of Alabama Press, 1991.

Murray, Gail S. "Rational Thought and Republican Virtues: Children's Literature, 1789–1820." *Journal of the Early Republic* 8 (1988): 159–77.

Mutschler, Ben. "The Province of Affliction: Illness in New England, 1690–1820." Ph.D. diss., Columbia University, 2000.

Nerone, John. *The Culture of the Press in the Early Republic: Cincinnati, 1793–1843.* New York: Garland, 1989.

Neuberg, Victor. "Chapbooks in America: Reconstructing the Popular Reading of Early America." In *Reading in America: Literature and Social History*, edited by Cathy N. Davidson, 81–113. Baltimore: Johns Hopkins University Press, 1989.

Newman, William R., and Anthony Grafton, eds. *Secrets of Nature: Astrology and Alchemy in Early Modern Europe.* Cambridge, Mass.: MIT Press, 2001.

Nichols, Charles L. "Notes on the Almanacs of Massachusetts." *Proceedings of the American Antiquarian Society* 22 (1912): 15–40.

Nickels, Cameron C. "Poor Richard's Almanacs: 'The Humblest of His Labors.' "

In *The Oldest Revolutionary: Essays on Benjamin Franklin*, edited by J. A. Leo Lemay, 77–89. Philadelphia: University of Pennsylvania Press, 1976.

Niebyl, Peter H. "The Non-Naturals: A Biographical Note and Translation." *Bulletin of the History of Medicine* 44 (1970): 372–77.

Nietz, John. *Old Textbooks: Spelling, Grammar, Reading, Arithmetic, Geography, American History, Civil Government, Physiology, Penmanship, Art, Music—As Taught in the Common Schools from Colonial Days to 1900.* Pittsburgh: University of Pittsburgh Press, 1961.

Nissenbaum, Stephen. *The Battle for Christmas.* New York: Alfred A. Knopf, 1997.

————. *Sex, Diet, and Debility in Jacksonian America: Sylvester Graham and Health Reform.* Westport, Conn.: Greenwood Press, 1980.

Nord, David Paul. *The Children of Isaiah Thomas: Notes on the Historiography of Journalism and of the Book in America.* Worcester, Mass.: American Antiquarian Society, 1987.

————. "The Evangelical Origins of Mass Media in America, 1815–1835." *Journalism Monographs* 88 (1984).

————. *Faith in Reading: Religious Publishing and the Birth of Mass Media in America.* New York: Oxford University Press, 2004.

————. "Free Grace, Free Books, Free Riders: The Economics of Religious Publishing in Early Nineteenth-Century America." *Proceedings of the American Antiquarian Society* 106 (1996): 241–72.

————. "Newspapers and American Nationhood, 1776–1826." *Proceedings of the American Antiquarian Society* 100 (1990): 391–406.

————. "Religious Reading and Readers in Antebellum America." *Journal of the Early Republic* 15 (1995): 241–72.

————. "A Republican Literature: Magazine Reading and Readers in Late-Eighteenth-Century New York." In *Reading in America: Literature and Social History*, edited by Cathy N. Davidson, 114–39. Baltimore: Johns Hopkins University Press, 1989.

————. "Teleology and News: The Religious Roots of America Journalism." *Journal of American History* 77 (1990): 9–38.

Norton, Mary Beth. *Founding Mothers and Fathers: Gendered Power and the Forming of American Society.* New York: Alfred A. Knopf, 1996.

Numbers, Ronald L. "Do-It-Yourself the Sectarian Way." In *Medicine without Doctors: Home Health Care in American History*, edited by Guenter B. Risse, Ronald L. Numbers, and Judith Walzer Leavitt, 49–72. New York: Science History Publications, 1977.

Nutton, Vivian. "Humoralism." In *Companion Encyclopedia of the History of Medicine*, 2 vols., edited by W. F. Bynum and Roy Porter, 1:281–91. New York: Routledge, 1993.

————. "Medicine in the Greek World, 800–50 BC." In *The Western Medical Tradition 800 BC to AD 1800*, edited by Lawrence I. Conrad, Michael Neve, Vivian Nutton, Roy Porter, and Andrew Wear, 23–52. Cambridge: Cambridge University Press, 1995.

O'Malley, Michael. *Keeping Watch: A History of American Time*. New York: Viking, 1990.

Page, Alfred B. "John Tulley's Almanacks, 1687–1702." *Publications of the Colonial Society of Massachusetts* 13 (1912): 207–23.

Paltsits, Victor Hugo. "The Almanacs of Roger Sherman, 1750–1761." *Proceedings of the American Antiquarian Society* 18 (1907): 213–23.

Pasley, Jeffrey L. *"The Tyranny of Printers": Newspaper Politics in the Early Republic*. Charlottesville: University Press of Virginia, 2001.

Patterson, K. David. "Amebic Dysentery." In *The Cambridge World History of Human Disease*, edited by Kenneth F. Kiple, 568–70. Cambridge: Cambridge University Press, 1993.

———. "Bacillary Dysentery." In *The Cambridge World History of Human Disease*, edited by Kenneth F. Kiple, 604–6. Cambridge: Cambridge University Press, 1993.

———. "Disease Environments in the Antebellum South." In *Science and Medicine in the Old South*, edited by Ronald L. Numbers and Todd L. Savitt, 152–65. Baton Rouge: Louisiana State University Press, 1989.

———. "Dysentery." In *The Cambridge World History of Human Disease*, edited by Kenneth F. Kiple, 696. Cambridge: Cambridge University Press, 1993.

Peitzman, Steven J. "From Bright's Disease to End-Stage Renal Disease." In *Framing Disease: Studies in Cultural History*, edited by Charles E. Rosenberg and Janet Golden, 3–19. New Brunswick: Rutgers University Press, 1992.

Pencak, William. "Nathaniel Ames, Sr., and the Political Culture of Provincial New England." *Historical Journal of Massachusetts* 22 (1994): 141–58.

Perlmann, Joel, and Dennis Shirly. "When Did New England Women Acquire Literacy?" *William and Mary Quarterly* 48 (1991): 50–67.

Porter, Roy. "Lay Medical Knowledge in the Eighteenth Century: The Evidence of the Gentleman's Magazine." *Medical History* 29 (1985): 138–68.

———. "The Secrets of Generation Display'd: *Aristotle's Master-piece* in Eighteenth-Century England." In *'Tis Nature's Fault: Unauthorized Sexuality during the Enlightenment*, edited by Robert P. McCubbin, 1–21. Cambridge: Cambridge University Press, 1985.

Porter, Roy, and Lesley Hall. "Medical Folklore in High and Low Culture: *Aristotle's Master-Piece*." In *The Facts of Life: The Creation of Sexual Knowledge in Britain, 1650–1950*, edited by Roy Porter, 33–64. New Haven: Yale University Press, 1995.

Potvin, Ronald M. "John Sherman's Book of Horoscopes, Ca. 1761." *Newport History* 66 (1995): 185–93.

Rather, L. J. "The 'six things non-natural': A Note of the Origin and Fate of a Doctrine and a Phrase." *Clio Medica* 3 (1968): 337–47.

Rawcliffe, Carole. *Medicine and Society in Later Medieval England*. Stroud, U.K.: Alan Sutton, 1995.

Raymond, Allan R. "To Reach Men's Minds: Almanacs and the American Revolution, 1760–1777." *New England Quarterly* 51 (1978): 370–95.

Reilly, Elizabeth Carroll. "Common and Learned Readers: Shared and Separate

Spheres in Mid-Eighteenth-Century New England." Ph.D. diss., Boston University, 1994.

———. *A Dictionary of Colonial Printers' Ornaments and Illustrations.* Worcester, Mass.: American Antiquarian Society, 1975.

Reilly, Elizabeth Carroll, and David D. Hall. "Customers and the Market for Books." In Amory and Hall, *Colonial Book in the Atlantic World,* 387–98.

Reiner, Jacqueline S. "Rearing the Republican Child: Attitudes and Practices in Post-Revolutionary Philadelphia." *William and Mary Quarterly* 39 (1982): 150–63.

Remer, Rosalind. "Preachers, Peddlers, and Publishers: Philadelphia's Backcountry Book Trade, 1800–1830." *Journal of the Early Republic* 14 (1994): 497–522.

———. *Printers and Men of Capital: Philadelphia Book Publishers in the New Republic.* Philadelphia: University of Pennsylvania Press, 1996.

Reynolds, David S. *Beneath the American Renaissance: The Subversive Imagination in the Age of Emerson and Melville.* Cambridge, Mass.: Harvard University Press, 1988.

Rogal, Samuel J. "Pills for the Poor: John Wesley's *Primitive Physick.*" *Yale Journal of Biology and Medicine* 51 (1978): 81–90.

Rogers, Naomi. "Women and Sectarian Medicine." In *Women, Health, and Medicine in America: A Historical Handbook,* edited by Rima D. Apple, 281–310. New York: Garland, 1990.

Roos, Anna Marie. "Luminaries in Medicine: Richard Mead, James Gibbs, and Solar and Lunar Effects on the Human Body in Early Modern England." *Bulletin of the History of Medicine* 74 (2000): 433–57.

Rorabaugh, W. J. *The Alcoholic Republic: An American Tradition.* New York: Oxford University Press, 1979.

Rosenberg, Charles E. "Body and Mind in Nineteenth-Century Medicine: Some Clinical Origins of the Neurosis Construct." *Bulletin of the History of Medicine* 63 (1989): 185–97.

———. "Catechisms of Health: The Body in the Prebellum Classroom." *Bulletin of the History of Medicine* 69 (1995): 175–97.

———. *The Cholera Years: The United States in 1832, 1849, and 1866.* Chicago: University of Chicago Press, 1962.

———. "Health in the Home: A Tradition of Health and Practice." In *Right Living: An Anglo-American Tradition of Self-Help Medicine and Hygiene,* edited by Charles E. Rosenberg, 1–20. Baltimore: Johns Hopkins University Press, 2003.

———. "Medical Text and Social Context: Explaining William Buchan's *Domestic Medicine.*" *Bulletin of the History of Medicine* 57 (1983): 22–42.

———. "The Therapeutic Revolution: Medicine, Meaning, and Social Change in Nineteenth-Century America." In *The Therapeutic Revolution: Essays in the Social History of Medicine,* edited by Morris J. Vogel and Charles E. Rosenberg, 3–26. Philadelphia: University of Pennsylvania Press, 1979.

Rosenberg, Charles E., and Carroll Smith-Rosenberg. "Pietism and the Origins of the American Public Health Movement: A Note on John H. Griscom and

Robert M. Hartley." *Journal of the History of Medicine and Allied Sciences* 23 (1968): 16–35.

Rothstein, William G. *American Physicians in the Nineteenth Century: From Sects to Science.* Baltimore: Johns Hopkins University Press, 1972.

———. "The Botanical Movements and Orthodox Medicine." In *Other Healers: Unorthodox Medicine in America,* edited by Norman Gevitz, 29–51. Baltimore: Johns Hopkins University Press, 1988.

Rouseau, G. S. "John Wesley's *Primitive Physic.*" *Harvard Library Bulletin* 16 (1968): 242–56.

Ruffin, J. Rixey. " 'Urania's Dusky Vails': Heliocentrism in Colonial Almanacs, 1700–1735." *New England Quarterly* 70 (1997): 306–13.

Ryan, Mary P. *Cradle of the Middle Class: The Family in Oneida County, New York, 1790–1865.* New York: Cambridge University Press, 1981.

Sagendorph, Robb. *America and Her Almanacs: Wit, Wisdom, and Weather, 1639–1970.* Boston: Little, Brown, 1970.

Sappenfield, James A. *A Sweet Instruction: Franklin's Journalism as a Literary Apprenticeship.* Carbondale and Edwardsville: Southern Illinois University Press, 1973.

Sappol, Michael. *A Traffic in Dead Bodies: Anatomy and Embodied Social Identity in Nineteenth-Century America.* Princeton: Princeton University Press, 2002.

Savitt, Todd L. *Medicine and Slavery: The Diseases and Health Care of Blacks in Antebellum Virginia.* Chicago: University of Illinois Press, 1978.

Schantz, Mark S. "Religious Tracts, Evangelical Reform, and the Market Revolution in Antebellum America." *Journal of the Early Republic* 17 (1997): 425–66.

Schudson, Michael. *Discovering the News: A Social History of American Newspapers.* New York: Basic Books, 1978.

Sellers, Charles. *The Market Revolution: Jacksonian America, 1815–1846.* New York: Oxford University Press, 1991.

Shapin, Steven. "How to Eat Like a Gentleman: Dietetics and Ethics in Early Modern England." In *Right Living: An Anglo-American Tradition of Self-Help Medicine and Hygiene,* edited by Charles E. Rosenberg, 21–58. Baltimore: Johns Hopkins University Press, 2003.

Shipton, Clifford K., and James E. Mooney, *National Index of American Imprints through 1800: The Short-Title Evans.* 2 vols. Worcester, Mass.: American Antiquarian Society and Barre Publishers, 1962.

Shryock, Richard H. *Medicine and Society in America: 1660–1860.* Ithaca: Cornell University Press, 1960.

———. "Sylvester Graham and the Popular Health Movement." In *Medicine in America: Historical Essays,* by Richard H. Shryock, 111–25. Baltimore: Johns Hopkins University Press, 1966.

Sidwell, Robert T. "The Colonial American Almanacs: A Study in Non-Institutional Education." Ph.D. diss., Rutgers University, 1965.

———. " 'Writers, Thinkers and Fox Hunters': Educational Theory in the Almanacs of Eighteenth-Century Colonial America." *History of Education Quarterly* 8 (1968): 275–88.

Sigerist, Henry E. "Faust in America." *Medical Life* 41 (1934): 192–207.

———. "On Some Further Editions of Faust's 'Catechism of Health.' " *Bulletin of the Institute of the History of Medicine* 2 (1934): 392–401.

Silver, Rollo G. *The American Printer, 1787–1825.* Charlottesville: University Press of Virginia, 1967.

———. *Typefounding in America, 1787–1825.* Charlottesville: University Press of Virginia, 1965.

Sklar, Kathryn Kish. "All Hail to Pure Cold Water!" In *Women and Health in America: Historical Readings,* edited by Judith Walzer Leavitt, 246–54. Madison: University of Wisconsin Press, 1984.

Slack, Paul. "Mirrors of Health and Treasures of Poor Men: The Uses of Vernacular Medical Literature in Tudor England." In *Health, Medicine, and Mortality in the Seventeenth Century,* edited by Charles Webster, 237–71. Cambridge: Cambridge University Press, 1979.

Smith, Dale C. "Quinine and Fever: The Development of the Effective Dosage." *Journal of the History of Medicine and Allied Sciences* 31 (1976): 343–67.

Smith, Ginnie. "Prescribing the Rules of Health: Self-Help and Advice Manuals in the Late Eighteenth Century." In *Patients and Practitioners: Lay Perceptions of Medicine in Pre-Industrial Society,* edited by Roy Porter, 249–82. Cambridge: Cambridge University Press, 1985.

Smith, Timothy L. *Revivalism and Social Reform: American Protestantism on the Eve of the Civil War.* Baltimore: Johns Hopkins University Press, 1980.

Snodgrass, Mary Ellen. *Signs of the Zodiac: A Reference Guide to Historical, Mythological, and Cultural Associations.* Westport, Conn.: Greenwood Press, 1997.

Spufford, Margaret. *Small Books and Pleasant Histories: Popular Fiction and Its Readership in Seventeenth-Century England.* Athens: University of Georgia Press, 1981.

Stahlman, William D. "Astrology in Colonial America: An Extended Query." *William and Mary Quarterly* 13 (1956): 551–63.

Starr, Paul. *The Social Transformation of American Medicine: The Rise of a Sovereign Profession and the Making of a Vast Industry.* New York: Basic Books, 1982.

Stern, Madeleine B. *Heads and Headlines: The Phrenological Fowlers.* Norman: University of Oklahoma Press, 1971.

Stokes, Melvyn, and Stephen Conway, eds. *The Market Revolution in America: Social, Political, and Religious Expressions, 1800–1880.* Charlottesville: University Press of Virginia, 1996.

Stowe, Steven. "Conflict and Self-Sufficiency: Domestic Medicine in the American South." In *Right Living: An Anglo-American Tradition of Self-Help Medicine and Hygiene,* edited by Charles E. Rosenberg, 147–69. Baltimore: Johns Hopkins University Press, 2003.

———. *Doctoring the South: Southern Physicians and Everyday Medicine in the*

Mid-Nineteenth Century. Chapel Hill: University of North Carolina Press, 2004.

Stowell, Marion Barber. *Early American Almanacs: The Colonial Weekday Bible*. New York: Burt Franklin, 1977.

———. "The Influence of Nathaniel Ames on the Literary Taste of His Time." *Early American Literature* 18 (1983): 127–45.

———. "Revolutionary Almanac-Makers: Trumpeters of Sedition." *Papers of the Bibliographical Society of America* 73 (1979): 41–61.

Sullivan, Robert B. "Sanguine Practices: A Historical and Historiographic Reconsideration of Heroic Therapy in the Age of Rush." *Bulletin of the History of Medicine* 68 (1994): 211–34.

Sutton, Walter. *The Western Book Trade: Cincinnati as a Nineteenth-Century Publishing and Book Trade Center*. Columbus: Ohio State University Press, 1961.

Tannenbaum, Rebecca J. *The Healer's Calling: Women and Medicine in Early New England*. Ithaca: Cornell University Press, 2002.

Tebbel, John. *The Creation of an Industry 1630–1865*. Vol. 1 of *A History of Book Publishing in the United States*. New York: R. R. Bowker, 1972.

Temkin, Owsei. *Galenism: Rise and Decline of a Medical Philosophy*. Ithaca: Cornell University Press, 1973.

Tester, S. J. *A History of Western Astrology*. Woodbridge, U.K.: Boydell Press, 1987.

Thomas, John L. "Romantic Reform in American, 1815–1865." *American Quarterly* 17 (1965): 656–81.

Thomas, Keith. *Religion and the Decline of Magic*. New York: Charles Scribner's Sons, 1971.

Thorne, Tanis. "The Almanacs of the San Francisco Bay Region, 1850–1861: A Neglected Historical Source." *Journal of the West* 17 (1978): 37–45.

Thulesius, Olav. *Nicholas Culpeper: English Physician and Astrologer*. New York: St. Martin's Press, 1992.

Tompkins, Jane. *Sensational Designs: The Cultural Work of American Fiction, 1790–1860*. New York: Oxford University Press, 1985.

Traister, Barbara H. "Medicine and Astrology in Elizabethan England: The Case of Simon Forman." *Transactions and Studies of the College of Physicians of Philadelphia*, 5th ser., 11 (1989): 279–97.

———. *The Notorious Astrological Physician of London: Works and Days of Simon Forman*. Chicago: University of Chicago Press, 2001.

Ulrich, Laurel Thatcher. *A Midwife's Tale: The Life of Martha Ballard, Based on Her Diary, 1785–1812*. New York: Alfred A. Knopf, 1990.

Valencius, Conevery Bolton. *The Health of the Country: How American Settlers Understood Themselves and Their Land*. New York: Basic Books, 2002.

Veits, Henry R. "George Cheyne, 1673–1743." *Bulletin of the History of Medicine* 23 (1949): 435–52.

Walker, William B. "Luigi Cornaro, a Renaissance Writer on Personal Hygiene." *Bulletin of the History of Medicine* 28 (1954): 525–34.

Wallace, Daniel J. "Thomsonians: The People's Doctors." *Clio Medica* 14 (1980): 169–86.

Walters, Ronald G. *American Reformers, 1815–1860.* New York: Hill and Wang, 1978.

Warner, John Harley. "The Selective Transport of Medical Knowledge: Antebellum American Physicians and Parisian Therapeutics." *Bulletin of the History of Medicine* 59 (1985): 213–31.

———. *The Therapeutic Perspective: Medical Practice, Knowledge, and Identity in America 1828–1885.* Cambridge, Mass.: Harvard University Press, 1986.

Warner, Michael. *The Letters of the Republic: Publication and the Public Sphere in Eighteenth-Century America.* Cambridge, Mass.: Harvard University Press, 1990.

Watson, Harry L. *Liberty and Power: The Politics of Jacksonian America.* New York: Hill and Wang, 1990.

Watson, Patricia Ann. *The Angelical Conjunction: The Preacher-Physicians of Colonial New England.* Knoxville: University of Tennessee Press, 1991.

Watts, Steven. *The Republic Reborn: War and the Making of Liberal America, 1790–1820.* Baltimore: Johns Hopkins University Press, 1987.

Wear, Andrew. *Knowledge and Practice in English Medicine, 1550–1680.* Cambridge: Cambridge University Press, 2000.

———. "Medicine in Early Modern Europe, 1500–1700." In *The Western Medical Tradition 800 BC to AD 1800*, edited by Lawrence I. Conrad, Michael Neve, Vivian Nutton, Roy Porter, and Andrew Wear, 310–16. Cambridge: Cambridge University Press, 1995.

———. "The Popularization of Medicine in Early Modern England." In *The Popularization of Medicine, 1650–1850*, edited by Roy Porter, 17–41. London: Routledge, 1992.

———. "Puritan Perceptions of Illness in Seventeenth-Century England." In *Patients and Practitioners: Lay Perceptions of Medicine in Pre-Industrial Society*, edited by Roy Porter, 55–99. Cambridge: Cambridge University Press, 1985.

Webster, Charles. "Alchemical and Paracelsian Medicine." In *Health, Medicine, and Mortality in the Sixteenth Century*, edited by Charles Webster, 301–34. Cambridge: Cambridge University Press, 1979.

Wells, Christa M. Wilmanns. "A Small Herbal of Little Cost, 1762–1778: A Case Study of a Colonial Herbal as a Social and Cultural Document." Ph.D. diss., University of Pennsylvania, 1980.

Wenrick, Jon S. "For Education and Entertainment: Almanacs in the Early American Republic, 1783–1815." Ph.D. diss., Claremont Graduate School, 1974.

Whitfield, Peter. *Astrology: A History.* New York: Harry N. Abrams, 2001.

Whorton, James C. "'Christian Physiology': William Alcott's Prescription for the Millennium." *Bulletin of the History of Medicine* 49 (1975): 466–81.

———. *Crusaders for Fitness: The History of American Health Reformers.* Princeton: Princeton University Press, 1982.

———. *Inner Hygiene: Constipation and the Pursuit of Health in Modern Society.* New York: Oxford University Press, 2000.

———. *Nature Cures: The History of Alternative Medicine in America.* New York: Oxford University Press, 2002.

———. "Patient, Heal Thyself: Popular Health Reform Movements as Unorthodox Medicine." In *Other Healers: Unorthodox Medicine in America,* edited by Norman Gevitz, 52–73. Baltimore: Johns Hopkins University Press, 1988.

Williams, Marilyn Thornton. *Washing "The Great Unwashed": Public Baths in Urban America, 1840–1920.* Columbus: Ohio State University Press, 1991.

Willis, Roy, and Patrick Curry. *Astrology, Science, and Culture: Pulling Down the Moon.* New York: Berg, 2004.

Wilson, Douglas L. *Honor's Voice: The Transformation of Abraham Lincoln.* New York: Alfred A. Knopf, 1998.

———. "Keeping Lincoln's Secrets." *Atlantic Monthly* 285, no. 5 (2000): 78–88.

Wilson, Leonard. "Fever." In *Companion Encyclopedia of the History of Medicine,* 2 vols., edited by W. F. Bynum and Roy Porter, 1:281–91. New York: Routledge, 1993.

———. "Fevers and Science in Early Nineteenth-Century Medicine." *Journal of the History of Medicine and Allied Sciences* 31 (1978): 386–407.

Wiltshire, John. *Samuel Johnson in the Medical World: The Doctor and the Patient.* Cambridge: Cambridge University Press, 1991.

Winkler, Louis D. "Pennsylvania German Astronomy and Astrology XIII: Health and the Heavens." *Pennsylvania Folklife* 26 (1976): 39–43.

———. "Pennsylvania German Astronomy and Astrology XIV: Benjamin Franklin's Almanacs." *Pennsylvania Folklife* 26 (1977): 36–43.

———. "Technical Aspects of Eighteenth-Century Common Almanacs." *The East-Central Intelligencer* 6, no. 3, n.s. (1992): 11–12.

Winship, George Parker. *The Cambridge Press, 1638–1692.* Philadelphia: University of Pennsylvania Press, 1945.

Winship, Michael. *American Literary Publishing in the Mid-Nineteenth Century: The Business of Ticknor and Fields.* New York: Cambridge University Press, 1995.

Winship, Michael P. "Cotton Mather, Astrologer." *New England Quarterly* 63 (1990): 308–14.

Wolf, Edwin. *The Book Culture of a Colonial American City: Philadelphia Books, Bookmen, and Booksellers.* New York: Oxford University Press, 1988.

Wosh, Peter J. *Spreading the Word: The Bible Business in Nineteenth-Century America.* Ithaca: Cornell University Press, 1994.

Wroth, Lawrence C. *The Colonial Printer.* Charlottesville: University Press of Virginia, 1964.

Young, James Harvey. *The Toadstool Millionaires: A Social History of Patent Medicines in America before Federal Regulation.* Princeton: Princeton University Press, 1961.

Zboray, Ronald J. "Antebellum Reading and the Ironies of Technological Innovation." In *Reading in America: Literature and Social History*, edited by Cathy N. Davidson, 190–96. Baltimore: Johns Hopkins University Press, 1989.

———. *A Fictive People: Antebellum Economic Development and the American Reading Public*. New York: Oxford University Press, 1993.

INDEX

213

Clough, Samuel, 28, 30, 32–33
cochineal, 179n56
color printing, 185–86n32
Columbian Almanac, 24–25, 80
*Columbian Calendar, or New-York and
 Vermont Almanack,* 69
Columbian Magazine, 76
Comic Almanac, 24, 25
common elder, 50
common school movement, 184n9
*Compendium of Physick, Chirurgery, and
 Anatomy* (Salmon), 35
Compendium Physicae, 34
Complete Dictionary of Astrology
 (Wilson), 37
Condie, D. Francis, 77, 91, 110, 184n4
Connecticut Almanack (Elliott), 6
contamination of food and water, 52,
 176n28
Continental Almanac, 24
Cornaro, Luigi, 68, 71, 85–86, 89, 180n2
country life, romantic view of, 84–85,
 183n46
cream of tartar, 47, 54, 63, 174n14
cubebs, 179n55
Cullen, William, 45, 56–57
Culpeper, Nicholas, 35, 44, 65, 68,
 170n57, 180n4
Cumberland Almanac, 81
cupping, 25, 63, 168n19
"Cure for Dropsy" (Appleton), 48
"Cure for Dropsy" (Zane), 46
"Cure for the Dropsy," 47

demand for almanacs, 8
demographic changes, and almanacs, 8–9
depletive measures, 51, 56, 57, 93
Dewees, William, 55, 60, 175n23, 177n46
diarrhea. *See* bloody flux
dietary advice: and bloody flux, 55, 57–58;
 Buchan on, 82; and moderation, 71,
 79–82; and poetry, 80–81; and
 rheumatism, 63; vegetarianism, 94
"Diet Drink for the Dropsy, A," 47
"Dietetic Maxims," 81
"Directions to Servants," 163n19
*Discourses on the Sober and Temperate
 Life* (Cornaro), 180n2
diuretics: cream of tartar, 47, 54, 63,
 174n14; and dropsy, 49, 173n9,

173n10, 173n12, 175n23; Glauber's
 salt, 176n33; gum guaiacum, 60, 62,
 179n57; ipecacuanha, 53, 54, 174n21,
 178n46; mustard seed, 47, 48, 62,
 174n13, 174n15; potash, 178n49; to
 restore balance, 44; Seneca snakeroot,
 60, 178n54; senna, 178n55; Squill pill,
 174n15
Domestic Medicine (Buchan), 49, 68, 77,
 84
Dr. Brandreth's Vegetable Universal Pills,
 100–101
Dr. Christie's Magnetic Fluid, 105
Dr. McIntosh's Italian Vegetable Pile
 Electuary, 101
dropsy, 42, 46–52, 173n8, 173–74n12,
 174n21; and bloodletting, 49, 175n23;
 and bodily equilibrium, 49; Buchan on,
 49; comparison of remedies, 48; "Cure
 for Dropsy" (Appleton), 48; "Cure for
 Dropsy" (Zane), 46; "Cure for the
 Dropsy," 47; "A Diet Drink for the
 Dropsy," 47; and diuretics, 49, 173n9,
 173n10, 173n12, 175n23; elimination of
 excess fluid, 47; forms of, 50
Dr. Reynolds' Imperial Health Pills, 101
Dr. Townsend's Compound Extract of
 Sarsaparilla, 101, 102, 104, 186n34
"Drunkard's Looking Glass" (Thomas),
 75
dwarf elder, 47, 173n11
dysentery. *See* bloody flux

Eagelmann, Charles Frederick, 27
eclectics, 51
Eisenstadt, Peter, 36
elderberry, 173n12
elecampane, 173n12
Eliot, Jared, 36
Elliott, Clark, 6
endemic disease, 52–53
English Physician; and Complete Herbal
 (Culpeper), 35
*Enquiry into the Effects of Spiritous
 Liquors upon the Human Body, and
 Their Influence upon the Happiness of
 Society, An* (Rush), 76
Erra Pater, 11, 18, 35, 167n6
Essay on Health and Long Life (Cheyne),
 86, 180n2, 183n51

THOMAS A. HORROCKS is associate librarian of Houghton Library for Collections, Harvard University. He received his PhD in history from the University of Pennsylvania and a graduate degree in library and information science from Drexel University. His previous positions were director of the Francis C. Wood Institute for the History of Medicine and director of the Library at the College of Physicians of Philadelphia, and director of the Center for the History of Medicine at the Francis A. Countway Library at Harvard Medical School. He and his wife, Elizabeth Carroll-Horrocks, live in Cambridge, Massachusetts.